Residential Satisfaction and Housing Policy Evolution

This book explores residential satisfaction and housing policy trends in developing nations by using subsidised low-income housing examples in South Africa, Ghana and Nigeria as case studies. While there has been much documentation on the formation of residential satisfaction and the evolution of housing policy in developed nations, relatively little has been written about these topics in developing nations.

This book provides readers with two major practical insights. The first is focused on the theoretical underpinning of residential satisfaction and the formation of residential satisfaction in subsidised low-income housing through the development of a conceptual framework, while the second is focused on housing policy evolution and its trends in South Africa. In this section of the book, comparative overviews of public housing in two West African countries are provided with an emphasis on the philosophical basis for its development in these countries. The central aim of the book is to provide readers with ideas on residential satisfaction formation and housing policy trends in South Africa.

The book is therefore of interest to researchers in housing, architecture, urban planning, geography, sociology and development studies.

Clinton Aigbavboa is Senior Lecturer at the University of Johannesburg, South Africa. He is an active researcher with an interest in the field of sustainable human development, with a research focus on the following areas: sustainable housing regeneration (urban renewal and informal housing), life-cycle assessment in the construction industry, leadership in low-income housing, post-occupancy evaluation and green job creation.

Wellington Thwala is Professor in the Department of Construction Management and Quantity Surveying at the University of Johannesburg, South Africa.

Routledge Studies in International Real Estate

The Routledge Studies in International Real Estate series presents a forum for the presentation of academic research into international real estate issues. Books in the series are broad in their conceptual scope and reflect an inter-disciplinary approach to Real Estate as an academic discipline.

Oiling the Urban Economy
Land, labour, capital, and the state in Sekondi-Takoradi, Ghana
Franklin Obeng-Odoom

Real Estate, Construction and Economic Development in Emerging Market Economies
Edited by Raymond T. Abdulai, Franklin Obeng-Odoom, Edward Ochieng and Vida Maliene

Econometric Analyses of International Housing Markets
Rita Li and Kwong Wing Chau

Sustainable Communities and Urban Housing
A comparative European perspective
Montserrat Pareja Eastaway and Nessa Winston

Regulating Information Asymmetry in the Residential Real Estate Market
The Hong Kong experience
Devin Lin

Delhi's Changing Built Environment
Piyush Tiwari and Jyoti Rao

Housing Policy, Wellbeing and Social Development in Asia
Edited by Rebecca L. H. Chiu and Seong-Kyu Ha

Construction and Application of Property Price Indices
Anthony Owusu-Ansah

Residential Satisfaction and Housing Policy Evolution
Clinton Aigbavboa and Wellington Thwala

Residential Satisfaction and Housing Policy Evolution

Clinton Aigbavboa and Wellington Thwala

Routledge
Taylor & Francis Group
LONDON AND NEW YORK

First published 2018
by Routledge
2 Park Square, Milton Park, Abingdon, Oxon OX14 4RN

and by Routledge
711 Third Avenue, New York, NY 10017

Routledge is an imprint of the Taylor & Francis Group, an informa business

First issued in paperback 2021

British Library Cataloguing-in-Publication Data
A catalogue record for this book is available from the British Library

Library of Congress Cataloging-in-Publication Data
Names: Aigbavboa, Clinton, author. | Thwala, Wellington, author.
Title: Residential satisfaction and housing policy evolution / Clinton Aigbavboa and Wellington Didibhuku Thwala.
Description: Abingdon, Oxon ; New York, NY : Routledge, 2018. | Includes bibliographical references and index.
Identifiers: LCCN 2018006459| ISBN 9781138500310 (hardback : alk. paper) | ISBN 9781351012676 (ebook)
Subjects: LCSH: Housing policy–Developing countries. | Housing policy–South Africa. | Housing–Resident satisfaction–Developing countries. | Housing–Resident satisfaction–South Africa.
Classification: LCC HD7391 .A5165 2018 | DDC 333.33/8091724–dc23
LC record available at https://lccn.loc.gov/2018006459

ISBN: 978-1-138-50031-0 (hbk)
ISBN: 978-1-03-209509-7 (pbk)
ISBN: 978-1-351-01267-6 (ebk)

Typeset in Goudy
by Swales & Willis Ltd, Exeter, Devon, UK

This book is dedicated to all homeless people in the world and particularly those in Africa who were rendered homeless by their neighbours.

Contents

Illustrations

Figures

Tables

Abbreviations

ACSI	American Consumer Satisfaction Index
ANC	African National Congress
BNG	Breaking New Ground
CHB	Central Housing Board
DHS	Department of Human Settlement
ePHP	enhanced People Housing Process
FCT	Federal Capital Territory
FHA	Federal Housing Authority
FMGN	Federal Mortgage Bank of Nigeria
FMWH	Federal Ministry of Works and Housing
FSP	Family Support Programme
GDP	gross domestic product
GHS	General Household Survey
GREDA	Ghanaian Real Estate Development Association
IDP	Integrated Development Plan
IHHSD	Integrated Housing and Human Settlement Development
IRDP	Integrated Residential Development Programme
LEDB	Lagos Executive Development Board
MoWH	Ministry of Works and Housing
NDP	National Development Plan
NGN	Nigerian naira
NGO	non-governmental organization
NHC	National Housing Code
NHF	National Housing Forum
NHP	National Housing Policy
NHSS	National Housing Subsidy Scheme
NHUDP	National Housing and Urban Development Policy
NLC	National Liberation Council
NSS	National Shelter Strategy
POE	post-occupancy experience
PPP	public–private partnership
RDP	Reconstruction and Development Programme

SCP	Sustainable Cities Programme
SHC	State Housing Corporation
SHI	Social Housing Institute
SHP	Social Housing Programme
SSNIT	Social Security and National Insurance Trust
TDC	Tema Development Corporation
UISP	Upgrading Informal Settlements Programme
UNDP	United Nations Development Programme

Preface

This book explores residential satisfaction and housing policy trends in developing nations with a special focus on South African housing development for the low socio-economic groups as a case study. While there has been much documentation on the formation of residential satisfaction in other housing topologies in the developed nations and the housing policy evolution as evident in the body of knowledge, relatively little has been written about the formation of residential satisfaction for the developing nation's subsidised low-income housing and the evolution of housing policy. Far fewer reference books are written about the developing nations and especially about African cities even though Africa is the current hotbed of residential housing development. The book adopts division into various parts and chapters to enable a proper categorisation of its content thereby allowing a better understanding of the subject matter. Each of the chapters commences with an introduction describing what to expect from the section and concludes with a summary highlighting major issues raised. As this is a research book, references are provided at the end of each chapter for further reading and expansion of knowledge. An index of important and key words is also provided at the end of the book for a quick reference to areas of interest.

This research book provides readers with two major practical insights. The first is focused on the theoretical underpinning of residential satisfaction and the formation of residential satisfaction in subsidised low-income housing through the development of a conceptual framework, while the second is focused on housing evolution and its trends in South Africa and other African countries. In this latter section of the book, a comparative overview on public housing in two West African countries is further provided with an emphasis on the philosophical basis for housing development in these countries. Generally, the central aim of the book is to provide readers with ideas on residential satisfaction formation and its achievement and housing policy trends to date in South Africa. The book is therefore of interest to researchers in architecture, urban planning, geography, sociology and development studies. Also, it allows researchers in housing studies to gain further insight into the formation of housing satisfaction as it has been considered a multi-faceted dimensional concept in the field of sustainable humane development. The book can be adopted as research guide, framework, aid, note or material for topics relating to housing satisfaction studies, housing policy evolution and trends, and the formulation of future housing policy in developing nations. We hope that all readers of this book will find it not only stimulating, insightful and impacting but also helpful in advancing their knowledge in the subject of housing theories and studies, thus adequately housing the poor and vulnerable in our societies.

Clinton Aigbavboa
Wellington Thwala

Part I
The fundamentals

Part I presents the fundamentals of the book. This part, which contains Chapter 1 of the book, is designed to give a quick overview of what this book is all about.

1 Introduction

Introduction

Residential satisfaction has been a major theme of discussion in various disciplines such as sociology, psychology, planning and geography (Marans & Rodgers, 1975; Galster & Hesser, 1981; Canter & Rees, 1982; Cutter, 1982; Weidemann & Anderson, 1985; Baillie & Peart, 1992; Nathan, 1995; Bruin & Cook, 1997). The focus of most of the social psychology scholars who have dominated satisfaction research varies from consumer satisfaction to job satisfaction to patient satisfaction (Yiping, 2005). An understanding of people's satisfactory evaluation of a product or a service is believed to be useful. Feedback could be identified and implemented to bring about improvements, which will increase the effectiveness of the product or service. As such, residential satisfaction research deals with the occupants' satisfaction of their housing units, and aims to inform public policy and planning intervention for future housing units to be developed.

Residential satisfaction describes the perceived gap between housing occupants' needs and aspirations and the reality of their current residential contexts (Galster, 1987). Housing satisfaction is also described as the degree of contentment experienced by an individual or a family member with regard to the current housing situation. Because of its subjective nature, housing satisfaction is termed a complex attitude (McCray & Day, 1977; Satsangi & Kearns, 1992; Lu, 1999). Residential satisfaction encompasses satisfaction with the dwelling unit and the entire neighbourhood, which is often employed to evaluate residents' perceptions of and feelings for their housing units and the environment (Onibokun, 1974; Ogu, 2002). The concept of housing satisfaction has also been used as a key predictor of an individual's perceptions of general 'quality of life' (Campbell, Converse & Rogers, 1976; Djebuarni & Al-Abed, 2000), while psychology scholars (Andrews & Whitney, 1976; Morris, Crull & Winter, 1976; Diaz-Serrano, 2006; Kleinhans, 2007) have affirmed that residents' perception of their environment defines the quality of their lives and most times determines their propensity to move to a new location. Hence, this book explores residential satisfaction and housing policy trends in developing nations with a special focus on South African housing development. While there has been much documentation on the formation of residential satisfaction in other housing topologies in the developed nations and the housing policy evolution as evident in the body of knowledge, relatively little has been written about the formation of residential satisfaction for the developing nation's low-income housing and the evolution of housing policy. Very few reference books have been written about the developing nations (especially African cities) even though Africa is the current hotbed of residential housing development. This book also presents a thorough background on residential theories and its formation.

The book is divided into four parts and eight chapters for guidance and ease of use. Part I consists of a chapter detailing the background information for the book with a contextual underpinning of the subject matter of the book followed by an understanding of the issues of housing adequacy. The subject of housing theories and policy development themes are discussed in Part II of the book. The second part of the book describes a generic overview of housing theories, theoretical perspectives on housing study, methodological issues with housing studies and policy development. This section of the book is further sub-divided into two chapters, namely: theoretical perspectives of housing studies research and housing policy evolution development. Part III of the book presents housing policy and development in two West African countries (Ghana and Nigeria) and one Southern African country – South Africa; three chapters have been allocated to deal with this concept. The first and second chapters in this section address housing demand and supply in both Ghana and Nigeria with an emphasis on the philosophical basis for housing development and the challenges facing housing developments. The third chapter in Part III is devoted to housing in South Africa with an extensive discussion on the evolution of its housing policy, housing policy progress in South Africa, programmes supporting housing developments in South Africa and the challenges of housing backlog in the country. This part addresses the second aim of the book, which is focused on a robust understanding of housing evolutions and its trends in South Africa and other African countries. Part IV of the book consists of two chapters that relate specifically to residential satisfaction theories and research. The chapters in this part discuss the theoretical and conceptual perspectives of residential satisfaction studies, thus addressing the first focus of the book, which speaks to the theoretical underpinning of residential satisfaction and the formation of residential satisfaction in housing through the development of a conceptual framework.

Overall, this housing research book provides readers with two major practical insights: the first is focused on the theoretical underpinning of residential satisfaction and the formation of residential satisfaction in subsidized low-income housing through the development of a conceptual framework, while the second is focused on housing evolutions and its trends in South Africa and other African countries. In this section of the book, a comparative overview on public housing in two West African countries is further provided with an emphasis on the philosophical basis for housing development in these countries. Generally, the central aim of the book is to provide readers with ideas on residential satisfaction formation and its achievement and housing policy trends to date in South Africa and in other African countries.

Understanding residential satisfaction

The motivation for the interest and popularity of residential satisfaction is twofold. First, residential satisfaction is recognized as an important component of an individuals' general quality of life; meaning that for most people, housing is the largest consumption item in their lifetime. Second, a home is the place where one most often finds refuge, rest and satisfaction. This means that the degree to which an individual's needs and aspirations are met by their housing condition is a concern for researchers but most importantly for housing developers, planners and specifically for housing policy-makers. This is because housing policy-makers in different national states are vested with the responsibility of policy formulation and implementation of housing delivery programmes for different groups in the society at large, and most especially for the low-income groups who have less opportunity to support and meet their housing needs. In housing programmes targeting the low-income groups, measures of residential satisfaction provide insights regarding occupants' experience of their housing, and these can be used to evaluate the success of the programmes devoted to housing delivery and set the tone for future developments.

Further, individuals' subjective evaluations of their housing determine the way they respond to the residential environment and form the basis of demand for public action (Dahmann, 1985; Nathan, 1995). In 'behavioral conceptualization' of migration, low levels of residential satisfaction precede housing and mobility behaviour (Speare, 1974). That is, when individuals feel dissatisfied with their current housing situation, they sometimes consider relocating and sometimes actually move to a different unit or location. However, Rory, Maarten and Peteke (2010), in their work on longitudinal analysis of moving desires, expectations and actual moving behaviour, revealed that housing dissatisfaction, and especially dissatisfaction with the neighbourhood, strongly increases the propensity to desire a move but not to expect a move, and also the propensity to desire *and* expect a move. However, other research works have found that dissatisfaction has a much smaller effect on expecting an undesired move. Hence housing dissatisfaction is closely associated with moving desires, but not with moving expectations, except when expectations are simultaneously stated with a desire.

Despite a sizeable amount of literature that has developed in this field, an understanding of how individuals form their residential satisfaction is still inadequate. An obvious sign of this inadequacy is the existence of inconsistent, sometimes even conflicting, research results about the factors that shape the residents' level of satisfaction with their housing and neighbourhood. This may be as a result of the differences in samples; most samples are not representative of the population being investigated and the way the key variables were defined, but it may also be because of how the data were analysed. This book is determined to present a robust theoretical perspective that should be considered in the construction of a better understanding of the variables that determine housing satisfaction.

The study of residential satisfaction in developed nations was fostered by two phenomena. The first is the post-war housing boom of the 1950s/early 1960s and the new residential environment through growth of suburban development (Campbell, Converse & Rogers, 1976). Second is the plight of central city residents under the active programme of slum clearance and central city rebuilding. Likewise, urban development in developed countries over the years is similar to the low-income and the large-scale inner-city redevelopment currently taking place in cities such as Johannesburg, Durban and Cape Town among others in South Africa and in other developing nations such as Lagos in Nigeria and Accra in Ghana. This has also fostered the increase in the study of how residential satisfaction is created in developing countries. There has been much discussion about residents' satisfaction in South Africa and in other developing economies, but the majority has centred on measuring residents' satisfaction in the informal settlement areas and privately owned low-income estates. Only a few studies have been done with regard to subsidized low-income schemes, with the major focus of the research being done on the post-occupancy evaluation of the residences, where residential satisfaction was treated as a sub-objective evaluation in these studies (Ria & Bontle, 2004; Darkwa, 2006; Aigbavboa, 2010). Also, the work of Westaway (2006) on the longitudinal investigation of satisfaction in a Soweto informal settlement (South Africa) was focused on the effect of satisfaction with personal and environmental quality of life. The study ascertained the group and time effects on satisfaction with personal and environmental domains of quality of life, and, likewise, determined personal and environmental predictors of life and neighbourhood satisfaction in the informal settlement. From the longitudinal study, it was found that the group from the squatter camp had the lowest levels of satisfaction with their personal and environmental quality of life. The group was found to be the most disadvantaged in this regard, when compared with the relocated, the awaiting relocation and the site tenure allocated groups.

Furthermore, Robin, Brian and Kingstone (2007) also measured the quality of life in three informal settlements in South Africa. In their work, they focused on the factors that are most important in improving the quality of life of residents in informal housing, as well as the main obstacles to a better quality of life. Likewise, Møller and Saris (2001) in their work on the relationship between subjective well-being and domain satisfaction in South Africa explored the effect of domain satisfaction on finances, housing and social contrast in relation with the developed countries. However, Ria and Bontle (2004). in their work on the post-occupancy evaluation of the Hope City Housing Complex (a private low-income housing estate), found that the residents of the housing estates were satisfied with the facilities in the dwelling units, the complex and the management components of the estate. Despite the residents being satisfied with their overall housing situations, it was observed that females were less satisfied than males. Regardless of the number of studies that have been conducted in this arena, there is a limited and comprehensive synchronization of literature on the theoretical perspective for the formation of residential satisfaction and the development of housing policy evaluation in Africa. This book hopes to fill the gap in this area.

Housing occupants' responses to residential satisfaction

Housing occupants responses that determine residential satisfaction towards a given housing situation have been a subject of dispute over time among many researchers. Social psychologists generally categorize people's responses to any social or physical object into three groups: the affective; the cognitive; and the conative/behavioral. Affective refers to a person's feeling towards and evaluation of some object, person, issue or event. The cognitive denotes his or her knowledge, opinions, beliefs and thoughts about the object. Lastly, conative refers to his or her behavioral intentions and actions with respect to or in the presence of the object. These three categories provide a useful framework in understanding and testing the theoretical development underpinning residential satisfaction research (Francescato, Weidemann & Anderson, 1987; Weidemann & Anderson, 1985). These categories also provide an understanding of the relationships between objective conditions, subjective experiences and the residents' level of satisfaction with their living environments. As a result, residential satisfaction is not only used as an indicator in evaluating housing policies, but also as a predictor of housing quality, propensity to mobility and the quality of life and well-being of the residents. High residential satisfaction levels have been considered an indication of the success of specific policies, programmes or designs. Hence, an understanding of the factors that facilitate a satisfied or dissatisfied response can play a critical part in making successful housing policy decisions.

Furthermore, there is no consensus about what type of evaluation residential satisfaction falls under. While some authors conceive residential satisfaction as a purely *cognitive* evaluation (Canter & Rees, 1982; Mandler, 1984; Oseland, 1990), others have held that it is *affective* (Weidemann & Anderson, 1985). However, authors such as Francescato, Weidemann and Anderson (1989) do not think that evaluation such as satisfaction can be neatly separated into *cognition* or *affect*. In addition, satisfaction studies have been approached from two main perspectives over time, namely satisfaction as a measure of the degree to which the environment facilitates or inhabits the goal of the user, called the purposive approach (Canter & Rees, 1982; Oseland, 1990), and those perspectives that conceive of satisfaction as a measure of the gap between consumers' actual and aspired needs, called the aspiration-gap approach (Galster, 1987). The implication of the purposive approach is that there is emphasis on goals or associated activities in relation to the attributes of the physical environment. This approach is entrenched in a cognitive view. However, it is useful because it assists researchers in understanding the degree to which different aspects and roles of users contribute to their satisfaction. In addition, people are not only goal-oriented but also they have affective relationships with the environment (or any psychological object), usually involving comparisons. This is the comparison between what the beneficiaries have and what they would like to have or have previously experienced. This is the proposition on which the aspiration-gap methodology is based and the more common conceptual frameworks of residential satisfaction (Galster, 1987; Morris & Winter, 1975; Weidemann & Anderson, 1985) have all conceived of residential satisfaction from this perspective. In their housing adjustment theory of residential mobility, Morris and Jakubczak (1988), theorize that individuals judge their housing condition according to normatively defined values, which are dictated by societal standards or rules for life conditions, and family/personal norms, which relate to a household's own standards for housing. This means that, on the one hand, when the housing norms are met, the household is likely to express a high level of satisfaction with the housing and the surrounding neighbourhood. On the other hand, an incongruity between the actual housing situation and housing norms results in a housing deficit, which gives rise to residential dissatisfaction, leading to some form of housing adjustments that may be either in situ, such as revising their housing needs and aspirations in order to reconcile the incongruity or to improve their housing conditions through remodelling, or else the residents may move to another place to bring their housing into conformity with their aspirations and needs (Morris & Winter, 1978). This concept is commonly known as the notion of 'housing deficit', which conceptualizes residential satisfaction as a dynamic process.

A more vigorous view of residential satisfaction is the conceptualization of residential satisfaction as an attitude or a multifaceted construct, which has cognitive, affective and conative dimensions (Francescato, Weidemann & Anderson, 1989). This definition of residential satisfaction is more comprehensive because it accounts for the low predictive strength of the construct in previous studies. Residential satisfaction has also been conceptualized as a multidimensional construct (Bonaiuto et al., 1999), focusing on different specific aspects of a place, such as the spatial features, human features and functional features. Various attributes of housing to which users respond in relation to satisfaction are categorized according to a number of dimensions. These attributes are also referred to as the 'referent of interaction' (Canter & Rees, 1982), while Francescato (2002) referred to them as the territory of the location. Generally, these attributes have been categorized in the literature as social/psychological, management/organizational and physical attributes. Social attributes include privacy, relationship with neighbours, safety and security, social densities, freedom of choice, social relations and personalization (Francescato et al., 1979; Rent & Rent, 1978; Spencer & Barneji, 1985). The management attributes usually examined are rules and regulations, maintenance, management staff and policies, participation and rents (Paris & Kangari, 2006). However, the physical attributes have received less attention in the literature. They usually include the lack or presence of certain facilities, spatial density, location and size of the bedrooms (Galster, 1987; Kahana et al., 2003; Peck & Stewart, 1985; Turkoglu, 1997). Other physical attributes used in the literature include the appearance of the building and the floor level (Kaya & Erkip, 2001).

However, physical attributes are not so simple to measure and data may not always be obtained about them with confidence (Francescato, 2002). This is why very few physical characteristics have been examined in most studies on residential satisfaction. An important physical characteristic, which is not often used in evaluating satisfaction, is the morphological configuration. Morphological configuration is referred to in architecture as typologies. These are the spatial and organizational forms of the building, based on certain physical characteristics. This is an important aspect of the design of buildings. However, usually it is the 'type of house' that is examined in satisfaction studies. The 'type of house' refers to terraces, apartments, single-family houses or duplexes. The differences between these house types are more or less functional, rather than morphological. This classification is not useful in all contexts of housing, where functional differences do not exist. However, differences in the morphological characteristics of buildings need to be captured for the purpose of evaluation. Some studies found that the type of site layout (site morphology) and the type of housing (low rise/high rise and detached/attached) were not predictors of satisfaction (Day, 2000; Francescato et al., 1979). However, there is enough evidence to suggest that the morphological configuration of the residence would significantly affect the level of satisfaction (Davis & Roizen, 1970; Gifford, 1997; Hourihan, 1984). For example, the length of the corridor of dormitories has been found to have a significant influence on the perception of crowding. In addition, whenever residential satisfaction has been examined, it usually focused on one (but rarely more than one) of the levels of the environment, which is also referred to as the scale of the environment (Aragones, Francescato & Garling, 2002) or levels of environmental interaction (Canter & Rees, 1982) with very little differentiation between the levels. In other words, the focus has been on satisfaction with a level (or scale) of the physical environment, such as the dwelling unit, the neighbourhood, the community or country of residence. In this book, morphological configurations of housing are separated from the physical attributes of the dwelling units.

Likewise, various demographic characteristics such as sex, age, length of residence, socioeconomic status, race and ethnicity, which influence housing satisfaction, have also been studied, which researchers have found that they also influence the satisfaction level with housing units. However, as noted earlier, not much evidence is available on residential satisfaction for low-income state housing schemes in South Africa. It is not certain whether the characteristics that predict satisfaction for residents in private medium-income and private low-income housing, informal settlements and rented apartments would also predict satisfaction for the beneficiaries of state-subsidized low-income housing units in a developing country context, using South Africa as a case study.

Housing adequacy issues

Housing production, access and affordability, and maintaining existing dwellings in habitable conditions have been the emphasis of government policies and programmes designed to help the poorest and those who cannot access housing in developing countries, most especially in South Africa. In spite of the national and international efforts aimed at developing appropriate shelter policies and strategies, no effective remedy has been found to cure housing ills as little consideration is given to the issue of the satisfaction of the beneficiaries/occupants of the housing projects (United Nations Centre for Human Settlements, 2000). There are at least two concerns about housing. One is quantitative – too few housing units for those needing them; that is, the number of houses provided do not meet the demands of the low-income group. The other concern is qualitative – the housing units being provided are unsuitable for the beneficiaries, that is,thc housing type not being satisfactory to the beneficiaries' housing needs, even though there is an improvement of comfort compared to most publicly funded beneficiaries' former housing situations. Quantitative problems come and go cyclically, depending on the economy and on the extent of population changes. However, qualitative problems always seem to stay with us. But their nature, however, changes from decade to decade. Qualitative concerns are very important as they influence the quality of life and affect the psychosocial aspects of the inhabitants.

Housing has been a major concern for all people worldwide, as it has always been considered as a basic human need. Housing fulfils physical needs by providing security and shelter from the weather and climate and fulfils psychological needs by providing a sense of personal space and privacy. Housing in South Africa emphasizes the provision of adequate, affordable and quality houses for all, with a particular emphasis on the low-income groups, as determined in the South African Constitution of 1996 and the Housing White Paper Policy Framework of 1994. Industrialization and urbanization have been some of the influencing factors contributing to the acute housing demand among the lower- and middle-income groups in cities and other larger urban agglomerations of many developing countries (Yong, 2008). However, the general demand for housing in the urban areas far outstrips supply, which at most times is due to the scarcity of suitable residential land and competing land uses in the urban areas of developing countries. Therefore, in spite of the developing country's government's commitment and effort in providing adequate, affordable and quality houses with emphasis on the development of low-income houses for the poor, the houses available are still not enough. Also, there are complaints about the housing products being delivered in the general housing sector not being able to fully meet the housing needs of the low-income group particularly.

Low-income housing provision has been a major focus of the government in post-Apartheid urban South Africa, as the government attempts to address the historical race-based inequalities, poor municipal service provision and contemporary rapid urbanization. The South Africa Housing White Paper of 1994 (Republic of South Africa, 1994), which has undergone several modifications, prioritized the needs of the poor, encouraged community participation and the involvement of the private sector, and committed to deliver one million houses in the first five years (Jenkins, 1999) after the democratic elections. The delivery of one million houses has since been surpassed but the housing needs of the poor and their participation in the process have not been fully incorporated into the developmental process, resulting in complaints about the delivered housing products. Since 1994, the low-income housing programme has mostly involved building serviced townships on urban peripheries, which in itself presents a myriad of environmental, social and political concerns. Despite this problem, by the end of 2015, the government had built and handed out more than three million houses, giving shelter to more than 13.5 million people (free of charge to individuals that have been aided by the state) and thereby providing better quality accommodation and some form of an asset over the past 20 years (DHS, 2015). Many problems with the process have become clear as the progression has unfolded. These problems include (Jenkins, 1999):

- New houses and infrastructure are of poor quality, and are rapidly deteriorating and require maintenance.
- New houses and Human Settlement Development continue placing the poor and low-income blacks in 'ghettos' on urban peripheries, far from jobs and services.
- People dislike the model of housing used, and would prefer larger houses (the main model was first changed in 1998 when the Department of Housing, now the Department of Human Settlement (DHS), increased the minimum size of new houses to $30m^2$, and this was further increased in 2004, during the launching of the Breaking New Ground Policy, to $40m^2$).
- The dominant model of freehold tenure inadequately deals with the dynamics of poverty, and several categories of the poor, such as temporary workers and many women, would be better served by rental accommodation as opposed to giving them houses.
- Because of these problems, people often sell or rent out their low-income houses bought through the subsidy, and move back to squatter or other informal settlements closer to economic activities.
- Environmental concerns regarding the new developments include increases in vehicular traffic caused by urban sprawl and land-use changes.

Recent studies on the post-occupancy experience (POE) of government housing subsidy beneficiaries have verified the above problems. A POE study found that most of the occupants in the South African government's Reconstruction and Development Programme (RDP) Housing Scheme are dissatisfied with the characteristics of the dwelling unit, such as the size of the unit and inadequacy of rooms in some units (Aigbavboa, 2010). Also, a Kuala Lumpur, Malaysia study of residential satisfaction of public low-cost flat dwellers found that most beneficiaries of the public low-cost flats were also dissatisfied with the characteristics of the dwelling unit, because there were no dining spaces and the bathroom and toilet were incorporated together in the units (Husna & Nurijan, 1987). The above studies revealed that good-quality housing is a reflection of the well-being of the community, which relates to the residents' acceptance of the houses and what housing provides for the people.

Determinants of good housing can be accessed through the investigation of the satisfaction levels experienced by the housing residents, through the objective and subjective measures of the right domains that can determine satisfaction in a given context. For instance, the concept of housing satisfaction has been used as an ad-hoc evaluative measure for judging the success of housing developments constructed by the public sector, which enhances the image of the housing provider, the public, and contributes towards a good housing environment (Marans & Rodgers, 1975).

However, the success of publicly funded housing schemes does not only depend on just the provision of housing units, but also on other factors that affect the needs and requirements of the beneficiaries. The failure of many laudable housing projects in developing countries is attributed to the lack of knowledge on the determinants of housing satisfaction. This is because beneficiaries' satisfaction reflects the degree to which individuals' housing needs are fulfilled, which acts as a guide to policy-makers to monitor the implementation of low-income housing policies and, in effect, the quality of life of the people. An understanding of how individuals form their housing satisfaction is important because their subjective evaluations determine housing adjustment and mobility behaviour and are the basis of demands for public action. This knowledge will also be used to design more effective housing programmes and to avoid problems that may result because of the perceptions of the planners and policy-makers, which do not always coincide with those of the residents.

Objectives of the book

Since there is some disagreement between researchers as to the relative importance of the variables that determine residential satisfaction, this book will assess the specific residential satisfaction variables that should be considered when planning for housing development that concerns the low-income groups in developing countries and most especially in South Africa. The principle components of the factors that affect the occupants' satisfaction will also be discussed.

A gap exists in the literature regarding the determinants of residential satisfaction in subsidized low-income housing in developing countries. This book will therefore contribute to existing knowledge by establishing the factors that determine residential satisfaction in subsidized low-income housing by establishing what should be considered when planning for development. Since the governments of developing countries, and most specifically the South African government, have been actively providing subsided public housing in different types of development projects in various locations, it is therefore important to assess whether or not these government development projects have met the needs and expectations of the users, particularly on the low-income housing development programmes that came into being after the draft and implementation of the new Housing Policy Framework in South Africa in 1994. Also, it is paramount for governments to know which attributes determine residential satisfaction in the constructed low-income housing. This study thus measured the success of the South African government body (DHS) that has been entrusted with the responsibility of delivering affordable quality housing for the low-income group. The study further provides a guide to the vital factors to consider in low-income housing development. For most individuals, housing is one of the largest investment items of their lifetime and, as a result, satisfaction with their housing situation is an important component of their quality of life and well-being.

This book provides readers with two major practical insights. The first focuses on the theoretical underpinning of residential satisfaction and the formation of residential satisfaction in subsidized low-income housing through the development of a conceptual framework, while the second focuses on housing evolution and its trends in South Africa. Comparative overviews of public housing in two West Africa countries are further provided with an emphasis on the philosophical basis for housing development in these countries. Generally, the central aim of the book is to provide readers with ideas on residential satisfaction formation and its achievement and housing policy trends to date in South Africa.

Summary

This chapter introduced the idea behind the conception of this research book with the emphasis on the explanation of why residential satisfaction in low-income housing is important. It has been shown that residential satisfaction is a very significant issue. It is important because it deals with the housing occupants' satisfaction, and aims to inform policy and planning intervention. Similarly, it has also been revealed that measures of residential satisfaction will provide additional insights regarding individuals' experience with housing, and can be used to evaluate the success of housing programmes. Also, occupants' objective and subjective evaluations of their housing units determine the way in which they respond to the residential environment and form the basis of any demands for public action. Despite the numerous empirical studies that have been conducted on residential satisfaction, there is still confusion on the attributes that determine residential satisfaction. Also, in spite of the sizeable amount of literature that is available in this field, an understanding of how individuals form their residential satisfaction in public-provided subsidized low-income housing is still inadequate. It is also clear from the background to this study that other studies that have been conducted on residential satisfaction in South Africa have centred on measuring residents' satisfaction in the informal settlement areas and privately owned medium- and low-income estates with only a few making reference to subsidized low-income housing as a sub-objective in the studies. Furthermore, the method used in these studies was not always completely successful. An obvious sign of this inadequacy is the existence of inconsistent, sometimes even conflicting, research results about the factors that shape individuals' satisfaction with their housing units and neighbourhoods. The main objective of this book, which discusses the theoretical underpinning of residential satisfaction and the formation of residential satisfaction in subsidized low-income housing through the development of a conceptual framework, was presented. While the second objective focused on housing evolutions and its trends in South Africa. To summarize, the central aim of the book is to provide readers with ideas on residential satisfaction formation and its achievement and housing policy trends to date in South Africa. The concept of housing theories and policy development is explained in Part II of the book.

References

Aigbavboa, C.O. (2010). *An evaluation of the post occupancy experience of housing subsidy beneficiaries in South Africa: A case study of Gauteng*. Johannesburg: University of Johannesburg.

Andrews, F. & Whitney, S. (1976). *Social indicators of well-being: America's perceptions of life quality*. New York: Plenum Press.

Aragones, J.I., Francescato, G. & Garling, T. (2002). *Evaluating residential environments: Choice, satisfaction and behaviour*. London: Bergin and Garvey.

Baillie, S.T. & Peart, V. (1992). Determinants of housing satisfaction for older married and unmarried women in Florida. *Housing and society*, 19(2):101–116.

Bonaiuto, M., Aiello, A., Perugini, M., Bonnes, M. & Ercolani, A.P. (1999). Multidimensional perception of residential quality and neighbourhood attachment in the urban environment. *Journal of environmental psychology*, 19(4):331–352.

Bruin, M. & Cook, C. (1997). Understanding constraints and residential satisfaction among low-income single-parent families. *Environment and behavior*, 29(4):532–553.

Campbell, A., Converse, P.E. & Rogers, W.J. (1976). *The quality of the America life: Perceptions, evaluations, and satisfaction*. New York: Russell Sage Foundation.

Canter, D. & Rees, K.A. (1982). Multivariate model of housing satisfaction. *International review of applied psychology*, 32:185–208.

Cutter, S. (1982). Residential satisfaction and the suburban homeowner. *Urban geography*, 3(4):315–327.

Dahmann, D.C. (1985). Assessments of neighbourhood quality in metropolitan America. *Urban affairs quarterly*, 20(4):511–535.

Darkwa, I. (2006). Post-occupancy evaluation of state-subsidised housing units in Kayamandi, Stellenbosch. Unpublished material.

Davis, G. & Roizen, R. (1970). Architectural determinants of student satisfaction in college residence halls. *Environment design and research association*, 2:28–44.

Day, L.L. (2000). Choosing a house: The relationship between dwelling type, perception of privacy and residential satisfaction. *Journal of planning education and research*, 19:265–275.

DHS (2015). History of the department. Available from: www.dhs.gov.za/content/depart ment-human-settlements-history (accessed 13 August 2015).

Diaz-Serrano, L. (2006). Housing satisfaction, homeownership and housing mobility: A panel data analysis for twelve EU countries (September 2006). IZA Discussion Paper No. 2318. Available at SSRN: https://ssrn.com/abstract=936331 (accessed 24 April 2018).

Djebuarni, R. & Al-Abed, A. (2000). Satisfaction level with neighbourhood in low-income public housing in Yemen. *Property management*, 18(4):230–242.

Francescato, G. (2002). Residential satisfaction research: The case for and against. In J.I. Aragones, G. Francescato & T. Garling (eds) *Evaluating residential environments: Choice, satisfaction and behaviour*. London: Bergin and Garvey.

Francescato, G., Weidemann, S. & Anderson, J.R. (1987). Residential satisfaction: Its uses and limitations in housing research. In W.V. Vliet, H. Choldin, W. Michelson & P. Popene (eds) *Housing and neighbourhood: Theoretical and empirical contributions*. Westport, CT: Greenwood Press, pp. 43–57.

Francescato, G., Weidemann, S. & Anderson, J.R. (1989). *Evaluating the built environment from the users' point of view: An attitudinal model of residential satisfaction*. New York: Plenum Press.

Francescato, G., Weidemann, S., Anderson, J.R., et al. (1979). *Satisfaction in HUD-assisted housing: Design and management*. Washington, DC: US Department of Housing and Urban Development.

Galster, G.C. (1987). Identifying the correlates of dwelling satisfaction: An empirical critique. *Environment and behavior*, 19(5): 539–568.

Galster, G.C. & Hesser, G.W. (1981). Residential satisfaction: An empirical critique. *Environment and behavior*, 13(6): 735–758.

Gifford, R. (1997). Environmental psychology: Principles and practices. Boston: Allyn and Bacon.

Hourihan, K. (1984). Context-dependent models of residential satisfaction: An analysis of housing groups in Cork, Ireland. *Environment and behavior*, 16:369–393.

Husna, S. & Nurijan, Y. (1987). Housing provision and satisfaction of low-income households in Kuala Lumpur. *Habitat international*, 11(4):27–38.

Jenkins, P. (1999). Difficulties encountered in community involvement in delivery under the new South African housing policy. *Habitat international*, 23(4):431–446.

Kahana, E., Lovegreen, L., Kahana, B. & Kahana, M. (2003). Person, environment, and person–environment as an infuences on residential satisfaction of elders. *Environment and behavior*, 35: 434–453.

Kaya, N. & Erkip, F. (2001). Satisfaction in a dormitory building: The effects of poor height on the perception of room size and crowding. *Environment and behavior*, 33:35–53.

Kleinhans, R. (2007). Does social capital affect residents' propensity to move from restructured neighbourhoods? ENHR 2007 International Conference on Sustainable Urban Areas. Holland, W05 – Poverty neighbourhoods.

Lu, M. (1999). Determinants of residential satisfaction: Ordered logit vs. regression models. *Growth and change*, 30(Spring):264–287.

McCray, J.W. & Day, S.S. (1977). Housing values, aspirations, and satisfactions as indicators of housing needs. *Home economics research journal*, 5:244–254.

Mandler, G. (1984). *Mind and body: Psychology of emotion and stress*. New York: Norton.

Marans, R. & Rodgers, S. (1975). *Toward an understanding of community satisfaction*. New York: Halstead Press.

Möller, V. & Saris, W. (2001). The relationship between subjective well-being and domain satisfactions in South Africa. *Social indicators research*, 55(1):97–114.

Morris, E.W. & Jakubczak, M. (1988). Tenure-structure deficit, housing satisfaction and the propensity to move: A replication of the housing adjustment model. *Housing and society*, 15(1):41–55.

Morris, E.W. & Winter, M. (1975). A theory of family housing adjustment. *Journal of marriage and the family*, 37: 79–88.

Morris, E.W. & Winter, M. (1978). *Housing, family and society*. New York: John Wiley and Sons.

Morris, E.W., Crull, S.R. & Winter, M. (1976). Housing norms, housing satisfaction and the propensity to move. *Journal of marriage and family*, 38(2):309–320.

Nathan, V. (1995). Residents' satisfaction with the sites and services approach in affordable housing. *Housing and society*, 22(3):53–78.

Ogu, V.I. (2002). Urban residential satisfaction and the planning implications in a developing world context: The example of Benin City, Nigeria. *International planning studies*, 7(1):37–53.

Onibokun, A.G. (1974). Evaluating consumers' satisfaction with housing: An application of a system approach. *Journal of American institute of planners*, 40(3):189–200.

Oseland, N.A. (1990). An evaluation of space in new homes. Proceedings of the IAPS Conference Ankara, Turkey, pp. 322–331.

Paris, E. & Kangari, R. (2006). Multifamily affordable housing: Residential satisfaction. *Journal of performance of constructed facilities*, 19(2):138–145.

Peck, C. & Stewart, K.K. (1985). Satisfaction with housing and the quality of life. *Family and consumer sciences research journal*, 13: 363–372.

Rent, G.S. & Rent, C.S. (1978). Factors related to residential satisfaction. *Environment and behavior*, 10:459–488.

Republic of South Africa (1994). *White paper on housing: A new housing policy and strategy for South Africa*. Pretoria: Government Printer.

Ria, V.W. & Bontle, M. (2004). *A post-occupancy evaluation of the hope city housing complex of the Greater Middelburg housing association*. Mpumalanga: University of Stellenbosch.

Robin, R., Brian, O. & Kingstone, M. (2007). Measuring quality of life in informal settlements in South Africa. *Social indicators research*, 81:375–388.

Rory, C., Maarten, V.H. & Peteke, F. (2010). *A longitudinal analysis of moving desires, expectations and actual moving behaviour*. Bonn: Forschungsinstitut zur Zukunft der Arbeit/ Institute for the Study of Labor.

Satsangi, M. & Kearns, A. (1992). The use and interpretation of tenant satisfaction surveys in British social housing. *Environment and planning*, 10(4):317–331.

Speare, A. (1974). Residential satisfaction as an intervening variable in residential mobility. *Demography*, 11:173–188.

Spencer, C. & Barneji, N. (1985). Strategies for sharing student accommodation: A comparison of male and female student responses to single and shared rooms. *Architecture and behaviour*, 2:123–135.

Turkoglu, H.D. (1997). Residents' satisfaction of housing environments: The case of Istanbul, Turkey. *Landscape and urban planning*, 39:55–67.

United Nations Centre for Human Settlements (2000). *Homelessness: A proposal for global definition and classification*. Nairobi: United Nations.

Weidemann, S. & Anderson, J.R.A. (1985). A conceptual framework for residential satisfaction. In I. Atman & R. Werner (eds) *Home environments*. London: Plenum Press, pp. 154–182.

Westaway, M.S. (2006). A longitudinal investigation of satisfaction with personal and environmental quality of life in an informal South Africa housing settlement, Doornkop, Soweto. *Habitat international*, 30:175–189.

Yiping, F. (2005). Residential satisfaction conceptual framework revisited – A study on redeveloped neighbourhood in inner-city Beijing. University of Colorado at Denver. An unpublished doctoral dissertation.

Yong, R.R. (2008). Housing satisfaction perceived by the residents of Projek Perumahan Rakyat (PPR) Sungai Bonus in Setapak, Kuala Lumpur. Kulliyyah of Architecture and Environmental Design International Islamic University Malaysia. An unpublished Master's dissertation.

Part II

Housing theories and policy development

Part II of this book presents a detailed understanding of housing theories and policy development. This part contains two chapters. Chapter 2 is devoted to a detailed discussion on the study of housing; while Chapter 3 explores the evolution of housing policy over time.

2 Theoretical perspectives of housing studies research

Introduction

An understanding of housing theory is imperative because it can be claimed that discussions of policy formulation and evaluation will be deprived of direction and reason unless there is a clear understanding of a solid theoretical basis. However, an understanding of the concept of housing practice and the nature of housing is needed in order to generate a useful housing theory. Therefore, this chapter presents an overview of housing research, housing theoretical frameworks and the most influential perspectives on housing, followed by a discussion on the methodological approaches to housing studies.

Housing research theory

Literature on housing has developed since the mid-1960s, and many housing or social scholars write from a position of commitment to a specific theoretical framework, be it neoclassicalism, institutionalism or neo-Marxism, among others. However, questions are raised questions as to whether the concept of housing in its essential nature can precisely fit into any single theoretical framework. Housing is a difficult thing to hypothesize about. This is because it is an inherently multifaceted commodity, with 'spatial fixity' a defining characteristic, and asset, investment and consumption dimensions to account for (Pugh, 1986; Sullivan & Gibb, 2006; Lux, 2003). The economics of housing remain a challenge to those who seek equity and efficiency improvements for today's society. Housing is not a simple category that can be viewed from a single perspective. On the one hand, housing is one of the basic human needs and the right to adequate housing has been classified as a basic social human right in most developed countries around the world, with most of the developing countries currently enshrining it into their constitutions. On the other hand, housing constitutes a special type of private property, traded on the market. Trade-offs between the social and economic aspects of housing may have to be made sometimes and these attempt to search for a consensus that assures both the effective functioning of the housing system as well as adequate housing for all social groups within a society (Lux, 2003). Furthermore, housing is also a field of inquiry; thinking in 'theory time' is a poor substitute for recognizing the role of real, non-abstract, historical time (Robinson, 1979). Moreover, conceptualizing from the spatial aspects of housing speaks of Maclennan (1982) informing us that it is a curious form of 'pointless economics'. Good theory, according to Maclennan, essentially involves jettisoning many of the assumptions usually made in neoclassical economics, which the work more difficult and 'messy'.

Further, housing is a multidisciplinary field, hence housing research draws on a number of disciplines and professions, including economics, geography, political science, planning and architecture, among others (van Vliet, 1998). Respective disciplines and professions tend to concentrate on a particular set of questions when studying housing and its formation. For example, economists, one the one hand, are inclined to concern themselves with issues of housing finance, dynamics of supply and demand, and house prices. Geographers, on the other hand, often explore spatial aspects of housing, together with the patterns of residential segregation and urban form, local and regional housing markets, urban regeneration and gentrification, and residential mobility. Likewise, architects usually focus on aspects of design, building materials and construction techniques. This emphasis of attention is neither mutually exclusive nor exhaustive. An inclination is shown within disciplines to employ certain types of questions according to the theories that characterize those disciplines more generally.

However, it should be noted that, most times, disciplinary labels apply to paradigms rather than to individuals. This is because the researchers may have been formally appointed in a certain discipline but their scholarly work may draw on conceptualizations or approaches originating from or dominating another discipline. A defining characteristic of a discipline is that it concerns itself with a diverse array of topics from a demarcated paradigm that helps specify the questions asked and that guides research design, choice of data collection methods and explanatory theory (van Vliet, 1998). In contrast, a field of study comprises a fairly clearly delineated subject matter, such as housing, but draws on the contributions from a wide range of disciplines. Hence, the next section of the book explains the various theoretical perspectives of housing studies as they have been conceptualized over time.

Theoretical perspectives of housing study

The theory of housing has its origin in the 'Paleolithic' period when *Homo sapiens* began to use natural materials such as stone, wood, leaves, animal skin and other similar items to create shelter from elements of weather (Ifesanya, 2003). Housing has been defined by different scholars in different ways depending on the emphasis and focus of analysis. However, the basic definition has been: housing as shelter, which is the provision of a basic human need (Sharipah, 2007). The initial form of housing was the post and beam construction of the Stone Age, when the principal and perhaps the only motivating factor for housing was fortification from external aggression and from climatic elements such as sun, rain, heat, cold and other extreme weather conditions (Ifesanya, 2003). This, nonetheless, cannot be referred to as housing, but ordinary shelter. The United Nations in 1978, however, defined housing not simply as a shelter, but also as a means of creating communities, placing great emphasis on the functions that housing performs, thus making housing a multi-dimensional concept.

As described above, housing in today's expression has become a multi-dimensional bundle of services, encompassing the need for privacy, aesthetic value, conformity to statutory standards, fiscal economy and other related issues of importance in contemporary society (Ifesanya, 2003). Housing must not be misunderstood or narrowed to describe a single unit of dwelling. The house is only a constituent part of housing, and its functionality and quality are determined by the surroundings, that is, the environment (Randava, 1979). Housing can also be a process of providing a large number of residential buildings on a permanent basis with adequate physical infrastructure and social services, planned decent, safe and sanitary neighbourhoods to meet the basic needs of the people. This fundamental perception of housing has since given way to an all-inclusive definition. Adequate housing offers a refuge for emotional and physical rest, and the stability found therein empowers families in their pursuit of a better quality of life. The importance of a decent place to live cannot be overstated, for with it comes stability and promise, family unity, hope and a foundation from which individuals reach their full potential. Adequate housing enhances healthy living and academic accomplishment (Hodgson, 1988, 1997, 1998); while emotional stability and psychological balance are constructed by having a decent and comfortable place to live.

Housing is one of the most important elements in our lives and community. It is both a shelter and a link to the neighbourhood and larger community. It likewise refers to both the physical product and the process of its attainment. Housing is mostly perceived according to its performance, and its usefulness varies with the level of comfort and hygiene it provides. The significance of people in housing is recognized not when housing complies with municipality or city by-laws, but when people come to live in it and it is acceptable to the community, which is a primary reason for writing this book. Housing also means privacy and is an expression of ways of life, aspirations and social relationships. In a nutshell, housing is the provision of comfortable shelter with available infrastructure, services and facilities that address the need of the occupants (Dwijendra, 2007). Furthermore, Li (2002) also defined housing as:

- a heterogeneous, durable and essential consumer good;
- an indirect indicator of status and income differences between consumers;
- a map of social relations within the city;
- an important facet of residential structure;
- a source of bargaining and conflict between various power groupings; and
- a source of profit to different institutions and agents involved in the production, consumption and exchange of housing.

Hence, these diverse classifications make the study of housing a complex issue open to various interpretations. Li (2002) thus classified these various perspectives as follows:

- political perspective;
- social perspective;
- developmental perspective;
- institutional perspective;
- radical perspective;
- comparative approach;
- historical approach;
- experiential perspective; and
- neoclassical perspective.

While this classification of housing gives a valid view, it would have been an all-inclusive view if the economic perspective was included as a separate entity, thus developing a framework that would have disentangled the multi-dimensional concept attached to housing. However, the diversity of approaches to the study of housing is partly a manifestation of the multifaceted nature of the topic. It should be noted that other renowned theoretical positions such as that of Mancur Olson's 1965 theory on collective choice and special group interest is also capable of explaining some important aspects and individual behaviour within a given housing system. The next section of this chapter provides a detailed overview of the three most influential approaches to the study of housing: the neoclassical, the institutional and the neo-Marxist (the radical) perspectives, with the discussion of two new separate views, the economic and social perspectives. The introduction of the economic perspective broadens the multi-dimensional concept attached to housing.

Neoclassical perspective

The neoclassical perspective on housing draws its theoretical guidance from neoclassical economics. Neoclassical economics describes a distinct and relatively homogeneous school of thought in economic theory that became prominent in the late nineteenth century and that now dominates mainstream economics. The term was first introduced by Thorstein Veblen in 1900 to describe developments in the discipline (of which Veblen did not entirely approve) associated with the work of social thinkers such as William Jevons, Carl Menger and Leon Walras. Neoclassical economics relies on subjective preferences for determining prices in order to escape from the so-called objective value theory of classical economics, according to which the value of goods could be established by reference to some basic commodity or the labour input required to produce such goods (Brennan & Moehler, 2010). However, it is largely concerned with the analysis of utility maximization on the part of individual consumers in an atomistic housing market (Li, 2002). Put at its simplest, neoclassical economics views society as collection of individuals whose nature is assumed to be given. The realization of individual preferences shapes the form of the economy and the nature of the society.

In the scholarship of economies, neoclassical economics makes four suppositions. First, the creation of goods and services reveals the preferences of consumers. Next, it is assumed that all households and organizations have perfect information. Third, from this basis of perfect information, households get the most out of utility and organizations and maximize profits. Last, the creation of goods and services is assumed to be flexible in that the factors of production can easily be interchanged. It should be borne in mind that the theoretical roots of these suppositions are in 'methodological individualism', which is the methodological position that aims to explain all economic phenomena in terms of the characteristics and the behaviour of individuals. Because everything ultimately reduces to what individuals do, methodological individualism states that any theory of how the economy runs should be built up from an understanding of how the individuals within it behave. It is this classic idea that underpins this book, in that the issue of housing should be understood from the occupants' point of view, which is referred in this book as 'methodological occupancy'. The neoclassical perspective's commitment to methodological individualism means that neoclassical economics puts clear boundaries around what it is attempting to explain (since theories cannot explain everything).

The neoclassical perspective is considered the orthodox approach to cities and housing formation and development because of the suppositions in 'methodological individualism'. Since housing has 'externality' value, one can locate housing in this theoretical framework by relating it to the economic theory of externality and public goods. However, the central tenets of the neoclassical approach include equilibrium, individual utility maximization and the absence of severe information problems (Arrow & Hahn, 1971; Hodgson, 1988, 1997, 1998). The assumptions and overall importance of the equilibrium of conditions continue to provide the footings of many studies of urban structure and housing (Li, 2002). In this dimension, the adjustment model of residential location in the determination of micro house prices is worthy of attention. This model suggests an association between the consumption of housing space and travel costs. The general hypothesis is that households trade off travel costs (which increase away from the city centre), against housing costs (which are shown to decrease from the city centre) in an attempt to maximize utility subject to an overall budget constraint (Kain, 1962; Alonso, 1964; Muth, 1969; Mills, 1972). The relationships between transport costs, housing costs and income and other trade-offs are joined together in this framework to predict the relationship of individual households and those of different income groups within the city (Li, 2002). Mills' (1972) model of urban structure effectively predicts the decline of land values and population density from the city centre, both of which are found in most large cities of North-West Europe and North America. Thus, individuals will always trade-off one commodity for another, but only in situations where there is some exogenous change (McMaster & Watkins, 1999; Li, 2002). Thus in the neoclassical theory, the individual's behaviour is explained by concentrating on the changes in the constraints to which he or she is exposed while preferences are assumed to be constant.

Basically, neoclassical economists have a habit of using their theoretical framework to explore principles of effectiveness, incentive and maximization of utility or minimization of costs. But when it comes to housing they are drawn into social and public policy where they face considerable problems. The most general criticism about this approach is that the model fails to consider the structuring of household's housing decisions. This is because households do not make choices in a vacuum. The preferences households express and the constraints that they experience are influenced by the nature of the wider social structure and by the more immediate effects of the specific character of certain systems of housing production and allocation. Also, another criticism of the neoclassical approach is that optimization is not practicable (McMaster & Watkins, 1999). This criticism is based on the grounds that the optimization process itself is costly and requires cognitive abilities that are scarce (Arrow, 1962).

Also, there is a fundamental paradox in the determination of the demand for information; its value for the purchaser (user or beneficiary) is not known until after he or she has the information (Arrow, 1962), but then the receiver has, in effect, acquired it without cost; given incomplete appropriability, the potential buyer will base his or her decision to purchase information on less than optimal grounds. Arrow's (1962) central criticism recognizes that information is costly to obtain, and that its value is uncertain *ex ante*, so the utility-maximizing individual faces a considerable conundrum. Today, market-based economic studies in housing policy are conscious of the effects of wider social factors and tend to have varied relative merits in the context of balancing economic and social values.

Institutional perspective

Institution is a term that is often employed in varied field of studies, but not frequently defined. Hodgson (1998) quoted Walton Hamilton's 1932 definition of an institution as, 'a way of thought or action of some prevalence and permanence, which is embedded in the habits of a group or the custom of a people'. Hodgson (1998) further informs that this is a broad definition that includes not only organizations, such as universities and firms, but also 'integrated and systematic social entities', such as money, language, law and religion. Hence, institutions represent a co-ordination of belief that is durable, although not unchanging.

It has long been accepted, even among neoclassical economists, that institutions matter. However, the challenge initially was finding a way to integrate institutions into housing analysis. At present, there has been a serious debate concerning the position and viability of existing institutional arrangements, including nation states. This is because many institutions have become 'shell-like', and have become inadequate to the tasks they are called upon to perform

(Giddens, 2002). However, a common set of institutions can be found in most societies, including public and private enterprises, public utilities, financial establishments, educational institutions, trade unions and government/quasi-governmental agencies. The relative strength of these institutions can vary, and also the manner in which they interact. An institution consists, primarily, of informal constraints, formal rules and the enforcement characteristics of both (North, 1990). These rules are separate from the players, or organizations such as schools, firms, trade associations and government agencies, which are also called institutions. These clarifications provide a strong background to discourage the loose but common-sense use of institutions only as organizations but not as rules.

Institutional economists believe that evaluation of policy is socio-political and that public policies are necessarily expressed through institutional arrangements (North, 1990). Contrasting with the neoclassical approach that accentuates preferences and value of the individual, the institutional perspective tends to focus on groups and organizations. This is because the institution arrangement believes that members of a group interact with each other on a regular basis, which is the premise that public participation is based upon. This regularity encourages the formation of shared values and commonly accepted rules and norms – institutions (Li, 2002). Likewise, a group's capacity to pursue its members' common interests depends on its collective power, which in turn is a function of the amount of resources at the group's disposal – wealth, position in the government and society, and the size of the group. Thus, the institutional approach to housing offers an alternative to the positivist theories, which reify, idealize and isolate economic structures and individual behaviour (Guy & Henneberry, 2002).

One way of theorizing the institutional perspective into housing analysis is to define a housing system or structures of building provision (Ball, 1996). The latter identifies historically contingent networks of relations (structures) associated with the provision of particular types of buildings. These networks, Ball (1996) claimed, are historically contingent, implying the pattern of networks is shaped by history and is an empirical question. When viewed from this perspective, the analysis of institutional power and behaviour of interest groups is a major strand of research to be explored. However, Bassett and Short (1980), using Marxist analysis, provided an analytical framework of the power relations and interactions among the institutions involved in the UK's public housing system, which was categorized as an institutional approach to housing.

Housing policies in most Western countries are best perceived as the state providing corrective measures to the housing market (Bengtsson, 2001). This means that institutional contracts serve as the main mechanism for distributing housing, and state intervention takes the form of corrective measures defining the economic and institutional settings of those institutional contracts. The emphasis on institutional power and behaviour leads to the development of strategies to contain or defuse conflict. Institutionalists realize that public policy economics is necessarily within a context of political power, conflicts of interests and the wider social and historical impacts, which affect the way institutions are developed (Li, 2002). Housing would reside in the context of political economy. Moreover, institutional scholars see the scope of political economy as widening and becoming increasingly relevant. They also recognize that various devices can be used to bring cohesion, including markets and the state's social, political, and economic roles.

Unlike the neoclassicalists, the institutionalists do not feel uncomfortable working with the 'political' and they often draw upon useful neoclassical methods and empirical findings. Unlike the neo-Marxists, the institutionalists do not look for a 'final' solution where conflicts disappear after the demise of capitalism. Rather, they perceive a continuously evolving society with well-designed institutional arrangements offering only temporary and tentative solutions, knowing that as society changes, so it will become necessary to revise institutional arrangements. Sometimes neoclassical economists criticize the institutional approach for its free-ranging characteristics and remoteness from deductive and prognostic techniques and thinking (Li, 2002) leading the neo-Marxists to conclude that the institutional perspective scholars are dealing with symptoms and offering mere prescriptions of justice without attention to class conflicts and recurring internal contradictions in capitalism. Institutional scholars are still striving to develop and strengthen their paradigm based on the criticism laid upon them.

In his work on transaction costs, institutions and economic history, North (1984) attempted to integrate the useful features of neoclassical and neo-Marxist approaches, in which three basic assumptions were hypothesized: individualism; specifying and enforcing the rules that underlie contracts is costly; and ideology modifies maximizing behaviour. North (1990) later put forth an explanation of institutional and organizational change that is endogenous. The main points in the work are:

- agents: entrepreneur, the decision-makers in organizations;
- sources: opportunities perceived by entrepreneurs;
- process: overwhelmingly incremental; and
- direction: determined by path dependence.

The explanation of institutional change provides profound implications for citizens and policy-makers to enable them to evaluate the gains and losses of alternative policies in a more accurate way (North, 1993). In this interplay institutional dynamics are created, meaning that political institutions are not only periodically contested but also the object of ongoing skirmishes as actors try to achieve advantage by interpreting or redirecting institutions in pursuit of their own goals, or by subverting or circumventing rules that clash with their interests (Streeck & Thelen, 2005). In summary, housing policy in an institutional perspective is about the interaction between rules, rule-makers and rule-takers. Here the interaction concerns a specific attempt to change rules that guides 'quality, quantity, price and ownership and control of housing' with regards to adequate housing.

Neo-Marxist perspective

The neo-Marxist perspective draws its foundations from the thought of Karl Marx (1818–1883), the founder of the Marxist tradition of political economy. The perspective is centred on the analysis of the contradictions of capitalism with a view to replace it with socialism. However, the radical road to socialism, such as that taken by Lenin and Mao Zedong in China, has not endured. Capitalism as an economic and political system has proven to be more durable and flexible than Marx maintained. In the modern social system, for example, the advent of communism does not appear to be imminent and it can be concluded that old Marxist theories may be dead but these have since been transformed and reworked into neo-Marxism.

The 'guiding thread' of Marxist analysis is the economic structure, or the approach of production consisting of the factors (techniques) of production and the relations (ownership) of production (Li, 2002). The guiding principles of Marx (1977) are listed here:

- 'In social production of their existence, men inevitably enter into definite relations, which are independent of their will, namely relations of production appropriate to a given stage in the development of their material forces of production.'
- 'The totality of these relations of production constitutes the economic structure of society, the real foundation, on which arises a legal and political superstructure and to which correspond definite forms of social consciousness.'
- 'The mode of production of material life conditions the general process of social, political and intellectual life ... At a certain stage of development, the material productive forces of society come into conflict with the existing relations of production ... from forms of development of the productive forces these relations turn into their fetters.'
- 'Then begins an era of social revolution. The changes in the economic foundation lead sooner or later to the transformation of the whole immense superstructure.'

Since housing is one of the three basic necessities a person requires for a nominal standard of living, Karl Marx and other Marxist scholars debate that the state should embrace the social obligation of housing provision to the disadvantaged sections of the society (Chereni, 2010). Hence, the state is seen as the main driver of the processes of shelter provision. Until the early 1990s, this thinking has been the motivation behind housing policies in Asian socialist countries and in some African countries that shared the same ideologies.

Volume III of Marx's (1976) *Capital* paid considerable attention to land rent, but with much debate. Marx's categories of rent go beyond merely the Ricardian residual value arising from differences in the fertility of the soil, which he called Differential Rent I. He introduced Differential Rent II arising from differences in outputs by varying the capital intensity on the same plot of land although there is some dispute over the usefulness of this rent category (Ball, 1977). Marx did not write a lot on housing and what he wrote is not closely integrated into his broader theories of economic structure and social change. Nevertheless, Engels (1970) provided an early analysis of what he called 'the housing question'. Engels' work opposed the suggestion that home-ownership is the answer to the housing problem, insisting that mortgage debts will 'chain' workers to the spot and prevent them from looking for employment elsewhere. Thus, insisting that the housing problem was inseparable from the capitalist mode of production, it could only be solved by the elimination of that mode of production, the abolition of the big city and the ending of the separation of town and country.

The neo-Marxists' perspective views the delivery of housing as the role of the state and not of the private sector. Their core argument is that, should this role be vested in the private sector, this will result in the commodification of housing. This is because of the basic tenets of neo-Marxism that the poor are regarded as a necessity for the purpose of capital accumulation. The neo-Marxist believes that the commodification of housing will therefore lead to inequalities and exploitation of the poor by capitalists. Classic neo-Marxism has the advantage of viewing housing in the broader political economy. Neo-Marxist thought is focused on the role of the state in the process of capital accumulation, including its role in housing (Smith, 1996). This is viewed in a twofold manner, namely: to support capital accumulation and to maintain social stability (legitimation). The neo-Marxist concept is further based on the fact that the poor are vulnerable to exploitation in the capitalist mode of housing delivery. That is, if housing is provided with the primary aim of serving as a means of poverty alleviation, then the state must be the exclusive provider of housing. This, they believe, will lessen the manipulation of the poor by capitalists as the state will be able to own land and therefore the poor will be in a position to be accommodated within well-located land and in close proximity to services and opportunities (Smith, 1996; Manikela, 2008). The neo-Marxists' belief is that the problems experienced in housing provision are solely due to capitalism. They see capitalism as dividing societies in terms of economic classes and the poor remain the most vulnerable and exploited (Manikela, 2008). Neo-Marxists also stress that the housing problems cannot be answered while the capitalist system is still in existence; it must be removed. They are the popular critics of what is termed the 'capitalist system of urban planning'. They claim that the urban planning system exercised by most capitalist countries has only served the bourgeois interests. They view the urban planning system as a means to segregate spatial land uses into economic class antagonism. According to the Marxists, urban development is just a reflection of mode of production in order to gain more economic surplus.

Nevertheless, the over-concentration on economic relationships, considered by neo-Marxists to be the most important basic relationship in society, has led to a number of criticisms. The main weakness of the neo-Marxist perspective is that Marxian categories are difficult to test empirically and the theories tend to be general rather than specific to housing. In particular, Marxism is not a theory that can be tested and possibly falsified, mainly because it sees the replacement of capitalism by communism as 'historically inevitable' (Popper, 1974).

Economic perspective

The economic perspective considers housing as private property because it is not accessible in a non-competitive manner and does not have the same features as other public goods (Truett & Truett, 1987). However, housing economists notes that the following important differences between housing and standard market commodities exist:

- Housing is a very heterogeneous, multifaceted and multidimensional good. This is because individual houses, apartments or flats differ in floor space, design, age, quality, standard, furnishing, tenure, size, number of additional spaces, building location, quality of the environment and accessibility among others. Likewise, it is also very challenging to measure the unit of output and the demand for housing in general because the rate/rent paid for a small flat can be the same as for a large family house, even under conditions of optimal distribution and market equilibrium. The above expressions have necessitated housing economists to introduce a theoretical construct called housing service. Housing service theory states that in a state of equilibrium, the price per housing service unit will be the same in all types of dwelling units (Lux, 2003). Therefore, households or individuals demand housing service rather than housing on the market.
- Housing is a durable good and as such it becomes subject to both consumption and investment. There are two types of housing markets as informed by Fallis (1985). In one, the consumer good, housing service, is exchanged and the price per unit of housing service is determined. In the other, the investment good, housing stock, is exchanged and the price per unit of the housing stock is determined. However, housing consumption and investment motives may conflict. For instance, the consumer may desire to maximize utility but the investor chooses from all the options a housing unit with a maximum net present value of expected future returns.
- Also, housing is a spatially fixed good and cannot be moved from one location to another. To buy a dwelling means not only a particular dwelling but also to buy the socio-economic status of the neighbourhood and a level of accessibility to a place of employment.

Housing constitutes a significant share of household expenditure as well as total wealth. Scholars have found that the mean expenditure share for shelter (i.e. housing) is about 20%, household income, supplies and furniture accounts for about 6%, transport (including gas and maintenance) is 16%, food and apparel are 15% each, utilities, fuels and public services accounts for 7%, health care is 6%, and the rest is made up of education, entertainment and miscellaneous items (Chetty & Szeidl, 2004). Also, researchers have found that the value of the residential capital stock is larger than that for business capital and, usually, the annual market value of residential investment is larger than that for business capital investment (Greenwood & Hercowitz, 1991). Clearly, housing is not just 'another' consumption good. Significant fluctuations in housing development prices would imply significant fluctuations in wealth, which thus affect potentially significant household wealth. For instance, Morris and Heathcote (2003) find that the market value of the United States residential property stock alone is approximately equal to the annual average gross domestic product (GDP).

Also, housing is usually associated with the high transaction cost of a potential move, that is, the finding and furnishing of a new dwelling. Moving involves considerable expense, not only monetary expenditure but also invested time and emotions that do not relate directly to the acquisition of a new dwelling. The housing market adapts to changes in household income very slowly, compared to potential adaptations, if the transaction cost equals zero. Such cost may range between 5% and 10% of the total price of a house, particularly where movement entails both selling and purchasing costs (Maclennan, 1982). However, it is suggested that at the city level that sufficient housing supply, underpinned by new housing investments both from the government or developers, helps to support a vibrant urban system and contributes to urban competitiveness (Monk, Tang & Whiteheadat, 2010).

The economic perspective of housing claims that housing accrues benefits, such as employment creation from investing in housing. Hence, the opportunity cost of investing in housing as compared to investing in employment creation directly would need to be estimated by measuring the value of the benefits of each investment. In principle, a house is a house, and housing as an investment is no different from any other kind of investment. In reality, housing wealth can be converted into additional income, and as a result alleviate income poverty among home-owners, especially in later life. Studies have shown that being a home-owner effectively shielded older people from different forms of poverty as home-owners have a significantly lower risk of being income poor, of being deprived and of being cumulatively deprived (Dewilde & Raeymaeckers, 2008). However, the poverty-reducing effect of being a home-owner diminished significantly as the home-ownership rate increased, because, as more households own their own home, there are more low-income homeowners. It is also argued that people use the equity in their house as part of their pension, or at least reduce savings levels because of their investment in a house (Muellbauer & Murphy, 2008). But it should be noted that not investing in housing will tend to amplify market inequality and social exclusion. Also, the impact of housing on a family include the opportunity that living in better housing could lead to a better economic position of the household. For instance, a move to an area of expanding employment could enable family members to get better paid jobs or to at least get jobs (Monk, Tang & Whiteheadat, 2010). This is particularly likely for social tenants who previously may have lacked a permanent address, causing them difficulty in accessing basic services that others take for granted such as overdraft facilities or even bank accounts. Thus, the macro-economy and the housing market are indeed interrelated and co-determined.

In delivering healthy and attractive communities, housing can contribute to the development of a knowledge-based economy and plays a vital role in attracting and retaining the most talented and skilled members of the workforce who will be the catalysts of economic growth in the future (Glossop, 2008). A study by Bramley and Morgan (2003) in Central Scotland also confirmed the pivotal role of new house-building in supporting city competitiveness. It is argued that new housing increases the competitiveness of cities in three main ways:

- by ensuring an adequate and responsive supply of housing;
- by providing a high-quality living environment; and
- by promoting urban vitality.

Likewise, new housing is principally important for mobile workers, especially those with higher skills, partly because of its relatively easy purchase process (Bramley & Morgan, 2003). However, with the over-arching benefits that come with the economic perspective of housing, standard macroeconomics textbooks either treat housing as one of many consumption goods, or neglect it all together. Mainstream macroeconomics, simply put, ignores the housing market. Conventional housing economics and urban economics research, for its part, virtually ignores interactions with the macro-economy. At best, some of the theoretical and empirical analyses for urban and housing economics include macroeconomic variables (such as inflation, economic growth, GDP, the unemployment rate etc.) as exogenous 'control variables'.

Social perspective – the right 'to adequate housing'

As previously stated, housing is professed to be a basic social need of human beings and its standard greatly influences the standard of welfare of the whole society. Housing insecurity can have far-reaching consequences for the labour market, as well as for the political stability of a particular country. In view of the increased acceptance of the theory of the welfare state after the Second World War, the right to adequate housing has become one of the fundamental social rights in all economically developed and developing countries and the responsibility for housing has progressively transferred from the occupants and family to the government of states and public finances (Lux, 2003).

The right to housing is a social right, constituting the third element of human rights, with the others being political and civil rights, which form the tenet of the social perspective. The right to housing is a basic human right essential to the fulfilment of a decent life. The key norm of the right to housing is equal and non-discriminatory access with respect to race, creed and sex among others. In a country like South Africa, housing earns the particular 'attention' of the state and is included directly in the constitution. South Africa has defined the right to housing in great detail in its constitution. The South Africa constitution contains justifiable socio-economic rights and enshrines everyone's right to have access to adequate housing. In the Bill of Rights in Chapter 2 of the Constitution, Section 26 outlines the following:

> 26 (1) everyone has the right to have access to adequate housing. (2) The state must take reasonable legislative and other measures, within its available resources, to achieve the progressive realisation of this right. (3) No one may be evicted from their home, or have their home demolished, without an order of court made after considering all the relevant circumstances. No legislation may permit arbitrary evictions.

The right to housing as one of the human rights is also expressed in a number of international documents, the oldest being the Universal Declaration on Human Rights, which the United Nations General Assembly adopted in December 1948. Article 25(1) of this document states that '[e]veryone has the right to a standard of living adequate for the health and well-being of himself and of his family, including food, clothing, housing and medical care and necessary social services'. In Principle 4 of the Declaration on the Rights of the Child, adopted in November 1959, it is stated: 'the child shall have the right to adequate nutrition, housing, recreation and medical services'. Likewise, Part II, Article 10 of the Declaration on Social Progress and Development, adopted in December 1969, states that 'the basic freedoms can be attained also by provision for all, particularly persons in low income groups and large families, of adequate housing and community services'. Furthermore, Article 11 of the International Covenant on Economic, Social and Cultural Rights adopted in 1966 states: 'the State Parties to the present Covenant recognizes the right of everyone to an adequate standard of living for himself and his family, including adequate food, clothing and housing, and to the continuous improvement of living conditions'. To substantiate the recognition of the obligations under these international documents, the United Nations Council for Human Rights has worked out numerous recommendations, explanations and commentaries supporting the adoption of the documents.

The social perspective of housing is mostly accepted as the right to 'adequate housing', which is understood as ensuring affordable housing for the disadvantaged and endangered social groups such as seniors citizens, children, physically handicapped individuals and victims of natural and other disasters. This right is a general awareness and acceptance of a housing price level in the society at large that will ensure the fulfilment of basic needs in the field of housing (Lux, 2003), as well as the likelihood of obtaining social support in cases when the family cannot ensure this fulfilment by its own means and the availability of housing. The continuous efforts to guarantee the greatest possible degree of general and financial affordability of housing is especially important in relation to groups of the population with little social power, that is, those who cannot by themselves ensure adequate housing on the free housing market (Lux, 2003).

International human rights law and most national states' local legislature and constitutions recognize people's right to an adequate standard of living including adequate housing. Despite the central place of this right within the global legal system, well over one billion people are not adequately housed. Millions around the world live in life- or health-threatening conditions, in overcrowded slums and informal settlements, or in other conditions that do not uphold their human rights and dignity. While millions are forcibly evicted, or threatened with forced eviction, from their homes every year. The elements that constitute the human right to housing (see the Habitat International Coalition, a network of non-governmental organizations – NGOs) according to international treaty obligations and other commonly accepted norms include:

- security of tenure;
- public goods and services;
- environmental goods and services (water, considered an essential prerequisite to the right to housing);
- affordability;
- habitability;
- accessibility;
- location;
- cultural appropriateness;
- freedom from dispossession;
- information, capacity and capacity-building;
- participation and self-expression;
- resettlement;
- safe environment; and
- security and privacy.

Key aspects of the right to adequate housing

The United Nations Committee on Economic, Social and Cultural Rights stated that the right to adequate housing should not be construed narrowly. Rather, it should be seen as the right to live somewhere in security, peace and dignity. The characteristics of the right to adequate housing are clarified mainly in the Committee's general comments No. 4 (1991) on the right to adequate housing and No. 7 (1997) on forced evictions as detailed below.

The right to adequate housing contains freedoms

These freedoms include:

- protection against forced evictions and the arbitrary destruction and demolition of people's home;
- the right to be free from arbitrary interference with one's home, privacy and family; and

- the right to choose one's residence, to determine where to live and to freedom of movement.

The right to adequate housing contains entitlements

These entitlements include:

- security of tenure;
- housing, land and property restitution;
- equal and non-discriminatory access to adequate housing; and
- participation in housing-related decision-making at the national and community levels.

Protection against forced evictions

These protections include:

- an opportunity for genuine consultation;
- adequate and reasonable notice;
- availability of information on the proposed eviction in reasonable time;
- presence of government officials or their representatives during an eviction;
- proper identification of persons carrying out the eviction;
- prohibition on carrying out evictions in bad weather or at night;
- availability of legal remedies; and
- availability of legal aid to those in need to be able to seek judicial redress.

Common misconceptions about the right to adequate housing

While most governments of nations such as the South African government are heavily involved to some degree in housing construction, the right to adequate housing clearly does not oblige the government to do certain things that citizens can do for themselves, unless enshrined in the nation's constitution. However, the following demonstrate what the right to housing is not:

- The right to adequate housing does not require the state to build housing for the entire population.
- The right to adequate housing is not only a programmatic goal to be attained in the long term.
- The right to adequate housing does not prohibit development projects that could displace people.
- The right to adequate housing is not the same as the right to property.
- The right to adequate housing is not the same as the right to land.
- The right to adequate housing includes ensuring access to adequate services.

According to United Nations figures, one billion urban inhabitants live in inadequate housing, mostly in slums and squatter settlements in developing countries. As pointed out by many civil society organizations and experts, corporate globalization and its negative effects on the life of the poor have had the greatest contribution to the global challenge of adequately housing the poor.

Methodologies in housing studies

With regards to the growing interest in theoretical housing issues, there remains a strong propensity for housing scholars to incline themselves in their own empirical and policy issues, with almost complete disinterest in 'abstract' questions (Kemeny, 1992). This contemporary approach to housing studies was further illustrated by Marston (2002). Marston (2002) posited that where theory is used in contemporary housing research, it tends to be a mid-range version of political economy theory, for instance the concept of a 'housing system', competing definitions of housing need, or comparative and state-centred social policy. These concepts have an important place, particularly comparative studies that confront us with our own assumptions about what's 'natural'. However, very few empirical studies are explicit about the epistemological foundations or the theoretical frameworks that inevitably inform them.

A principal reason that this trend continues is that most housing scholars have tended to ignore the definitions of housing policy-makers. Housing scholars bend to this mind-set because 'policy problems' are taken to be objective facts, rather than contested realities (Saugeres, 1999; Wang, 2004). Within this mind-set, much of the focus of this type of housing research is theoretical empirical work focused on addressing policy problems defined by governments and their instrumentalities (Wang, 2004). Nevertheless, this mind-set does not mean that researchers leave an empty space for the theoretical basis of their research; in actual fact, the paradigm indicates that there is hidden theoretical evidence for these housing studies rarely to be challenged.

There are two major methods for planning the theoretical background in housing study. One stresses the similarities and the other emphasizes the differences. An example of a study on the different methods is the famous Esping-Andersen's (1990) welfare-state typology. In the book titled *The Three Worlds of Welfare Capitalism*, the capitalist world is characterized into three different types of welfare-system regime: the liberal, the corporate and the social-democratic. In the liberal welfare-state regime, the state constructs a safety net directed at the lowest-income population and it is carefully separated from the free market. This is a system currently practised in South Africa to house the lower income groups. The other system, the corporatist, does not consider the conceding of social rights harmful to the market mechanism. The corporatist system believes that rights are attached to class and status, as also claimed by the neo-Marxist scholars, but the philosophy background is against the Marxian school of thought. The neo-Marxist believes that the market mechanism controlled by the capitalist should not be the deciding factor for housing provision.

The socio-democratic system, rather than tolerate a dualism between state and market, between working class and middle class, pursues a welfare state that would promote an equality of the highest standards not an equality of minimal needs as was pursued elsewhere (Esping-Andersen, 1990). The advantage of the welfare-state approach is 'a safeguard against notions that housing systems will inevitably converge to a single type', which is far from the reality the global world has conceded to (Brandsen, 2001).

Likewise, a typical representative of the focus on the similarities is the neoclassical scholars who concentrate on the dynamics of the supply and demand of housing in a market mechanism, which most of the time brings about trade-offs. The supposition is based on the universality of the market mechanism and the identical behaviour of its participants. This has been criticized in various ways. The critiques mainly stress three different points in neoclassical economics theory, which are: the neglect of historical and geographical variations; the neglect of relationships other than economic ones; and the neglect of the active roles of the participants, which has been seen to be a more sustainable way of delivery development that affects the citizens of a particular state. The debate between these two groups forms the basis of the methodological background in housing studies. Hence, the next section of this chapter explores the two most dominant methodologies that have been discussed in varied ways: the positivist and social constructionist methodologies that have been adopted over time in housing studies.

Positivist methodology

Before social scientists and housing scholars shifted to the social constructionist approach in the 1990s, housing studies were dominated by positivist thinking. Positivist methodology brought the trend of paying little attention to theorization. The positivist methodology in the UK, for instance, was decisively influenced by Fabianism. Fabianism refers to a tendency in English thinking based on the technique of empirical research that emerged in the late nineteenth century, which is essentially non-revolutionary, pragmatic and rational, with a belief in government intervention and the perfectibility of the welfare state (Marshall, 1998; Jacobs & Manzi, 2000). This method emphasizes the scientific qualities of housing research by verifiable quantitative methods, which it thinks will convince the decision-makers. Consequently, this methodology has moulded the motivation and expectation attached to housing studies over time. For many housing scholars, their studies are carried out principally to improve policy practice, the expectation being that new research can apprise policy-makers in their efforts to resolve social problems. While the absence of an explicit theory remains a defining characteristic of mainstream housing research, it primarily relies upon a positivist epistemology (Jacobs & Manzi, 2000).

Positivist methodology was initiated from separate movements in nineteenth-century social science and early twentieth-century philosophy (Kincaid, 1998). Fundamental positivist ideas were that philosophy should be scientific; that metaphysical speculations are meaningless; that there is a universal and a priori scientific method; that the main function of philosophy is to analyse that method; that this basic scientific method is the same in both the natural and social sciences; that the various sciences should be reducible to physics; and that the theoretical parts of good science must be translatable into statements about observations (Kincaid, 1998). In housing research and the philosophy of housing studies, positivism has supported the emphasis on quantitative data and precisely formulated secondary theories. This belief was criticized on several grounds because: the theory/observation peculiarity is difficult to draw in any sharp way; efforts to translate theoretical terms into observational ones often presupposed theoretical terms in the course of describing the observational data (Kincaid, 1998). Also, theoretical terms can be applied in indefinite ways to observations, and even if the theory/observation distinction could be drawn, every scientific test involves background theoretical assumptions, thus showing that observational evidence has no absolute epistemic ontological status. The above criticisms have led to doubts about the positivist idea of a unified science because if theoretical terms cannot and need not be reduced to observational ones, then it seems implausible that the various sciences are reduced to physics or that they must then be a good science. These criticisms certainly undercut positivist doctrines in the social sciences. They have also led many to conclude, somewhat implausibly, that any standards of good social science are merely matters of rhetorical persuasion and social convention (Kincaid, 1998).

The duty of the housing researcher within this paradigm is one of discovering objective facts, presenting them in a descriptive format with the expectation that policy-makers will take notice and act accordingly. However, research within this pragmatic tradition achieves a level of complexity in its analysis of social phenomena, but the primary purposes are to establish facts and to recommend effective action once problems are acknowledged. Most housing studies have been quantitative and problem-solving oriented over time. In turn, the positivist methodology reinforces the ignorance of theorization in housing study, or, put another way, gives housing study the characteristic of being conservatively aligned to the policy of the regime it is serving. Not surprisingly, the conceptual categories used in housing research are seldom examined within this paradigm; instead they depend on the collection of material evidence to support policy recommendations. The resulting research product is often methodologically conservative (Wang, 2004). Besides, it is difficult to pursue new lines of research or, for that matter, to develop different conceptualizations of the policy process. Thus, the positivist methodology has had an impact on the approach used in housing research over time. Housing issue debates tend to be steered within an agenda dominated by two competing ideologies: either policy should be formulated to strengthen market mechanisms, or the role of the state should be extended (Jacobs & Manzi, 2000; Wang, 2004). This still remains the situation today. Because government funds are critical to housing research, housing studies are generally are conducted through the positivist methodology with a heavy reliance on quantitative survey and secondary data analysis, which is still being adopted in most studies today. Despite the criticism that has been levied on this methodology, most research on housing is based on a positivist approach either because of its roots in policy-sponsored work or in economic or psychological analysis.

Social constructionist methodology

Since the late 1990s, increasing attention has been given to the inadequacy of the positivist approach. This has necessitated the implementation of the social constructionist methodology in housing research. For instance, the re-emergence of research drawing upon social constructionist epistemology marks an attempt to enlarge the scope of housing studies (Jacobs & Manzi, 2000). Hence, more and more scholars have begun to make use of the methodological insights offered by explanations rooted in constructionism.

A constructionist epistemology proposes that an individual's experience is an active process of interpretation rather than a passive material apprehension of an external physical world (Jacobs & Manzi, 2000). Social constructionism is an amalgamation of different strands of work that have different emphasis, although they sometimes share the same fundamental assumptions. It is not a clear unified tradition of thought with an agreed research modus operandi (Clapham, 2009). In contrast, it is a dispersed field that draws on different traditions and in which there are many differences of approaches (Clapham, 2009). Social constructionism as an epistemology has its origin in a number of theoretical developments.

Jacobs and Manzi (2000) gave an in-depth account of the philosophical basis and development of social constructionist approach in housing studies, arguing that a major claim advanced by those adopting a social constructionist epistemology is that actors do not merely provide descriptions of events, but are themselves constituents of wider policy discourses and conflicts. Viewing society and social policy as malleable and subject to power struggles, constructionists do not accept social facts as permanently 'accomplished'. This emphasis on contestation is important in offsetting any tendency by actors to objectify social phenomena or reify abstractions into material realities. Social constructionism therefore offers an altogether different conception of reality from the one advanced by positivism, as well as a basis from which to understand the contexts and the processes of housing. An important goal of constructionist research is therefore to examine how certain issues become defined as 'problems' and to identify the collective strategies developed to confront these issues. Within a housing context, what becomes a 'problem' is, to a considerable extent, contingent on how interest groups compete with one another to gain acceptance of a particular definition, while rejecting others (Kemeny, 1984). In this respect, problems are constructed as policy-makers attempt to establish their policy agendas in response to changing economic and social conditions and in accordance with their own needs.

Though there are many aspects in social constructionism housing research, it has largely been confined to four areas, the most popular being what is termed the 'social construction of social problems'. The emphasis on the 'social construction of social problems' is trying to understand different definitions of social problems such as homelessness by using investigative policy histories. The problems are perceived not to have 'objective' foundations, but are constructed on the shifting sands of public rhetoric, coalition building, interest-group lobbying and political expediency (Jacobs, Kemeny & Manzi, 2004). The strength of the method is in its probing of existing ways of thinking in policy (Clapham, 2009). One can infer that it opens the eyes of policy-makers to query existing assumptions of policy.

The second area of social constructionist housing research is focused on interaction, but is far less advanced than the social problems construct. For example, the work on the social construction of housing management (Clapham, Franklin & Saugeres, 2000) has taken an explicitly 'interactionist' stance. Also, what is being socially constructed through interaction is a relationship and an occupational role, which is a variant of the social problems tradition. Most times, it is not a social problem that is being purported but a small part of social reality as constructed through interaction between individuals in different positions in social space. In this way, the analysis is uniquely social constructionist in a way that other research as epitomized in discourse analysis may not be (Clapham, 2009). The symbolic interactionist component of social constructionism places prominence on discovery of the life-worlds of individuals and groups and describing the world as they see and experience (Clapham, 2009).

The third area of social constructionist housing research methodology is in international comparative research. The focus of this is on how and why social problems are defined differently in different countries. This approach has led to a questioning of theories of national housing policy that have laid emphasis on the convergence of policy and instead suggested a notion of continuing separation (Kemeny & Lowe, 1998). There is the general notion of culture, that countries should retain an individual housing structure that is in agreement with the country's political structure and in particular the type of welfare policy pursued by the country. This approach builds on the philosophies of the three worlds of welfare (Esping-Andersen, 1990). Most housing research has sought to place housing within this framework and to map the relationships between housing and other elements of the welfare state. A social constructionist approach to international comparative housing research can abate the 'ethnocentrism inherent in much research of this kind' (Haworth, Manzi & Kemeny, 2004).

The fourth type of social constructionist research has been in developing an all-inclusive view of the housing field. Despite this area being part of the methodology, most social constructionist housing research has been focused on specific research topics rather than trying to describe a social constructionist view of the housing field and its relationships to other fields.

There are many general criticisms of social constructionism reflecting the many other sociological approaches. A common criticism of social constructionism is its relativism. Relativism is a fundamental contradiction at the heart of the social constructionist approach; if all discourse is socially constructed and there is no such thing as objective truth then social constructionism itself is only one discourse among many and cannot claim superiority over any other approach (King, 2004). Another criticism is that humans only achieve their humanity through social interaction. Social constructionism sees individual subjects as empty vessels filled up through discourse. However, it should be noted that in research associated with the meaning of home, there has been an understanding of the importance of emotions in influencing the relationship between people and their physical environment. Though people may have a strong emotional relationship with home, their relationship to the physical fabric of the house is mediated through their physical characteristics. Hence, without an understanding of the influence of embodiment on meaning, social constructionism can offer only partial explanations. Clearly, the importance of the social constructionist methodology is that it moves forward to challenge the 'given' context of previous housing studies, and tries to bring forward alternative understandings to the question. Therefore, a housing study is no longer providing answers to given questions, but should challenge and redefine the given question.

Summary

This chapter has outlined a number of issues upon which housing research studies should rest. Housing by its nature is multifaceted as observed from the literature. It consumes natural resources and produces impact on the natural environment. It constitutes a major economic activity and impacts on the general economy. It is an important component of social development and quality of life. It is often used by government to achieve political and economic ends. It is also a cultural attribute, manifesting the aesthetic value and the way of life for human beings in their particular settings. Thus, a holistic perspective of housing studies is therefore needed if we wish to chart the future of housing development although housing research has tended not to engage with the theoretical debates about methods and focus. Rather, research has either been based on a general shared assumption or on one particular approach. The most important point to stress in conclusion is that the central objective of housing policy must be the stimulation of environments that give dignity to people's lives. It is not simply the provision of shelter.

Housing is a difficult thing to hypothesize about. This is because it is an inherently multifaceted commodity, with 'spatial fixity' a defining characteristic, and asset, investment and consumption dimensions to account for. The economics of housing remain a challenge to those who seek equity and efficiency improvements for society to this day. Housing is not a simple category that can be viewed from a single perspective; hence, various theoretical perspectives of housing studies were discussed in this chapter in order to provide a background to how housing is viewed across all walks of life. A major tenet of the chapter was the discussion of the right to adequate housing, which has its foundations in global treaties and national constitutions that seek to adequately house the poor and the needy in a basic standard of housing. Owing to the varying understandings of adequate housing, the chapter further explained what adequate housing is not and the various aspects of the right to housing. The methodological dimensions of housing studies were also discussed in this chapter. This section of the chapter explained the important studies, particularly comparative ones, that confront us with our own assumptions about what's 'natural' when studying housing and, as such, the positivist and social constructionist methodology should be considered.

The purpose of this chapter was to provide an understanding of housing theories and methodologies. This is imperative because the discussions of policy formulation and evaluation will be deprived of direction and reason, unless there is an understanding of a clear theoretical basis. However, an understanding of the concept of housing practice and the nature of housing is needed in order to generate a useful housing theory.

References

Alonso, W. (1964). *Location and land use*. Cambridge, MA: Harvard University Press.

Arrow, K.J. (1962). *Economic welfare and the allocation of resources for invention in the rate and direction of inventive activity: Economic and social factors*. National Bureau of Economic Research. Priceton, NJ: Princeton University Press.

Arrow, K.J. & Hahn, F.H. (1971). *General competitive analysis*. Edinburgh: Oliver & Boyd.

Ball, M. (1977). Differential rent and the role of landed property. *International journal of urban and regional research*, 3(3):380–402.

Ball, M. (1996). *Housing and construction: A troubled relationship*. Bristol: Policy Press.

Bassett, K. and Short, J. (1980). *Housing and residential structure: Alternative approaches*. London: Routledge and Kegan Paul.

Bengtsson, B. (2001). Housing as a social right: Implications for welfare state theory. *Scandinavian political studies*, 24(4):255–275.

Bramley, G. & Morgan, J. (2003). Building competitiveness and cohesion: The role of new housebuilding in central Scotland's cities. *Housing studies*, 13(4):447–471.

Brandsen, T. (2001). Bring actors back in: Towards an institutional perspective. *Housing, theory and society*, 18:2–14.

Brennan, G. & Moehler, M. (2010). Neoclassical economics. Available from: http://moehler.org/publications/ (accessed 24 June 2015).

Chereni, S. (2010). Dynamics of housing land allocation in Bulawayo: Implications for low-cost housing. Available from: www.urbanlandmark.org.za/conference/2010_abstracts/abstract_chereni.pdf (accessed 20 May 2015).

Chetty, R. & Szeidl, A. (2004). Consumption commitments and asset prices. Paper presented at the 2004 SED Meeting. Harvard University Working Paper.

Clapham, D. (2009). Social Constructionism and Beyond in Housing Research. Paper for ISA Housing Conference Glasgow.

Clapham, D., Franklin, B. & Saugeres, L. (2000). Housing management: the social construction of an occupational role. *Housing theory and society*, 17(2):68–82.

Dewilde, C. & Raeymaeckers, P. (2008). The trade-off between home-ownership and pensions: Individual and institutional determinants of old-age poverty. *Ageing and society*, 28(6):805–830.

Dwijendra, N.K. (2007). Quality of low cost housing settlement project. Bali, Indonesia: Architecture Department, Faculty of Engineering, Udayana University.

Engels, F. (1970). *On the housing question*. Moscow: Progress Publishers.

Esping-Andersen, G. (1990). *The three worlds of welfare capitalism*. Cambridge: Polity Press.

Fallis, G. (1985). *Housing economics*. Toronto: Butterworths.

Giddens, A. (2002). *Runaway world: How globalization is reshaping our lives*. London: Profile Books.

Glossop, C. (2008). *Housing and economic development: Moving forward together*. London: Centre for Research and Market Intelligence, Housing Corporation.

Greenwood, J. & Hercowitz, Z. (1991). The allocation of capital and time over the business cycle. *Journal of political economy*, 99:1188–1214.

Guy, S. & Henneberry, J. (2002). *Developers and development: Perspectives on property*. Oxford: Blackwell Sciences/RICS Foundation.

Haworth, A., Manzi, A. & Kemeny, J. (2004). Social constructionism and international comparative housing research. In Keith Jacobs, Jim Kemeny and Tony Manzi (eds) *Social constructionism in housing research*. Aldershot: Ashgate, pp. 159–185.

Hodgson, G.M. (1988). *Economics and institutions: A manifesto for a modern institutional economics*. Cambridge: Polity Press.

Hodgson, G.M. (1997). The ubiquity of habits and rules. *Cambridge journal of economics*, 21:663–684.

Hodgson, G.M. (1998). The approach of institutional economics. *Journal of economic literature*, 36:166–192.

Ifesanya, O. (2003). Developing affordable housing delivery in Nigeria. Ado-Ekiti, Nigeria: Department of Quantity Surveying School of Environmental Studies Federal Polytechnic.

Jacobs, K. & Manzi, T. (2000). Evaluating the social constructionist paradigm in housing research. *Housing, theory and society*, 17(1):1735–1742.

Jacobs, K., Kemeny, J. & Manzi, M. (2004). *Social constructionism in housing research*. Aldershot: Ashgate.

Kain, J.F. (1962). The journey to work as a determinant of residential location. Papers and proceedings, Regional Science Association, pp. 137–160.

Kemeny, J. (1984). The social construction of housing facts. *Scandinavian housing and planning research*, 1:149–164.

Kemeny, J. (1992). *Housing and social theory*. London: Routledge.

Kemeny, J. & Lowe, S. (1998). Schools of comparative housing research: From convergence to divergence. *Housing studies*, 13(2):161–196.

Kincaid, H. (1998). *Positivism in the social sciences: Routledge encyclopedia of philosophy*. London: Routledge.

King, P. (2004). Relativism, subjectivity and the self: A critique of social constructionism. In K. Jacobs, J. Kemeny and T. Manzi (eds) *Social constructionism in housing research*. Aldershot: Ashgate, pp. 32–48.

Li, Z. (2002). *Development and contradictions of Wuhan's public housing system*. Singapore: National University of Singapore.

Lux, M. (2003). *Housing policy: An end or a new beginning?* Budapest: Open Society Institute.

Maclennan, D. (1982). *Housing economics: An applied approach*. New York: London: Longmans.

McMaster, R. & Watkins, C. (1999). The economics of housing: The need for a new approach. PRRES/AsRES/IRES conference, Kuala Lumpur, 26–30 January.

Manikela, S.J. (2008). *Understanding the peripheralisation of low-income housing delivery in the Mbombela Local Municipality in Faculty of Engineering and the Built Environment*. Johannesburg, South Africa: University of the Witswatersrand.

Marshall, G. (1998). *A dictionary of sociology*, 2nd edn. Oxford: Oxford University Press.

Marston, G. (2002). Critical discourse analysis and policy-oriented housing research. *Housing, theory and society*, 19:82–91.

Marx, K. (1976). *Capital*. New York: International Publishers.

Marx, K. (1977). *A contribution to the critique of political economy*. Moscow: Progress Publishers.

Mills, E.S. (1972). *Studies in the structure of the urban economy*. Baltimore: Johns Hopkins Press.

Monk, S., Tang, C. & Whiteheadat, C. (2010). What does the literature tell us about the social and economic impact of housing? Available from: www.scotland.gov.uk/socialresearch (accessed 21 April 2016).

Morris, D. & Heathcote, J. (2003). Housing and the business cycle. Available from: www.federalreserve.gov/pubs/feds/2004/200411/200411pap.pdf (accessed 11 May 2014).

Muellbauer, J. & Murphy, A. (2008). Housing markets and the economy: The assessment. *Oxford review of economic policy*, 24(1):1–33.

Muth, R.F. (1969). *Cities and housing*. Chicago: University Press.

North, D.C. (1984). Transaction costs, institutions, and economic history. *Journal of institutional and theoretical economics*, 1:407–417.

North, D.C. (1990). *Institutions, institutional change and economic performance*. New York: Cambridge University Press.

North, D.C. (1993). *Institutional change: A framework of analysis*. New York: Cambridge University Press.

Popper, K. (1974). *Replies to my critics: The philosophy of K. Popper*. La Salle, IL: Open Court.

Pugh, C. (1986). Housing theory and policy. *International journal of social economics*, 13 (4/5):3–104

Randava, H. (1979). *Origin of urban planning: Architectural handbook*. New York: McGraw Hill.

Robinson, R. (1979). *Housing economics and public policy*. Basingstoke: Macmillan.

Saugeres, L. (1999). The social construction of housing management discourse: Objectivity, rationality and everyday practice. *Housing, theory and society*, 16:93–105.

Sharipah, N. (2007). Quality affordable housing: A theoretical framework for planning and design of quality housing. *Journal of techni-social*, 2(1):1–10.

Smith, N. (1996). *The urban frontier: Gentrification and the revanchist city*. London and New York: Routledge.

Streeck, W. & Thelen, K. (eds) (2005). *Beyond continuity: Institutional change in advanced political economies*. Oxford: Oxford University Press.

Sullivan, T. & Gibb, K. (2006). *Housing economics and public policy*. Oxford: Blackwell Science Ltd.

Truett, L.J. & Truett, D.B. (1987). *Macroeconomics*. St Louis: Timer Mirror/Mosby College Publishing.

van Vliet, W. (1998). *The encyclopedia on housing*. London: Sage Publications.

Wang, L. (2004). A social perspective on the reformed urban housing provision system in China: Three cases in Beijing, Xi'an and Shenzhen. Trondheim: Norwegian University of Science and Technology.

3 Housing policy evolution and development

Introduction

Globally, housing policies have been used as an attempt to try and address housing problems, especially with respect to the low-income earners, with the view of helping them access better housing. The evolution of housing policy in developing countries has been studied and identified in different ways. Hence, this chapter presents an overview of housing policy development and evolution, followed by a discussion of the objectives and purpose of housing policy. Also explored in this chapter is the place of housing policy instruments in order to resolve housing issues in different national states.

What is housing policy?

A policy is a guiding principle used to set direction in an organization (Anderson, 2005). It can be a course of action to guide and influence decisions. Policies are used as a guide to decision-making under a given set of circumstances within the framework of objectives, goals and management philosophies as determined by management (Anderson, 2005). Likewise, policy may also refer to the process of making important organizational decisions, including the identification of different alternatives such as programmes or spending priorities, and choosing among them on the basis of the impact they will have. Also, a policy can be understood as political, management, financial and administrative mechanisms arranged to reach explicit goals (Jiboye, 2011). Furthermore, it is a plan of action, a statement of aim and ideas (Agbola & Alabi, 2000). There are two types of policies. The first consists of rules, frequently used as employee policies, formulated by the management of an organization guiding the conduct of all employees. The second is mini-mission statements, frequently associated with procedures, which is the category that housing policy falls into (wishful thinking and strategic intention) (Anderson, 2005). Policy is not usually used to denote what is actually done; this is normally referred to as either procedure or protocol. However, a policy will contain the 'what' and the 'why', while procedures or protocols contain the 'what', the 'how', the 'where' and the 'when'. Policies are generally adopted by the board of an entity of governance within an organization, a national state or an arm of the state to guide decision-making. Policies are thus well reasoned, carefully articulated presented documents (Olatubara, 2002).

Thus, a housing policy is a guideline provided by government through the negotiation of various bodies in a country as put together by the government, which is intended at meeting the housing need and demand of the people through a set of suitable approaches including fiscal, institutional, legal and regulatory frameworks (Agbola, 1998). Housing policies provide a guide that defines action and sets goals and, in most cases, specifies strategies for achieving the goals. It further institutes guidelines and limits for discretionary actions by individuals liable for implementing the overall plans of action. Other scholars define it as a system of courses of action, regulatory measures, laws and funding priorities concerning a given topic promulgated by a governmental entity or its representatives. Some housing policy decisions (written or implied) prompt the overall past work of government, while others are goal statements or prescriptions of elemental rules for the conduct of personal or organizational affairs (Duruzoechi, 1999). Housing policy is fundamentally necessary in any country as a guide or control on the various actors in the housing sector.

Furthermore, housing policy as a governmental action is generally the principled guide to housing action taken or to be taken by the administrative or executive branches of a state with regard to a class of issues in a manner consistent with law and institutional customs. In general, the foundation of any housing policy is the pertinent national and subnational constitutional law and implementing legislation. Housing policy is sometimes embodied in constitutions, legislative acts and judicial decisions (Schuster, 2008). The main goals of any housing policy is to achieve the best possible use of existing housing resources in order to ensure adequate housing for the people, guide the location of new housing and be responsive to the housing needs of 'special groups' such as the low-income earners.

Housing policies are typically legislated through official written documents and they often come with the endorsement or signature of the executive powers within the country or organization to legitimize the policy and show that it is considered enforced. Housing policies often have standard formats that are particular to the country or organization issuing the policy. While such formats differ in form, housing policy documents usually contain certain standard components including:

1 A purpose statement, outlining why the policy is being issued, and what the desired effect or outcome of the policy should be.
2 An applicability and scope statement, describing who the policy affects and which actions are impacted by the policy. The applicability and scope may expressly exclude certain people, organizations or actions from the policy requirements. Applicability and scope are used to focus the policy on only the desired targets, and avoid unintended consequences where possible.
3 An effective date that indicates when the policy comes into force. Retroactive policies are rare, but can be found.

4 A responsibilities section, indicating which parties and organizations are responsible for carrying out individual policy statements. Some policies may necessitate the formation of new institutions, functions or actions to effectively execute the goals.
5 Policy statements showing the specific regulations, requirements or modifications to organizational behaviour that the policy is creating. Policy statements are extremely diverse depending on the national state or organization and intent, and may take almost any form.
6 Background, indicating any reasons, history and intent that led to the creation of the policy, which may be listed as motivating factors. This information is often quite valuable when policies must be evaluated or used in a confusing situation.
7 Definitions, providing clear and unambiguous definitions for terms and concepts found in the policy document.

All housing policies usually have a cycle. A housing policy cycle is a system used for the evaluation of the development of a policy item. The policy cycle is also referred to as a 'stagist approach', 'stages heuristic' or 'stages approach'. It is thus a rule of thumb rather than the actual reality of how policies are created, but has been influential in how housing scholars looked at policy in general. This refers to models that bring some order and coherence to the policy-making process, continue to influence the practice of policy-making – at least as a process. It was developed as a theory from Harold Lasswell's work. A typical housing policy cycle includes the following stages:

- Agenda setting (problem identification) – The recognition of certain subject as a problem demanding further government attention.
- Policy formulation – Involves exploring a variation of options or alternative courses of action available for addressing the problem (appraisal, dialogue, formulation and consolidation).
- Adoption of the policy – Government decides on an ultimate course of action, whether to perpetuate the policy status quo or alter it (the decision could be 'positive', 'negative' or 'no-action').
- Implementation – The ultimate decision made earlier will be put into practice.
- Evaluation of the policy – Assesses the effectiveness of a public policy in terms of its perceived intentions and results. Policy actors attempt to determine whether the course of action is a success or failure by examining its impact and outcomes.

An eight-step policy cycle is developed in detail in *The Australian Policy Handbook* by Peter Bridgman and Glyn Davis (now with Catherine Althaus in its fourth and fifth editions):

- issue identification;
- policy analysis;

- consultation (which permeates the entire process);
- policy instrument development;
- building coordination and coalitions;
- program design: decision-making;
- policy implementation; and
- policy evaluation.

Policy cycles are usually considered as adopting a classical approach. Hence some postmodern academics challenge cyclical models as unresponsive and unrealistic, preferring systemic and more complex models (Young & Enrique, 2009). Young and Enrique (2009) consider a broader range of actors involved in the policy space that includes civil society organizations, the media, intellectuals, think tanks or policy research institutions, corporations and lobbyists, among others. Housing policy addresses the intent of the state or any organization, whether government, business, professional or voluntary. It is intended to affect the 'real' world, by guiding the decisions that are made. Whether they are formally written or not, most organizations and national states have identified and formulated policies in almost all relevant aspects of the economy such as the housing sector.

Evolution of housing policy framework

While there is no universally established definition of housing policy as observed from the previous section, there are, however, two established views of what housing policies need to be. These two viewpoints are the static and the dynamic views (Malpass & Murie, 1999). The first is associated with how things are done as a matter of routine, characterized by general rules and conventions governing practice. It reflects recognized positions on housing topics. This is very significant in many African countries, where there are no specific policy documents, although the practice has changed in some countries, yet there are entrenched practices in housing. The second, vigorous view of policy tends to be more prevalent where there is overt action to resolve a housing problem. This implies specific actions, relating to a problem defined in a specific way, in pursuit of some objectives. This view of policy involves change towards some end and also needs a policy process. The policy process includes: problem formulation, planning, execution and evaluation (Malpass & Murie, 1999). However, most of the housing policy formulated in African countries either end up not being implemented or when they are implemented, they are never evaluated.

Globally, housing policies have been used as an attempt to try and address housing problems, especially with respect to the low-income earners, with the view of helping them access better housing (Harris & Giles, 2003; Mukiibi, 2011). The evolution of housing policy in developing countries has been studied and identified in different ways. Scholars have identified the following as the definite timeframe in the evolution of housing policy (Harris & Giles, 2003):

- the period of public housing provision (1945–1960s);
- sites-and-services (1972–1980s); and
- market enabling (1980s–present).

This grouping is based on the policy recommendations from international agencies and focuses less on policies that nations pursued, as can be seen from the current adoption of the Cities Without Slums agenda and the Millennium Development Goals by developing countries (Harris & Giles, 2003). In each period, scholars have supposed that the policies adopted by national governments in the developing world matched the recommendations of international agencies. The assumption was based on meagre evidence and is challenged by the earlier statements made by informed observers. For instance, about 40 years ago the United Nations' Bureau of Social Affairs observed that several countries in Latin America had been providing public housing regardless of the United Nations' preference for self-help (Harris & Giles, 2003). However, established global organizations such as the United Nations and the World Bank, among others, began to influence the housing policy agenda of nations in the developing world after the Second World War. The most significant among these organizations were national agencies of the United States and United Kingdom, inclusive of the United Nations.

Housing policy framework for development planning has changed in important ways over the last six decades. According to UN-Habitat (2006), the initial planning concepts of the top-down strategies have gradually given way to market- and people-based solutions, process approaches and a strong emphasis is repeatedly being placed on building capacities and institutions through the policy. Thus, current housing policies of nations of the world have been influenced by these dynamics. Table 3.1 shows a summary of housing policy developments since the 1960s. The early focus of a housing policy framework was on physical planning and public housing, which quickly gave way, first to 'self-help' housing projects, which were used to service the middle-income households. This proved to be an unsustainable option over time to address the needs of the poor due to the high subsidies that were involved. This later evolved into the 'enabling approach', which concentrated on maximizing the contributions of all the stakeholders in housing production within a supportive legal and regulatory framework (Erguden, 2001; UN-Habitat, 2006).

However, in reality, the evolution of housing policy is never so neat or linear as this, and there are always instances in which agencies or governments seek to return to ways of doing things that have long been discredited. This is principally the case where there is political pressure to show quick results through, for instance, large-scale evictions of squatters or construction of public or subsidized private housing (UN-Habitat, 2006). For instance, the Botshabelo Accord of 1994 in South Africa, which sought support for the construction of one million housing units each year through the commercial private sector, is a good example. However, due to a lack of resources and neglect in policy to utilize rental housing alternatives, which could mobilize private capital, a mere

Table 3.1 The evolution of housing policy

Phase and approximate dates	*Focus of attention*	*Major instruments used*	*Key documents*
Modernization and urban growth: 1960s– early 1970s	Physical planning and production of shelter by public agencies	Blueprint planning: direct construction (apartment blocks, core houses); eradication of informal settlements	
Redistribution with growth/ basic needs: mid-1970s–mid-1980s	State support to self-help ownership on a project-by-project basis	Recognition of informal sector; squatter upgrading and sites-and-services; subsidies to land and housing	Vancouver Declaration (Habitat I. 1976); Shelter, Poverty and Basic Needs; World Bank evaluations of sites-and-services (1981–1983); UNICEF Urban Basic Services
The enabling approach/urban management late 1980s–early 1990s	Securing an enabling framework for action by people, the private sector and markets	Public/private partnership; community participation; land assembly and housing finance; capacity-building	Global Shelter Strategy to the Year 2000 (1988); Urban Policy and Economic Development; Cities, Poverty and people; Agenda 21 (1992); Enabling Housing Markets to Work (World Bank, 1993)
Sustainable urban development mid-1990s onwards	Holistic planning to balance efficiency, equity and sustainability	As above, with more emphasis on environmental management and poverty- alleviation	Sustainable Human Settlements Development: Implementing Agenda 21 (UNCHS, 1994)
Habitat II: 1996	'Adequate shelter for all' and 'Sustainable human settlements development'	Culmination and integration of all previous policy improvements	The Habitat Agenda; Global Report on Human Settlements

Source: UNCHS (1995: 15) and expansion to include Istanbul+5.

10% were actually built and none went to the poor (Bolnick, 1996) in the first two years. However, the initial projection has since been exceeded.

In spite of the evolution, there is a common agreement today on the enabling approach in the formulation of housing policy. However, UN-Habitat (2006) argues that changes continue to show up between scholars who place more faith in markets to deliver both efficiency and equity goals, and those who emphasize sustainable human development as an agenda within which markets must be carefully managed. On the other hand, capacity-building for a developed urban management, institutional reform especially in the public sector, and 'local ownership' over policy decisions have significance in both approaches (Erguden, 2001). Both systems have also identified the key roles of NGOs and other civil society groups in the housing process both as care-givers and in other roles, such as community participation and support, and both place gender equity and other issues of difference at the centre of policy choices (UN-Habitat, 2006).

Forms of housing policy

Forms of housing policy/provision can be defined by the processes through which such provision is achieved. A useful systematic tool for identifying and examining these processes is the concept of structures of provision, which is based on the identification of social relations and interactions of agents involved in all aspects of housing provision, such as production, exchange and consumption (Healey & Barret, 1990; Ball & Harloe, 1992). However, there are a limited number of ways in which governments can act to improve housing conditions, especially for low-income and disadvantaged households universally. But, at times, governments can build (provide) housing inexpensively, usually to rent. They can help households build their own homes, through the subsidization of materials and other help where most needed, or they can try to make the housing market more efficient by delivering affordable homes.

In any major city, there are many forms of housing stock through which people seek shelter. For example, the forms in operation in South Africa include private-sector housing catering to a range of income groups; public-sector housing of various forms, frequently housing more than one family; shacks, which are both 'legal' and 'illegal'; garages; backyard shacks in formal housing areas; shacks in the relatively undeveloped landscape; single-quarter migrant hostels among others. Nevertheless, three main forms of housing policy exist universally. They are:

- public housing;
- aided self-help; and
- enabling the building industry (popularly referred to as market-enabling strategy – a World Bank-sponsored approach).

In the next section, these forms of housing provision mechanisms will be discussed briefly.

Public housing

Public housing is a form of housing tenure in which the property is financed and owned by a government authority, which may be central or local and operated by public-housing authorities for low-income families and for elderly and handicapped individuals. For example, in China the government provides public housing through various sources, such as new housing, abandoned properties and old flats, which are rented at a very low price. This is called 'low-rent house' or 'low-rent housing'. Also, in Hong Kong, the government offers public housing through flats that are rented at a lower price than the market price, and through the home-ownership schemes, where homes are sold to the public at a lower price, with a special emphasis on the low-income earners. The houses are built and managed by the Hong Kong Housing Authority and the Hong Kong Housing Society (Hong Kong Census and Statistics Department, 2006).

Public housing was established to provide decent, safe and affordable rental housing for eligible low-income families, which would otherwise occupy housing units of much reduced quality. This is supported by the notion that housing carries several positive externalities, for example that housing affects children depending on the quality of the housing unit. It comes in all sizes and types, from scattered single family houses to high-rise apartments for low-income and elderly families. The aim of public housing is not only the provision of housing for low-income families but also for stimulating the economy through the construction and finance sectors. Publicly sponsored construction offered governments a means of nurturing the local building industry, providing on-the-job training in the handling of modern construction materials and methods (Leigh & Mitchell, 1980; Harris & Giles, 2003). They are effective vehicles for consolidating political support, which is obvious in the South African low-income housing setting. The medium makes it possible for governments to reward followers, whether by the judicious allocation of building contracts and jobs, or through the allocation of constructed housing units.

Public housing is called different things in different countries. In the United Kingdom it is often referred to by the British public as 'council housing' often on 'council estates', based on the historical role of district and borough councils in running public housing. In Sweden, it is called the Million Programme, a term for an ambitious housing programme executed in Sweden between 1965 and 1974 with the aim of building one million new dwellings in ten years. In Canada, public housing is usually a block of purpose-built subsidized housing operated by government agencies, which are often referred to as projects or community housing. While in South Africa, it was initially referred to as the Reconstruction and Development Programme (RDP) Housing Scheme, a major policy document developed by Nelson Mandela's government in 1994 to bridge the inequity that followed the Apartheid regime. It is now known as Breaking New Ground (BNG) housing, named after the revision of the 1994 version of the Housing Act. The provision of the housing is based on different programmes as directed by the National Housing Policy (NHP) in South Africa. There are several methods of developing public housing, of which the peculiarities of the system are mostly country specific and to a large extent determine if the occupants will be satisfied with the houses received. For instance, in the US, four systems are mostly in use, which are (Leigh & Mitchell, 1980):

- conventional method;
- the turnkey method;
- a nonconventional means of acquisition of existing units; and
- leasing.

While in South Africa, there are different systems, which are discussed further in Chapter 6 of the book.

The United States was the first country to have an established public-housing sector, with the introduction in 1937 through the Housing Act also known as Wagner–Steagall Act. Since public housing is limited, governments all over the world usually set eligibility standards based on the following:

- annual gross income;
- whether you qualify as elderly, a person with a disability, or as a family;
- citizenship or eligible immigration status of the particular country.

When the eligibility statuses are met, the administration also check an applicant's background to make sure that they will be good tenants in the rental option, and in the non-rental option, the applicant must have been on the waiting list, on which the names of all eligible persons are kept.

In general, occupants can stay in public housing as long as they comply with the lease in the rental option. While with the other option of outright ownership without any contributions as operated in South Africa, occupants are given ownership once the houses are allocated to them. However, in some other countries, such as the US, on re-examination of a family's income, if it is found that the income is sufficient to obtain housing on the private market, the Housing Authority will determine whether the family should stay in public housing or not. However, no occupant is required to move unless there is affordable housing available on the private market.

However, this system of housing provision is not sustainable to the government of nations because of the numerous limitations that are usually encountered. A major problem with public-housing delivery is its cost to the state. Also, there is the problem of the lack of skills and resources to handle the production rate. As a result of this, international agencies and various countries that had adopted the form of housing provision soon concluded that public housing could not solve the housing problem (Harris & Giles, 2003), meaning that public housing is not a solution to the general housing problem. However, Harris and Giles (2003) assert that an International Labour Organization study claimed that public housing was fine 'in principle' but that high costs often make it a 'low priority' to government of certain nations.

Aided self-help

The term aided self-help was coined in about 1948 by Jacob Crane as a result of the limitations that surrounded the public-housing provision. Aided self-help housing generally revolves around the idea that governments might help families to build their own homes (Harris, 1998). After 1945, aided self-help housing was propagated by agencies of the United States, in the first place by Jacob Crane and later by the United Nations and the British colonial office. However, Crane (1949) used the expression 'aided self-help' for the first time in 1945, and linked it at first with rural projects and equal to 'minimum urbanization'. Crane (1949) claims that the government can build very few excellent houses, which will actually accomplish almost nothing as measured against the problem, or instead undertake an 'aided self-help' programme. Other early advocates of self-help were Abrams, Mangin and Turner, who mostly had positive views on a family's power to build a house through self-help. Self-help provides a household with a medium of upward mobility (Bredenoord & van Lindert, 2010). Initial experiences with aided self-help housing took place mostly in Western countries and were based on the notion that governments should assist families to build their own dwellings. Throughout the developing world, millions have been building their own homes, where they have title to land without government aid. Generally, the people's power to construct their homes with or without assistance happens almost everywhere in the world especially in the developing countries.

Furthermore, aided self-help housing was practised in South Africa, before the First World War. A site-and-service scheme with plots and services was first developed at Pimville (currently Soweto) near Johannesburg. The 'sites-and-services approach' was later revitalized after the Second World War in South Africa. Massive land invasions and squatting during the 1940s obliged the city of Johannesburg to convert many into controlled sites and service camps (Harris, 1998). However, after the abolishment of the Apartheid rule, self-help was later replaced with the People Housing Process, now the enhanced People Housing Process (ePHP), to address limitations that were observed in the first 12 years of its implementation. Aided self-help housing is usually implemented to help alleviate housing problems at minimum costs. According to Bredenoord and van Lindert (2010) aided self-help housing was above all liberal, having a social component, but predominantly perceived in contrast to public housing. The 'aid' or 'assistance' in 'aided self-help housing' is usually (Bredenoord & van Lindert, 2010):

- land for construction
- urban services;
- knowledge-development; and
- the option to construct a house step-by-step, which is also called the 'incremental' housing process.

However, the scarcity of land and increasing land prices make sites-and-services projects relatively hard to develop. For instance, where can suitable and sufficient land be found to be divided into parcels and be sold or allocated for aided self-help housing? Another concern is how to improve individual houses and even whole neighbourhoods without constraints? Moreover, the growing demand for new urban land is causing financial and organizational difficulties for local governments, which necessitated some countries to formulate urban land laws. A major feature of aided self-help is the freedom a shelter offers; if it was constructed without using loans, the responsibility to pay-off every month is restricted or even zero, which is the best for the poor and disadvantaged families in the society.

Self-help is usually linked to informality, since the possibility of realizing a mass public-housing system is difficult with all the limitations. Also, because the customary housing sector cannot provide enough dwellings for the low-income groups, most have to resort to the informal housing market, where the self-help principle is a significant feature (Bredenoord & van Lindert, 2010). However, aided self-help housing is present almost everywhere, in formal as well as informal developments, except in countries that have shown a strong economic development and where large-scale or industrial development is adopted. In real life, self-help housing is present: it happens on a larger scale and is unavoidable for many in developing countries where there is little or no support from the government, despite the criticism and constraints. The advantages that comes with the aided self-help housing are that it costs much less than public housing and that it stimulates owner-occupancy, which many believed would boost social stability, give people pride in their homes and a stake in the society, while encouraging savings and investment (Harris & Giles, 2003). Furthermore, it is a way of assuring residential satisfaction since occupants are involved in the construction and are more likely to accept any defects since they had responsibility for the construction, compared to the allocation of public housing that has already been constructed.

During the implementation stage of the aided self-help housing form, owner-builders use methods and materials with which they are familiar, unless obliged to do otherwise. Owner-builders produce homes that most experts regard as temporary and that some judged as substandard. Critics of this housing form charged that self-help produced instant slums. Hence, Ward (1982) argues that self-help housing failed to become a significant housing solution in most countries of the South because of this limitation. Also, Burgess (1982) claims that there are six constraints of self-help housing and Marcuse (1992) even claimed they were ten. With time, however, it became clear that the vision and the power of self-help cannot be over-valued (Bredenoord & van Lindert, 2010). Other opponents further argued that the process of learning with self-help would be ineffective and that most families can only master the process when they have almost completed the house (UNCHS, 1995). However, families having some experience with initial self-help housing have a better chance of managing construction-related work. It is obvious that the disabled, single-parent households and elderly people cannot participate, except by getting help from others. A good condition for the success of self-help is if people with the same attitude take the initiative and receive added help from the government or support organizations. Another problem of self-help housing is that the initial target group is not always fully serviced, since aided self-help housing increases and becomes more exclusive. UNCHS (1995) asserts that self-help housing is the most affordable and intelligent way of providing sustainable shelter because it is based on minimum standards and incorporates a substantive amount of 'sweat' equity and can be cost-reducing. Also, it can be useful because individuals and communities are engaged in it and acquire valuable skills; it can also be practical because it answers to people's needs and levels of affordability.

Market-enabling strategy

Housing provision can also be promoted by helping the building industry to become more efficient at providing decent and affordable housing. This strategy may involve:

- the provision of better building materials and methods (Harris & Giles, 2003);
- the training of tradesmen and entrepreneurs;
- assistance to small savings and mortgage-lending institutions; and
- efforts to guarantee secure tenure.

This form of housing provision through the private market mechanism has been on the agenda of housing studies since the mid-1970s (World Bank, 1975). Throughout the 1980s, through the recommendations of scholars and housing practitioners, there was an almost universal acceptance of reducing the role of the government in direct provisory roles in the economy and increased reliance on the private sector (World Bank, 1988). In different capacities, most countries, irrespective of ideology, political structures or levels of development, have pursued this policy (World Bank, 1988; Keivani & Werna, 2001). Subsequently, the extension of the role of the private market in the provision of housing has become increasingly the focus of attention.

This strategy was particularly promoted during the 1980s by the World Bank and its associated writers who developed an enabling strategy for public-sector support of private market activity in housing provision particularly in developing countries (World Bank, 1988). The World Bank (1984) paper on 'housing and financial institutions in developing countries' set the tone for this strategy universally. The policy document lay emphasis on the need for developing countries' governments to encourage financial innovation in the provision of housing finance to households on a financially viable basis, as far up as the upper level of the informal sector, and to develop specific programmes for the lower-income households, who could still contemplate some form of house ownership with the major focus centred on urban infrastructure and services (World Bank, 1984). These concerns were taken over by the Vienna Recommendations in 1986, and from there keywords such as 'enabling environments', 'co-operation', 'efficacy' and 'financial sustainability' were developed. The responsibility of governments was to shift from being a housing provider to a policy 'enabler' in order to incorporate shelter as an integral part of the national macroeconomic plans. By the late 1980s, this form of housing delivery was widely promoted as the 'enabling strategy' (World Bank, 1993). The strategy was new to the housing delivery sector with the notion that a bundle of measures might be defined as a coherent strategy. Taken individually, however, many of the interventions themselves were not, and neither was the underlying assumption that governments should help the market work its 'magic' (Harris & Giles, 2003).

The 'market-enabling strategy' approach meant that housing provision policies were to become self-sustainable, and therefore all participants involved in the process should interact, co-ordinate, re-organize and revise their roles towards the new approach (Duran, 1995). The role of communities in the decision-making process was emphasized so that they could determine their own set of priorities and the pace and extent of the development process. Likewise, at the national level, the government's role is to lean towards policy-making and institutional support, which is aimed at concentrating on the highest priority needs, while the private sector is to play a leading role.

Although the need for recognizing the importance of supporting and encouraging the construction sector has been understood by many developing countries, few questions have been asked about its implications upon the poor, who create the biggest demand for houses in many developing countries. This policy could leave the poor completely dependent on the success or failure of the free market and the private sector. This is because the approach encourages governments to 'enable' the housing market to work but they also propose the gradual abolition of subsidies, albeit, not in all economies. The ability of a free-market economy to provide cheap housing with reasonable profit margins remains to be proven. For instance, in South Africa subsidies are the only means available for the lower-income sector to acquire housing as a result of the socio-economic problems facing the lower-income groups. This approach of the enabling strategy, however, has been subject to much argument and has been criticized for its over-concentration on the private markets and rejection of alternative/complementary modes of housing provision from serious policy consideration (Keivani & Werna, 2001). While private markets can and should be supported, they cannot form the attention of the enabling strategy in most developing countries. As an alternative, a comprehensive approach to enabling strategies, which combines adjustments to overall supply and demand conditions with the identification and inclusion of different modes and agents of housing provision in a holistic integrated policy, will better serve the dire need of housing provision in the under-developed and developing countries of the world and most especially to the low-income group and the disadvantaged.

Intentions of housing policy

It is impossible to put enough emphasis on the importance of creating a housing policy that will provide a framework for an affordable and decent living environment for all people. As discussed previously, housing impacts on almost all dimensions of an individual's and a family's life. From a societal approach, widespread conditions of inadequate housing contribute considerably to social instability, as witnessed by the 'tragic violence in South African black townships, and to general the attitudes of despair and de-socialization' (Dewar, 1996). A major feature that makes the issue of housing multifaceted is that 'housing' does not simply relate to the provision of shelter. This is because in obtaining shelter the individual gains access to a number of different products. Housing has the potential to contribute to an improved quality of life and this should direct the formulation of a housing policy.

Most countries universally set their housing policy objectives based on the current housing situation prevalent in the economy at that time. Thus, there is no country with the same wordings of housing policy objectives, but each has unique features that most times follow in the same line of thinking as proposed by the international housing agencies responsible for monitoring of shelter provision. However, the main products associated with a housing policy decision, and the objectives that should be associated with it in an ideal situation, are access to land, access to a good habitable socio-economic location, access to adequate services, access to adequate shelter and access to an adequate external, social and physical environment. All of these factors have some relevance in any housing policy formulation and do not represent a sequential list of priorities that must be satisfied on a one-to-one basis, but all must be present to some degree or other for any housing policy to succeed, which is the reason for its formulation. If all are present, and all of the objectives satisfied, the situation would be optimal. It is obvious that the decisions facing individuals in the arena of housing are intricate and priorities will vary widely with individual circumstances (Dewar, 1996). It follows from this that no single ideal approach or package exists and that centralized, external agencies cannot decide on priorities. The clear implication is that the more individuals can determine their own priorities, the better the situation, and the greater the range of choices available to people, the more they are assisted. Thus, it should be recognized that housing policy objectives require a framework that locates the housing issue within its broader urban context – a framework of broader issues that should inform the direction of housing policy in the specific context of any country.

The effectiveness of a housing policy is about the ability of the policy to achieve its purposes. The effectiveness of a housing policy, therefore, cannot be judged in isolation from what it is expected to do. It would be completely wrong to design a new housing policy or to propose changes to an existing policy or to implement a housing policy without a clear view about the purpose of the housing policy (new or revised). This should logically be examined within the context of the overall purpose of housing policy and the place of the entity's overall goal within the policy. Hence, the primary purpose of any housing policy should be to provide the whole population adequate and secure housing by unblocking and unleashing all potential energies and resources from a wide variety of sources, which can play a role in improving living conditions. Possible but not exhaustive lists of housing policy purposes according to Oxley (2009) are:

- help low-income groups access decent housing;
- help low-income households have adequate post-housing expenditure incomes;
- improve the quality of housing consumed by low-income groups;
- increase housing choices for households with unmet housing needs;
- increase the supply of housing in the society;
- improve the quality of urban neighbourhoods;
- improve the functioning of urban labour markets;
- promote community cohesion;
- improve the functioning of the macro-economy; and
- promote environmental sustainability.

In most nations of the world, housing policies are becoming increasingly integrated with a wide range of social and economic objectives, which means that housing policy is reaching further down the list above than was the case in past decades. A housing policy that has broad goals is much more multifaceted than one that solely emphasizes housing low-income groups (Oxley, 2009). Therefore, any finance and other economic systems that will enhance the actualization of the policy must be compatible with the goals of policy in the given country. When housing policy focuses on the purpose of helping low-income and disadvantaged groups to access decent housing, the setting of the appropriate standards for decent housing is a key element in the success of the policy. Hence, meeting the need for decent housing in that particular context will mean that governments have to create policies that will bridge the gap between what is needed and what is demanded. If the standards of decent housing are set too high and what is needed is too great, housing policies will be extremely expensive. It has been argued that setting standards at inappropriate levels has been one of the failures of policies in developing countries (UN-Habitat, 1994, 2006).

Housing policy instruments

Housing policy instruments may be defined as the set of techniques by which governmental authorities wield their power in attempting to ensure support and effect or prevent (Vedung, 1998) the provision of affordable housing to the citizens. Over time, ranges of housing policy instruments have been developed to respond to policy imperatives of housing delivery. However, most times, it is not anticipated that any instrument will be discontinued or terminated, but when the instrument can no longer meet the need it was designed for, it is usually discontinued, modified or terminated. Rationally, most existing instruments that are not meeting the policy goals are sometimes supplemented by additional instruments to provide flexible solutions to demand-side needs. No one singular policy instrument has been found to fulfil the housing policy goals of a nation's housing policy. Most housing arrangements include a mix of conditional subject and conditional object subsidies (Oxley, 2009). When housing problems are regarded as demand-side affordability problems, the greater the preference to use conditional subject subsidies (Oxley, 2009). Likewise, the more the emphasis is on supply-side housing shortage problems, the greater the preference for conditional object subsidies. Although housing finance systems can support housing suppliers directly by means of conditional object subsidies, they can also support suppliers indirectly by conditional subject subsidies that underpin the rental revenue stream (Oxley, 2009).

A fundamental mix of housing policy instruments aimed at securing greater provision of housing stock ranges from:

- rent regulation;
- allocation and rental policies in current social housing;
- support for the construction of new social flats provided by municipalities or non-profit housing associations;
- housing allowances;
- tax relief and interest subsidies for ownership housing; and
- housing subsidies for special social groups in the society etc.

According to Lux (2003), social housing represents the subsidies aimed at decreasing the cost of housing, while housing allowance represents the subsidies aimed at increasing income of households from the pillars of public housing policies in most countries' housing policy instrument. Housing allowances are sometimes regarded as demand-side subsidies and social housing as a set of arrangements that involves supply-side subsidies (Oxley, 2009). Given that they go to individuals, the demand-side subsidies are also termed subject subsidies and the supply-side subsidies, given that they support buildings, are termed object subsidies (Oxley, 2009). However, there are, in practice, very few examples of either pure subject or pure object subsidies. Pure subject subsidies represent income supplements with no housing-related conditions attached, where households would be able to spend the additional resources on whatever they wished. Pure object subsidies are used to build new dwellings without any conditions about who occupied the dwellings and how they were priced.

There are many variants of conditional subject subsidies and conditional object subsidies found throughout the world. It is the conditions that make them unique in any set of environments and the conditions that make them successful or not successful. It is ultimately the conditions, how they are used and what effects they have, that is at the essence of the choice of policy instruments (Galster, 1997). For instance, one housing allowance system with one set of conditions is very different from another with another set of conditions. The conditions attached to housing allowances usually include considerations of the size of the household, household income and housing costs. There may also be conditions associated with the size and quality of the housing occupied, which is mostly determined by the allocated amount of finances for each respective building. The relationship between the amount received and these items can vary within a country. There are thus occasionally locational elements to the conditions. The conditions also specify who gets the resources: the household or the housing supplier. The application of the conditions turns what is superficially termed a demand-side subsidy into a measure with important supply-side features. The conditions usually have substantial influences on the way that housing allowances affect housing quality and quantity.

Most times, new housing policy instruments tend to focus attention on sectors that have been previously neglected. These instruments are inclined to place greater emphasis on flexibility and responsiveness to local circumstances particularly the physical context within which housing is to be delivered. This usually is a natural consequence of an increased focus on the development of sustainable human settlements as opposed to the delivery of 'commoditized housing units'. For example, in South Africa, there is consequently a greater emphasis on the process of housing delivery emphasizing planning and engagement, the quality of the housing product not only in terms of location but also in terms of final housing form and the long-term sustainability of the housing environment leading to a focus on institutional capacity, which were observed as the problems with housing delivery in the first decade of applying different housing policy delivery instruments when the new housing policy was formulated in 1994. Nevertheless, there is no explicitly 'best' housing policy instrument in all circumstances. Every policy instrument has its own comparative advantages to a degree as determined by the particular country's housing market context and by the goals of the particular housing policy.

Summary

The most important point to stress in conclusion is that the central objective of housing policy must be the stimulation of environments that give dignity to people's lives. It is not simply the provision of shelter. Against this criterion, the record of housing policy and implementation in South Africa in recent decades has been really poor. Thousands of millions of rands have been spent on housing development but the environments that have resulted are almost unfailingly sterile, monotonous, hostile and inconvenient. In order for the money spent not to be wasted, there is a need to conduct a post-occupancy evaluation of the constructed houses and evaluate the residential satisfaction of the housing occupants so that errors made can be corrected for future development. A narrow focus on the individual housing unit and the provision of shelter, which is the prevalent disposition, gives rise to a particular mind-set and approach. This ensures the generation of poorly performing, sterile environments. Significant improvement demands a paradigm shift – a shift that places not the individual unit but collective spaces, institutions and facilities at the centre of 'housing research'. The next section of the book discusses housing theories and development in two West African countries and one Southern Africa country – South Africa.

References

Agbola, T. (1998). *The housing of Nigerians: A review of policy development and implementation.* Ibadan, Nigeria: Development Policy Centre.

Agbola, T. & Alabi, M. (2000). Sustainable housing delivery, lesson from international experience. National workshop on sustainable housing delivery in Nigeria; challenges for public/private partnership, 5–7 June 2000, Sheraton Hotel Abuja, Nigeria

Anderson, C. (2005). What's the difference between policies and procedures? Available from: www.bizmanualz.com/information/2005/04/26/what's-the-difference-between-policies-and-procedures.html (accessed 24 June 2014).

Ball, M. & Harloe, M. (1992). Rhetorical barriers to understanding housing provision: What the 'provision thesis' is and is not. *Housing studies*, 7(1):3–15.

Bolnick, J. (1996). The grass speaks: People's dialogue and the South African homeless people's federation (1994–1996). *Environment and urbanization*, 8(2):153–170.

Bredenoord, J. & van Lindert, P. (2010). Pro-poor housing policies: Rethinking the potential of assisted self-help housing. *Habitat international*, 34:278–287.

Burgess, R. (1982). Self-help housing advocacy: A curious form of radicalism. A critique of the work of John F.C. Turner. In P. Ward (ed.) *Self-help housing: A critique*. London: Mansell, pp. 55–97.

Crane, J.L. (1949). Huts and houses in the tropics. *Unisylva*, 3:99–105.

Dewar, D. (1996). *The urban housing issue*. Sandton, South Africa: The Free Market Foundation.

Duran, C.O. (1995). The impact of current global housing strategies on the development of the housing sector in Colombia. Available from: www.ucl.ac.uk/bartlett/development/publications/2016/Dec/%2371.-Impact-of-Current-Global-Housing-Strategies-On-Development-of-The-Housing-Sector-In-Colombia (accessed 1 May 2018).

Duruzoechi, N.F. (1999). *Housing development and public policy*. Owerri, Nigeria: Alphabet Nigeria Publishers.

Erguden, S. (2001). Low cost housing, Policies and constraints in developing countries. Spatial information for sustainable development, international conference, Nairobi, Kenya.

Galster, G. (1997). Comparing demand-side and supply-side housing policies. *Housing studies*, 12(4):561.

Harris, R. (1998). The silence of the experts: 'Aided self-help housing', 1939–1954. *Habitat international*, 22(2):165–189.

Harris, R. & Giles, C. (2003). A mixed message: The agents and forms of international housing policy, 1945–1973. *Habitat international*, 27(2):167–191.

Healey, P. & Barret, S. (1990). Structure and agency in land and property development processes: Some ideas for research. *Urban studies*, 27(1):89–103.

Hong Kong Census and Statistics Department (2006). *Population by-census*. Hong Kong: Census and Statistics Department.

Jiboye, A.D. (2011). Achieving sustainable housing development in Nigeria: A critical challenge to governance. *International journal of humanities and social science*, 1 (No. 9 Special Issue – July 2011):1–7.

Keivani, R. & Werna, E. (2001). Modes of housing provision in developing countries. *Progress in planning*, 55(2):65–118.

Leigh, W. & Mitchell, M. (1980). Public housing and the black community. *The review of black political economy*, 11(1):53–75.
Lux, M. (2003). *Housing policy: An end or a new beginning?* Budapest: Open Society Institute.
Malpass, P. & Murie, A. (1999). *Housing policy and practice*. 5th edn. Houndmills, Basingstoke: Palgrave.
Marcuse, P. (1992). Why conventional self-help projects won't work. In K. Mathéy (ed.) *Beyond self-help housing*. London: Mansell, pp. 15–22.
Mukiibi, S. (2011). An evaluation of factors that have influenced housing policy development in Uganda. Second international conference on advances in engineering and technology, Uganda.
Olatubara, C.O. (2002). Housing policy and its impact on the populace: The elusive solution to housing problem. Continuing professional development workshop on housing policy and its impact on the populace, Ogun State, Nigeria, Nigeria Institution of Estate Surveyors and Valuers, Ogun State Branch.
Oxley, M. (2009). Financing affordable social housing in Europe. In X.Q. Zhang (ed.) *The human settlements financing tools and best practices series*. Nairobi, Kenya: United Nations Human Settlements Programme.
Schuster, W.M. (2008). For the greater good: The use of public policy considerations in confirming chapter 11 plans of reorganization. *Houston law review*, 46:467.
UNCHS (1995). *The future of human settlements: Good policy can make a difference*. Nairobi: UNCHS (A/CONF.165/PC.3/CRP.2).
UN-Habitat (1994). *Case studies of innovative housing finance institutions*. Nairobi: UNCHS.
UN-Habitat (2006). *Shelter for all: The potential of housing policy in the implementation of the habitat agenda. HS/488/97* E. New York: United Nations/Earthscan.
Vedung, E. (1998). Policy instruments: Typologies and theories. In M.-L. Bemelmans-Videc, R.C. Rist and E. Vedung (eds) *Carrots, sticks & sermons: Policy instruments & their evaluation*. New Brunswick, NJ: Transaction Publishers, pp. 21–58.
Ward, P.M. (ed.) (1982). *Self-help housing: A critique*. London: Mansell.
World Bank (1975). *Housing sector policy paper*. Washington, DC: World Bank.
World Bank (1984). *Housing and financial institutions in developing countries*. Washington, DC: World Bank.
World Bank (1988). *World development report 1988*. New York: Oxford University Press for the World Bank.
World Bank (1993). *Housing: Enabling markets to work*. Washington, DC: World Bank.
Young, J. & Enrique, M. (2009). *Helping researchers become policy entrepreneurs*. London: Overseas Development Institute.

Part III

Housing policy and development in Africa

Part III of this book presents housing policies and other housing issues in two West African countries (Ghana and Nigeria) and in one Southern Africa country – South Africa. This part contains three chapters:

- Chapter 4 – Ghana;
- Chapter 5 – Nigeria; and
- Chapter 6 – South Africa.

4 Housing development in Ghana

Introduction

Provision of adequate housing is one of the major challenges faced by most African countries. In this chapter, housing policies and other housing issues in Ghana are discussed. The roles played by the different bodies such as the government and NGOs in the provision of housing will be discussed. This is because in most West Africa countries like Nigeria and Ghana, the ownership of affordable good-quality housing has been a problem. This justifies major public- and private-sector intervention. Unlike South Africa, most African countries have refused to include the right to housing in their national constitution, knowing all too well the role of housing in national development. This chapter of the book reviews housing in Ghana. The chapter provides a historical overview of housing provision in Ghana. It attempts to systematically bring to focus the challenges of housing delivery by reviewing past and present housing schemes. The policies and agencies supporting housing delivery in Ghana are also explored, such as the government, the private sector and others. Lastly, a summary of the lessons learnt to date is presented. This chapter sets out a background review on housing in developing countries and a summary of the literature presented.

Housing in developing countries

The need to provide adequate, suitable and equitable housing has remained a major priority of every government in the developing world. Hitherto, since the problem of housing is complex and pressing, no developing nation has been able to provide adequate housing of an acceptable standard for all its citizens. Besides, it is worth noting that the minimum housing standard differs from one country to another, depending on geographic and economic conditions. The United Nations, recognizing the seriousness of the housing problem, declared 1987 as the International Year of Shelter for the homeless. This was in recognition of the fact that there are no encouraging signs of the housing problem for the world's population in the developing being solved soon.

Housing is usually regarded as the most valuable asset for all people in the developed world and most especially in the developing countries. However, some scholars have advanced the argument that it is incorrect to assume that housing is a priority for everyone (Alder, 2002; Chambers, 1995), even in the developing countries. This stems from the fact that the urban poor do not give high priority to security of tenure in general. They give even less consideration to the possibility of land-ownership in the city. For instance, the Kenyan study of home-ownership among Nairobi's urban poor found that a high significance is placed on personal security (Adler, 2002). Besides, the urban poor are more apprehensive of other issues that directly influence their ability to earn a living, plus access to health and education services. Indeed, the opportunity to earn an income or keep a job are often more imperative concerns among the low-income groups than owning a house. In most cases, when they are given the opportunity to own a dwelling, most choose to sell or rent it as soon as they obtain the title deed (Adler, 2002). However, a significant number of people in the developing countries prioritize housing as their most urgent need. It must however be acknowledged that income generation or livelihood is usually the highest priority for people in developing countries (Skinner, 1989) but often that is linked to housing, with the house also being a workplace in many developing countries.

Housing has a tremendous social and economic impact on the total living environment of the world. It has direct and immediate influence on the health, education, economy, environment, political and social life of any society. Thus, home-ownership assumes high priority and offers home-based subsistence livelihood activities (Ahmed, 2011). But the shortage of housing in developing countries most especially for people of low-income groups has been termed a problem of 'colossal magnitude' (Alaghbari et al., 2009). The extent of the housing needs of the populace in these countries rises phenomenally by the day on account of rapid population growth and urbanization occurring in these countries, and the lack of a commensurate increase in housing stock (Olotuah, 2006). In many developing countries, the urban housing crisis is growing relentlessly even though a number of new policies, programmes and strategies is being engaged by the public and private sectors in addressing this problem (Ibem, Anosike & Azuh, 2011). The governments of developing countries have recognized that the bulk of those in dire need of housing is in the low-income categories and that some require special housing programmes to be able to live in decent housing, outside of the programmes currently in place.

In developing countries, the low- and moderate-income majority build their own homes incrementally over a period of 5 to 15 years, largely without the support of formal-sector, private and public institutions (Ferguson, 2001). The term 'housing' in developing countries is used as a verb because households must actively perform most of the tasks to gain access to land and construct adequate shelter during a longer time period, regardless of the many interventions that have sprung up in most developing countries. Whereas the term 'housing' has become a noun in the high-income industrialized countries, because it is a product delivered mainly by a sophisticated network of private firms and public institutions. Most developing countries lack social safety nets of all kinds as reported in much of the literature. The low- and moderate-income households constitute a greater majority in these countries, which live in a world of few windfalls and many lay-offs from jobs along with income changes, disease and other events. In developing countries, a home of one's own represents a precious refuge. Indeed, the literature on housing in developing countries often shows that housing ranks above education and health services as a priority. Thus, households in developing countries value home-ownership more than households in advanced industrialized countries. In fact, in most developing nations when a family does not have a house they can call their own, that family is regarded as the poorest of the poor.

However, acquiring access to a home and to the components that comprise housing and housing policy – land and property rights, building materials, basic services, regulations, subsidies and credit – are extraordinarily difficult for most households in developing countries (Angel, 2000). Poor land records and dysfunctional legal systems and regulatory bodies typically cloud ownership rights for a large number of households. De Soto (2000) states that investment in housing in developing countries has been severely hindered by regulation, that investment in informal housing has been further slowed down by confusing property rights, and that titling land with ambiguous property rights will sharply stimulate investment in low- and middle-income housing. De Soto (2000) was quite right with the first point, as shown by the inelasticity of the formal housing sector supply and the high price of titled land in most cities in developing countries. With regards to the second point, he may or may not have been right, but on the third point he was largely wrong. This is because titling by itself appears to do little to solve land market problems. The land titling process is costly and time consuming, titling land that is illegally occupied raises legal and compensation problems, titling may conflict with traditional property rights, and titling a property is not enough to obtain a mortgage.

De Soto's (2000) idea of making capitalism work for the poor through formalizing their property rights in houses, land and small businesses is very logical, but many of his policy recommendations may be inappropriate for the poorest and most vulnerable, and could have negative impacts on their security and well-being. This is because titling does not necessarily increase tenure security or certainty; in many cases, it does the opposite. Also, formalization of property rights does not promote lending to the poor. Rather than turning their property into 'capital', formalization could increase the rate of homelessness. Formalization through registered title deeds creates unaffordable costs for the poor in developing countries. However, developing countries' informal property systems supports a vibrant rental market so formalization could undermine this, producing unintended negative consequences for the poor and disadvantaged.

One of the major features of developing countries is the increasing inequality between the urban and rural areas. This feature has its roots in the neoclassical economic theories, which acknowledged that development can be accelerated by concentrating investments in the cities and that rural poverty will be ameliorated by the trickle down of benefits from the urban industrial growth. With the so-called growth-centred strategy, the developing countries have continued to witness imbalances in the living conditions between the urban and rural dwellers. Thus, development theories over the years have been searching for alternative strategies that would not only accelerate growth but also spread the benefits of development to all areas. Therefore much of the housing crisis in the developing countries is predominantly an urban one. Rural people living at reasonably low densities are often able to meet their own housing needs, though at a less sophisticated level than city dwellers (Akpomuvie, 2010). It is in the cities where the legal acquisition of land is far beyond the means of most people where the traditional forms of housing are often not acceptable, and where the population is increasing that the problem of housing is more acute. Furthermore, housing in developing countries is characterized by some general features. The first is the relatively high house prices to income ratio. In countries with less elastic supply for whatever reason, asset prices are usually a bit up. The poor housing finance performance is responsible for the inelastic housing supply and the resulting high house price to income ratio (Malpezzi, 1990). Most developing countries' housing stocks are dominated by rental tenant units. About 40% of the world's urban dwellers are said to be renters; with two-thirds of the developing country cities' housing stock being in rental (Farzana, 2004). Another feature of housing in developing countries is the domination of the informal housing supply because of deficiencies in formal housing. Formal housing, on the one hand, is that which has the legal approval of the planning agency prior to its development and has been developed within the framework of government housing policy rules, regulations and controls and meets the minimum required standard of environmental quality and infrastructure. On the other hand, informal housing is illegal and is composed of unauthorized colonies and squatter settlements, which have mostly emerged because of non-availability or unaffordability of housing in the formal housing market (Farzana, 2004).

The building materials industries in developing countries frequently suffer from cartelization and inefficient production methods that result in high prices (Ferguson, 2001). The provision of water, roads, drainage and electricity occurs at a low level equilibrium. The government usually provides poor, incomplete services, while households refuse to pay a substantial share of these infrastructure costs. This vicious circle greatly limits the delivery of the infrastructure departments and companies, the capacity to extend their services to new areas and to improve their services in existing areas. Most national agencies in some developing countries set high building and subdivision standards, attempting to regulate local land use, and imposing transfer and other taxes on real-estate and mortgage transactions as an easy means of raising revenue, which has been a problem of housing development in this region of the world.

The greatest setback, however, often occurs with accessing credit. Widespread access to long-term, competitively priced mortgages has revolutionized housing in high-income industrialized countries over the past 60 years as opposed to that of developing countries (Ferguson, 2001). An overwhelming share of households in these countries has now acquired homes with market-rate mortgages from private-sector financial institutions. The reality of mortgage finance is the opposite in developing countries. Only a small minority of households – typically less than 20% of the population – can obtain a mortgage to finance their homes. This system is gradually changing as compared to the last 20 years in most developing countries. Regardless, many of the mortgages receive substantial subsidies from government in one form or another. Once these subsidies are taken into account, the private-sector mortgage market in which market-rate intermediation occurs often is extremely small (often less than 5% of new household formation) or is missing entirely (Bruce, 1998). Various factors lie behind the low levels of mortgage finance in developing countries. Much of the blame is attributed to inflation. High and explosive inflation destroyed the existing mortgage finance systems of many countries in the 1980s and 1990s, such as in Nigeria, Ghana and Kenya. Likewise, the repayment of international debt has contributed to the stabilizing of inflation and interest rates in some of these countries, but a considerable improvement has not been shown in the housing sectors of most developing countries. This macro-financial stability provides the opportunity for reconstruction of mortgage finance systems, as is currently being done in countries such as Nigeria and Ghana.

In spite of the remarkable increase in literature on the demand for housing attributes in developed countries over the last decade, there exists little or no scholarly studies estimating the parameters of the demand for housing attributes in developing countries. Very little is known about the working of housing markets in this region and the state of affairs of housing in developing countries could be attributed to the difficulty associated with obtaining data on the operations of the housing market in developing countries (Arimah, 1992). The apparent belief that housing markets in developing countries are inhibited by socio-cultural and political institutions raises doubts as to the applicability of microeconomic models to such markets, and the fact that data from such markets are unreliable. Nonetheless, it is still possible to undertake an analysis of the demand for housing in a developing country. This is because public policy in terms of government intervention, which is the often-cited reason for housing market imperfections, in the form of public housing programmes and rent control, is quite ineffective in preventing substantial market transactions (Koenigsberger, 1986). Also, most policy-makers and executors in developing countries have a genuine lack of understanding about the operations of the housing market, as well as the fact that housing programmes in developing countries aimed at improving huge housing problems are usually formulated based on ad hoc notions of 'needs' and 'standards' without due consideration of the actual demand for housing (Arimah, 1992). This has led to the general failure of housing programmes in many developing countries.

Around the world and most especially in the developing countries, no nation can claim to have solved the housing problems of their people as shown by various authors' reports that highlighted various countries' related housing issues. The following examples illustrate the housing shortages that prevail:

- In Ethiopia, the Ministry of Works and Housing in 2008 stated that studies conducted in the last five years found a housing shortage of between 900,000–1,000,000 in urban centres and that only 30% of the existing urban housing stock is in good or fair condition.
- For the Metropolitan Region of Sao Paulo, the urban housing deficit is approximately 611,936 units (UN-Habitat, 2010).
- The housing shortage in Nigeria is estimated to affect between 17 and 20 million people and it is indicated that more than R600 billion (NGN12trillion) will be required to finance the housing deficit.
- In Pakistan, in 2011, the level of urbanization was 36.2%, while there were 21.7 million houses in the country, which has a population of 186 million. Pakistan is facing shortage of 9 million residential houses, which is growing with the ratio of 600,000 annually. In 2008, the yearly estimated housing demand was 570,000 units. Actual supply was 300,000 units, leaving a shortfall of 270,000 units every year. The consequence of this situation is that almost half of the total urban population now lives in squatter or informal settlements.
- In 2014, the urban housing shortage in India plunged from 24.7 million at the beginning of the eleventh five-year plan in 2007 to 18.78 million for the next five-year plan from 2012 to 2017.
- Bell (1996) emphasized that the burden of the cumulated housing shortage in Algeria is still high – it was estimated at 763,176 in 2009 and 994,357 in 2010 with a population of 33.8 million in 2007– and it is expected to reach nearly 2 million dwellings by 2025. In Mexico, Centro de Investigacion Documentacion de la Casa and Sociedad Hipotecaria Federal in 2006 established that 1.8 million new housing units and 2.7 million housing improvements are needed in a country with a population of 103.3 million people.
- In Kenya, the government of Kenya showed that the country has a deficit of units of 127,700 in urban and 303,600 in rural areas.
- In Uganda, the Uganda Bureau of Statistics estimates that Uganda has a housing deficit of 550,000 units. About 160,000 of this backlog is in urban areas and Kampala alone has a housing deficit of 100,000 units.
- In South Africa, in spite of the delivery of 3 million houses between 1994 until 2015, the South Africa National DHS showed that the backlog is still 2.7 million.

The above-mentioned situation calls for concern. This concern was reflected by Tibaijuka (2005) who stated that the need for housing production in developing countries' cities is estimated at around 35 million per year. Breaking this figure down, Tibaijuka added that some 20 million units are required to meet demographic growth and new household formation, while the remaining 15 million units are to meet the requirements of the homeless and people living in inadequate housing. Summing this up, some 95,000 new urban housing units are needed to be constructed each day to ensure acceptable housing conditions.

Globally, the housing conditions of the poor are deteriorating with the developing world accounting for the worst rate of deterioration. According to the latest UN-Habitat publication regarding urban development and management, the absolute number of slum dwellers continues to grow due to the fast tempo of urbanization. UN-Habitat states that the number of people living in slum conditions is now estimated at 863 million, in contrast to 760 million in 2000 and 650 million in 1990, and that number could double by 2030 if developing nations do not reverse this course and start giving the issue serious attention. These figures indicate that the housing challenge in the developing countries of the world is enormous.

Ghana – background

The modern-day Ghana was created from the British Gold Coast colony, established in 1874, and the UK-administered Trusteeship Territory of Togoland, incorporated in 1956 following a referendum. Anxiety for independence grew strongly after the Second World War. From the early 1950s, self-government was introduced with elections in 1951, 1954 and 1956. In 1957, Ghana became the first sub-Saharan country in colonial Africa to gain its independence. The earliest Europeans to arrive were the Portuguese in the fifteenth century. Upon their arrival, they found so much gold between the River Ankobra and the Volta, they subsequently named it 'da Mina', meaning 'The Mine' (Republic of Ghana, 2011).

The Republic of Ghana is a country located on the coast of West Africa. Ghana is located on the Gulf of Guinea, only a few degrees north of the Equator, therefore giving it a warm climate. The country covers an area of 238,500 square kilometres (92,085 square metres). It is surrounded by Togo to the east, Cote d'Ivoire to the west, Burkina Faso to the north and the Gulf of Guinea (Atlantic Ocean) to the south.

The Ghanaian population is estimated to be about 28,308,301 million, up from about 24.2 million in 1995 and 6.7 million in 1960 (Ghana Statistical Service, 2017). However, according to the Central Intelligence Agency, the *World Factbook* report of July 2016, the population is estimated at 26,908,262, which represents a growth rate of 2.18%. According to the Ghanaian Statistical Services, the most populous region is Ashanti, with a population of 4,780,280, representing 19.4% of the country's total population followed by Greater Accra, with a population of 4,010,054 (16.3%). The least populous regions are Upper West with 702,110 persons constituting 2.8% of the total population and Upper East with 1,046,545 persons or 4.2% of Ghana's population. The United Nations projected that by the year 2025 about 60% of the Ghanaian population will reside in urban areas (United Nations, 1995). The rapid rate of urbanization in Ghana is sustained not only by the high fertility rate, but also by the continuing rural–urban migration. In the period ranging from 1948 to 1960, urban population increased in Ghana by almost one million. Today, migration is not quite as rapid, but it still continues. In the 1980s, the average annual growth of the population for the country was about 3.2%, but for the urban areas, it was about 4.2% (Berry, 1995), of which much of the difference is attributed to rural–urban migration.

Housing in Ghana

The need to provide adequate, suitable and equitable housing has remained a major priority of every Ghanaian government. Even though housing is a basic necessity of life, more than half of the Ghanaian population lives in inadequate houses (Government of Ghana, 2005) where they have no access to adequate sanitary facilities, water or warmth to meet their daily physical needs. Adequate housing is seen as one of the effective means to alleviate rural and urban poverty, which has further external and internal effects. The lack of adequate housing has lowered the life expectancy of the homeless according to the European Federation of National Organizations Working with the Homeless, as they are exposed to serious health risks, which gravely affect their contribution to society.

In Ghana, the housing situation is said to be inadequate but improving. Many households, particularly those in the cities and other urban areas, continue to live in overcrowded and unsanitary conditions. Their houses lack basic amenities such as toilets, kitchens, bathrooms and refuse facilities. The shortage of houses, especially in the urban areas, has given rise to very high occupancy rates, exorbitant rent, unstable tenancies and poor living conditions. These factors, combined with issues of land litigation, high cost of urban residential land, multiple sale of urban land, high cost of building materials, and shortage of infrastructure and services, underline the difficulties of housing delivery in Ghana.

Since Ghana's independence, provision of housing has remained central to the development agenda of the various governments. Various policies, programmes and institutions have sought to address issues, such as land-ownership, land-title regulation and the provision of affordable housing units to the working and non-working population. However, a number of these housing approaches was negatively affected by the lack of funds, a poor macroeconomic environment and lack of private-sector participation (Bank of Ghana, 2007). Thus, compared with other advanced countries, Ghana's housing industry remains rudimentary. According to the Ghana National Shelter draft policy document, housing tenancy in the country ranges from home-ownership to weekly tenancy. More than half (57.4%) of the national housing stock is owner-occupied. Rental units represent 22.1% of the stock while rent-free and 'perching' constitute 19.5% and 1.0% respectively (Government of Ghana, 2005). According to the draft policy document, quite a number of people live in houses rent-free. These houses are usually called *ebusua fie* (family home), often for the extended family, long after the original owners have died. A large number of extended family members and even some 'strangers' live rent-free in these homes (UN-Habitat, 2010).

In recent times, however, and within the context of the improved macroeconomic environment characterized by low inflation rates, low interest rates and relatively stable exchange rates, activity in Ghana's housing sector is gaining momentum. Although housing demand and supply gaps that are driven by a rapidly growing middle-class as well as increased urbanization remain, the rising mortgage debt outstanding to GDP ratio (as asserted by the Bank of Ghana) provides evidence that the sector has recorded moderate growth over the past seven years in particular, albeit from a low base. The gradual improvement in housing supply notwithstanding, the sector still faces a number of challenges, such as land acquisition, prolonged land-title and registration processes, high costs of rental units and house prices that require policy intervention.

Philosophical basis for housing development in Ghana

Unlike housing development in Nigeria, which is underpinned by its constitution, the philosophical basis for housing development in Ghana is not completely supported constitutionally. The foundation is found in separate Ghana Development Plans as deemed necessary by the previous and even the current government as a follow-up to their manifestos before being elected into government. For instance, the present government involvement in housing provision is a result of the manifesto's declaration, which states that 'every Ghanaian must have a home, though not necessarily own a house, as a meaningful expression of the right to shelter'. The government manifesto agenda further states that 'housing, especially for the low and lower-middle income earners, will be one of the government's top priorities'.

However, Chapter Five of the Ghanaian Constitution, usually referred to as the fundamental human rights and freedom chapter, which contains the central passage on human rights sets out a range of rights to which every person in Ghana is entitled. Among these rights is that every person has the right to own property either alone or in association with others and that no person shall be subjected to interference within the privacy of his or her home, property, correspondence or communication except in accordance with the law and as may be necessary in a free and democratic society for public safety or the economic well-being of the country, for the protection of the rights or freedoms of others. Unlike the Nigerian Constitution and South Africa, which expresses that the government is entrusted with the responsibility to harness the resources of the nation to serve the common good of all and promote national prosperity based on an efficient, dynamic and self-reliant economy, the Ghanaian Constitution is completely silent on this. However, among the rights enshrined in Chapter Five of the Ghanaian Constitution, the right to housing or adequate housing as a responsibility of the government is also not included. However, the fact that the constitution is limited in its conception of human rights should not, in principle, be a challenge to the protection of rights since the framers of the constitution purposefully made the provisions on rights expandable. For instance, the Ghanaian Constitution states in Article 33(5):

> The rights, duties, declaration and guarantees relating to the fundamental human rights and freedoms specifically mentioned in this chapter shall not

> be regards [sic] as excluding others not specifically mentioned which are considered to be inherent in a democracy and intended to secure the freedom and dignity of man.

The constitution accordingly makes room to include into the legal framework those rights that are articulated and protected outside the national space, and those that might exist in the future. Despite Ghana being a signatory to numerous international and regional treaties that enforce the right to adequate housing such as the African Charter, there is no visible manifestation of those rights by the government in the provision of housing to the citizens. In effect, the governments of Ghana past and present only make housing a priority in their political development agenda; none has tried to include it as a right in the constitution. Therefore, the national philosophy for housing development in Ghana is the political manifestos of the ruling parties, which are not sustainable in the long run since they are not a legal framework. Thus, the Ghanaian Constitution does not contain justifiable socio-economic rights that directly enshrine everyone's right to have access to suitable and adequate housing.

History and development of housing policy in Ghana

There has been continuous government support in the housing sector in Ghana since the colonial era. In the first-half of the twentieth century, the colony of the Gold Coast, including Ashanti and the Northern Protectorate, had a fairly standard attitude towards housing construction for the time up to independence in 1957 (Graham & Korboe, 1998). It started with a motivation to house the British civil servants in some 'splendour' and separate from the local people. This was to prevent the spread of the tropical illnesses such as malaria, yellow fever and other debilitating diseases, which had no cure at that time. After this, nothing was done to improve the housing conditions of the local population. However, the public-housing schemes embarked upon by consecutive governments through the State Housing Company Limited have only been successful in providing housing for the few who are relatively rich (Wiredu, 2000). The huge public investments in housing throughout the years have produced less than the expected results, which is obvious in the severe shortage of housing in Ghana up to date.

Public-housing delivery has undergone socio-political transformation in Ghana's history. The pre-independence era witnessed the direct involvement of government in public housing. The emphasis on developing the housing industry gained prominence in Ghana from the late 1950s to the early 1960s as it attained independence from colonial rule (Bank of Ghana, 2007). To date, all housing schemes initiated by various governments from pre- to post-independence eras were unsuccessful due to a host of factors and, as such, the history of housing delivery in Ghana is 'de-facto, a tale of failed economic policies' (Decardi-Nelson & Solomon-Ayeh, 2009; Agyemang, 2001).

As previously noted, the housing interventions during the pre-independence era took the form of provision of staff houses for the senior public officers of the colonial governments in many parts of the country, especially in regional capitals, towns and mining areas through direct funding by the colonial government (Agyemang, 2001). The available housing schemes initiated by major companies in the then Gold Coast only provided accommodation for the expatriates, senior officers and junior workers and were not extended to the rest of the population. It was only in the 1920s and after the incidence of the 1939 earthquake in Ghana (Agyemang, 2001) that housing issues became more paramount. However, the main developments in housing improvement waited until after the Second World War when the new emphasis was on colonial development, driven by the need to show some gratitude to the heroic soldiers returning from the battle fronts to their colonial homelands.

The Gold Coast government's first recorded and direct involvement in housing was in the 1920s when the Dispossessed Person's Housing Scheme was introduced to provide housing for the natives dispossessed as a result of various government development programmes. Under the scheme, which began in 1923, affected persons were given a building materials loan to commence the construction of their own houses. By 1933, 118 loans had been approved and disbursed. The scheme was discontinued in 1933 because the Gold Coast government perceived it to be very expensive. This was during the tenure of Governor G. Guggisberg's reign (9 October 1919 to 24 April 1927). From that time onwards, little attention was paid to housing the native population until the 1939 earthquake (Agyemang, 2001). The 22 June 1939 earthquake in Accra, the now capital city of Ghana, called for the direct intervention of the government in the provision of affordable housing for the affected population. The government provided funding to build 1,000 two-bedroom unit houses for the affected people in various locations (Kwofie, Adinyira & Botchway, 2011). By 1955, only 1,250 units were completed, which still exist up to date, but now are occupied by civil and public servants and the armed forces. The housing provided through the earthquake intervention scheme was subsidized rental properties, and the tenants were given the opportunity to acquire them through hire-purchase.

Further, the Alan Burns government (29 June 1942 to 2 August 1947) also introduced a four-year development plan in 1943 of which housing was considered a top priority. The plan sought to implement the construction of inexpensive but well-built houses with as much local material content as possible on a limited budget (Agyemang, 2001). In 1946, two new housing schemes (Schemes A and B) under the government plan and policies were published. New housing Scheme A was under the direction of Department of Social Welfare. Under this scheme, three-, two- and one-bedroom apartments were to be constructed and rented to all people at economic cost. Only employees were required to pay non-economic rents. Scheme B was termed Town and Council Housing and was to be concentrated in Accra, Kumasi and Sekondi-Takoradi. Under this scheme, persons could apply for financial assistance to build within the municipality using their own design or adopting a pro-forma building plan from the Department of Social Welfare of which the plan and the contractor responsible for the housing construction had to be approved by the town council.

In the post-independence era, several interventions have been undertaken in the Ghanaian housing industry in an attempt for the new government to address the housing situation of those that were deprived of housing during the pre-independence period. However, all attempts made were considered unsuccessful by experts and stakeholders. Under the reign of Dr Kwame Nkrumah (6 March 1957 to 24 February 1966), the first president of Ghana, three development plans were formulated all aimed at the provision of adequate housing for the citizenry. The first development plan was the five-year plan from 1951 to 1956. This plan established the Tema Development Corporation (TDC) and the State Housing Corporation (SHC) (Agyemang, 2001; Bank of Ghana, 2007). The main objective of the TDC was to provide affordable housing for the low-income workers of the newly created Tema Province. The activities of the TDC led to the creation of the communities of Tema such as the communities one to eight, thus contributing over 2,255 housing units. The Schockbeton Housing Scheme was also established, which was targeted at the provision of 168 houses in Accra, Kumasi and Sekondi-Takoradi. This scheme was specifically under the consultancy of a Dutch firm, which introduced pre-cast materials perceived to be cheaper but which later became more expensive than estimated, hence this led to the abandonment of the whole scheme.

Likewise, the Roof Loan Scheme, which sought to grant loans and assistance to public-sector workers under the recommendation of the United Nations, also made contribution to the provision of housing units in Ghana. However, due to inefficiencies with the system only 2,517 units out of the originally proposed 6,700 housing unit were constructed (Decardi-Nelson & Solomon-Ayeh, 2009). The established SHC was to provide housing for the workers in the civil and public-service class and also to provide long-term housing finance. The activities of the SHC were expanded to cover all nine regions of the country. Its activities were monitored under the Ministry of Works and Housing (MoWH) with direct funding of its projects from the central government and, in 1995, it was converted into a limited liability company and operated as a commercial enterprise. Its schemes operated with the flexibility of workers owning their home through years of gradual monthly payment from salary deductions (Agyemang, 2001).

The Kwame Nkrumah second development plan was instituted to continue provision of housing from 1959 to 1964. This was to support the United Nations Commission's recommendations and initiated programmes for the government to provide housing units for the citizenry. The plan sought to continue and expand the Roof Loan Scheme, which was focused on assistance from employers to employees through the provision of housing loans and self-help housing sites and services (Decardi-Nelson & Solomon-Ayeh, 2009). The shortfall of this plan was that there was no needs assessment and, as a result, there was no indication of projected targets and outputs in the development plan (Agyemang, 2001). Despite the development plan's version to provide housing for all Ghanaians, Nkrumah's vision on housing was to house those in urban areas where shortage was at its peak due to uncontrolled urbanization. However, he was not able to see this plan to its end before he was replaced by a different government in 1966. Generally, the first Republican (Kwame Nkrumah) government used housing provision as a way of intervening in population distribution through housing in towns where employment opportunities were planned.

After the collapse of the Nkrumah's government, the National Liberation Council (NLC) under the leadership of Joseph Ankrah (24 February, 1966–3 April 1969) took over control and immediately adopted a two-year development plan, which was run through the existing systems put into place by the formal government. The NLC's plan through the TDC and the SHC was to produce 2,000 housing units annually. However, only a total of 1,000 units was realized. Out of the produced houses, 2.7% were one-room apartments. According to the housing location, 63.6% were constructed in Accra, 9% in Kumasi, 7.5% in Sekondi-Takoradi and 11.3% in the Cape Coast. The main objective of this scheme was to ensure that housing was generated by the productive sectors of the economy through a rational and balanced approach (Decardi-Nelson & Solomon-Ayeh, 2009). The development plan was also targeted at the clearance and slowing down of the growth of slums in the urban areas.

The Kofi Busia (1 October 1969 to 13 January 1972) administration also showed commitment to alleviating the housing crisis confronting the nation especially in the major Ghanaian cities by introducing a one-year development plan. The initial one-year development plan (1970–1971) of the second republic, later proceeded to a seven-year development plan. The main objective of this plan was aimed at a housing occupancy rate of ten persons per house as against a housing occupancy rate of six persons per household as recommended by the United Nations. The plan was also aimed at the construction of an estimated 26,000 housing units per year. However, the plan failed to specify the housing units with their associated cost. At its end, the scheme added under a quarter (764 – SHC, 1,012 – TDC = 1,776) of the targeted 8,000 units, which was mostly attributed to a lack of funds (Decardi-Nelson & Solomon-Ayeh, 2009).

When the National Redemption Council under I.K. Acheampong (13 January 1972–9 October 1975) took over government in 1972, it quickly established the National Low-Cost Housing Committee under the auspices of the MoWH. This plan initially received a capital injection of 10 million cedis to construct low-cost housing for low-income households in the urban areas across the ten Ghanaian regions. The plan had an annual projected delivery of 2,300 units (Decardi-Nelson & Solomon-Ayeh, 2009). By June 1975, the scheme had only realized a total of 5,466 units at a cost of 47,602,678 cedis. The scheme was, however, abandoned in 1976 because of its failure to serve the targeted population due to its associated high cost (Decardi-Nelson & Solomon-Ayeh, 2009). For instance, the original estimate indicated a cost of between 2,000 and 4,000 cedis per unit depending on the size, but upon completion of 5,466 units, the average per unit cost stood at 8,709 cedis. Furthermore, 6,000 units cost a total sum of 62.6 million cedis, thus increasing the average cost to over 10,433 cedis. The government acknowledging its limitation with funding sought to encourage the private sector to complement its effort (Agyemang, 2001).

The Hilla Liman (24 September 1979 to 31 December 1981) government also recognized the enormity of the housing problems and thus contributed to the building of 1,990 rental units through the SHC and 228 by the TDC (Benjamin, 2007; Decardi-Nelson & Solomon-Ayeh, 2009). However, because of the poor economic performance in Ghana with the growing energy crisis, rising costs of oil, excessively high rise in imported building materials, decline in external funding, the Ghanaian construction industry was brought to a halt, which impeded the construction of houses as planned by the Liman administration. It was against this background that the Liman government sought to invest in the development of the use of local materials leading to the establishment of the Tile and Brick Factory (Benjamin, 2007).

The Jerry J. Rawlings era (31 December 1981 to 7 January 2001) saw the implementation of many schemes in an attempt to solve the housing problems that other past administrators could not solve. Among the introduced housing schemes were the National Shelter Strategy (NSS), Ghana Vision 2020 and the Structural Adjustment Programme and Economic Recovery Programme.

The NSS, initiated in 1986, led to the formation of the NHP Committee by the MoWH to examine the housing situation in Ghana. The intention was to establish an appropriate government policy and action plan that sought to provide adequate and decent housing units in order to improve the quality of life of the people in urban and rural areas (Bank of Ghana, 2007). The focus of this committee was on constraints in housing delivery, especially in the area of housing finance, land, physical planning, infrastructure, building materials, design and construction, and coordination delivery efforts. The report of the committee culminated in a national housing policy and action plan covering the period 1987 through to 1990. Prior to the formation of the action plan, the MoWH had identified the need for a comprehensive NSS and an enhancement of the Ministry's planning capacity to implement housing policies. The strategy sought to implement a revised national housing sector policy and action plan for short-, medium- and long-term strategies for Ghana, with emphasis on rural communities in order to assist them to improve their existing shelter or improve access to the means for providing their own shelter as well as to develop non-conventional housing delivery systems that encourage community participation at all levels and with emphasis on local authorities playing a substantial role in the management and development of housing. In summary, the NSS was to create an enabling environment and framework to enhance housing provision rather than the full participation of the government to the delivery of housing.

The Ghana Vision 2020 scheme had the first medium-term development plan (from 1997 to 2000) target of the provision of affordable low-income housing units, which are within the reach of the poor in order to improve their living conditions (Bank of Ghana, 2007). The scheme introduced a new facility under the Social Provident Scheme, which permitted contributors to withdraw part of their contributions to purchase a house. Unfortunately, due to lack of funds, low private-sector participation and political will, none of the housing strategies under this plan were implemented or look likely to be implemented with 2020 fast approaching.

No considerable additions had been made to public housing from 1985 to 2000. Nevertheless, the John A. Kuffour government (7 January 2001–7 January 2009) also pursued the reduction of the crisis situation of the housing sector through the initiation of a plan to build about 20,000 affordable housing units in 2001. In 2007, building of about 4,500 units from bedsits to one- and two-bedroom apartments started at various locations. This represented the new government's effort to ease the housing problems in the country. The main target group of this scheme was civil and public servants. Unfortunately, by the expiration of the Kuffour government not a single unit was completed and most have been taken over by squatters. The scheme was discontinued by the new government in 2009.

The government of John Evans Atta Mills (7 January 2009 to 24 July 2012) drove for the provision of housing in Ghana, which is fully enshrined in the Coordinated Programme of Economic and Social Development Policies, 2010–2016, an agenda for shared growth and accelerated development for a better Ghana. The Coordinated Programme of the Economic and Social Development Policies is a strategic blueprint for directing national priorities in the medium-term that provides a framework for channelling national aspirations towards accelerated industrial development. On careful scrutiny, the agenda is an expanded manifesto of the National Democratic Congress presented in 2004 entitled 'A Better Ghana'. The agenda is operationalized to guide the execution of development policy and related activities at all levels of the governance structure (Government of Ghana, 2010). The present government recognizing the ever-increasing population growth, rural–urban migration and the re-classification of settlements from rural to urban and other population growth dynamics, which have contributed to the rapid urbanization of Ghanaian towns and cities, refuses to make a commitment to the exact number of housing units to be constructed. Instead, a different approach was adopted to provide an enabling environment for all stakeholders to participate in the housing delivery process. The government stated that a special effort would be made, together with local and international private-sector partners, to launch a new national housing initiative to begin the rationalization of the housing market in order to provide affordable housing for Ghanaians.

The involvement of the quasi-government institutions in the Ghanaian housing delivery cannot be overlooked. Towards the end of the 1980s, the Social Security and National Insurance Trust (SSNIT) expanded on its programmes to build housing for its staff across the country. Though this was originally targeted at its staff, it was later expanded in 1988 in a significant investment in housing at 'social' not market prices, providing a cheaper option for the general public to also benefit from the scheme. However, at the end of construction, the SSNIT did not attain its objective for the poor and low-income earners/groups. The project, however, benefited the middle- and upper-income classes (Benjamin, 2007). Also, another of the SSNIT's notable schemes was the 1,637 units at Sakumono, where its success led to it being repeated across the country in Anaji- Takoradi, Koforidua, Wa, Adenta-Accra and Kumasi among others (Amoa-Mensah, 2003). Conversely, in 1999, when Ghana's financial crisis hit its peak, the SSNIT was unable to continue operating its social rental units at a loss in so much that its reduced rents were higher than what most Ghanaians could afford. Being saddled with huge operational and maintenance costs, the SSNIT began the process of divesting most of its real-estate assets. To date, it has sold around 92% of its housing units.

Likewise, the SHC, after its recapitalization in 1995, adapted a new approach to housing delivery. Under this scheme, prospective home-owners were given the opportunity to finance their own home after first making a down payment of about 20–25% of the cost of the building. This has come with little success, as many of the units overran in time and cost. This scheme was carried out in all the regions where the SHC operates. Also, the Ghanaian Real Estate Development Association (GREDA) was formed to help improve the dismal housing deficit, especially through the adoption of best practices in construction and management. Notwithstanding the expansive role of the GREDA in recent times, housing supply has not increased any further (Bank of Ghana, 2007; Ahadzie, 2008). Since its formation in 1988, GREDA has delivered a total of 10,954 housing units (Mahama, 2004). The delivery from GREDA annually, at its peak, averaged 2,500 units, constituting less than 10% of the total annual delivery. This is a drop in the ocean, compared to the then annual housing requirement of 199,000 units. The actual delivery was purported to be between 25,000 to 30,000 units.

Housing policy in Ghana

From the above analysis of the history and development of housing policy in Ghana, it can be inferred that the main policy directions in Ghana have been in the direct supply of quite a small number of dwellings and a number of measures to influence demand. These have included provision of low-income housing for the civil servants and others; rent subsidies and subsequent purchase of government-built dwellings; subsidised interest rates for borrowers from the few institutions concerned with housing finance; and a very successful rent-control regime starting in 1943 and only relaxed in 1987 (Graham & Korboe, 1998). The NSS and the Ghana Vision 2020 represent the current direction of urban housing policy in Ghana with United Nations assistance through the MoWH. Its six main objectives are:

- improving the quality of shelter;
- improving the environment of human settlements;
- making shelter programmes more accessible to the poor;
- promoting private-sector involvement through an enabling-policy environment;

- encouraging rental housing; and
- promoting orderly growth with infrastructure in place.

Until the early 1980s, housing was regarded as a social service in Ghana, which was to be enjoyed by both the rich and poor. In the light of high incidence of poverty, income inequality and acute housing shortages in Ghana, the consideration of housing as a social policy became a matter of critical necessity. Housing provision in Ghana reflected these beliefs until it was realized that this approach had left the government-approved bodies seriously indebted and liable, and unable to house the poor. There was a general shift in the national ideology in Ghana in the early 1980s when the economy was liberalized that resulted in a re-orientation of the approach to housing delivery. Housing is now seen as an economic commodity, which is produced and sold for profit. The corresponding institutional response was the metamorphosing of the SHC into a limited liability company, which is expected to now show maximum returns on investments in housing. However, public housing has not met and is still not meeting the housing demand in Ghana. Besides, the supplied houses are widely unsuitable for the users. Grave housing inequalities are therefore visible in Ghanaian urban areas in the form of slums and squatter settlements.

Challenges facing the provision of housing in Ghana

The foregoing discussions reveal that the housing industry in Ghana is inundated with an array of challenges. Currently, Ghana is facing an acute housing problem with a housing deficit in excess of 400,000 units. The most vulnerable groups are the urban and rural poor whose houses are mostly constructed with sub-standard materials with little or no basic services and infrastructure, including proper drainage and waste-disposal systems. The key challenges mitigating against effective housing delivery in Ghana include the following:

- poverty – land cost and its accessibility;
- finance – high cost of mortgage;
- infrastructure development;
- development approval procedures;
- availability and cost of building materials;
- institutional co-ordination; and
- a lack of adequate governance for shelter provision.

In view of this, the ultimate goal of the country's shelter policy is to provide adequate, decent and affordable housing that is accessible and sustainable with infrastructural facilities to satisfy the needs of Ghanaians. Other factors also responsible for the inadequate provision of housing in Ghana include (Bank of Ghana, 2007):

- absence of a clearly defined national housing policy;
- managerial inefficiencies;

- high cost of building materials;
- lack of access to sustainable capital/finance; and
- lack of control and regulatory policy framework for rent.

Housing in Ghana: needs, demand and supply

Provision of housing in Ghana has witnessed fragmented and unsustained effort from individuals, private developers and governments. This situation has contributed to the huge housing deficit currently experienced in Ghana. The shortage of housing continues to be one of the most critical socio-economic challenges facing the country at the present moment. The rapid increase in population has resulted in a large housing deficit, especially in urban areas. This has manifested in overcrowding and the development of slums. According to the government of Ghana, there is insufficient housing stock to meet the ever-increasing demand for housing in urban areas. Recent estimates indicate that there is a housing backlog of more than one million units nationwide. It is further estimated that to replace this shortfall, annual national housing delivery should be approximately 120,000 housing units. However, the supply capacity nationally is 42,000 units per annum. Thus more than 60% of the national requirements will remain unsatisfied each year. Demand for housing is higher in the major cities of the country, such as Accra, Kumasi and Tema, among others.

The main sources of housing demand in Ghana include:

- locally resident Ghanaians;
- non-resident Ghanaians;
- expatriates living in Ghana;
- corporate organizations; and
- foreign nationals.

An increasing number of people from the West Africa sub-region also contribute greatly to the demand for housing in Ghana. The Ghanaian housing supply source has a long history as enumerated above. The government through the state-owned housing corporation has played a significant role in housing delivery, albeit not enough to cater for the entire low-income earners and poor groups. However, under the Government Liberalization Policy since 1992 and the current agenda for shared growth and accelerated development for a better Ghana, the state has significantly reduced its role in the housing sector and encouraged the participation of the private sector to provide housing. The SSNIT, a para-statal organization, has over the years developed a number of high-income and middle-income housing either directly or through joint ventures.

Lessons learnt from Ghanaian housing studies

The lessons learnt to date from the Ghanaian housing studies are not far from those achieved by the Nigerian government, which are:

Ahadzie, D.K. (2008). Management practices in Ghanaian house building industry. Unpublished material.

Ahmed, I. (2011). An overview of post-disaster permanent housing reconstruction in developing countries. *International journal of disaster resilience in the built environment*, 2(2):1–27.

Akpomuvie, O.B. (2010). Self-help as a strategy for rural development in Nigeria: A bottom-up approach. *Journal of alternative perspectives in the social sciences*, 2(1):88–111.

Alaghbari, W., Salim, A., Dola, K. and Ali, A.A.A. (2009). Housing shortage for low-income in Yemen: Causes and suggestions, *International journal of housing markets and analysis*, 2(4):363–372.

Alder, G. (2002). Ownership is not a priority among the urban poor: The case of informal settlements in Nairobi. *Habitat debate*, 5(3):1–5.

Amoa-Mensah, K. (2003). Housing in Ghana: A search for sustainable options as the way forward for enhanced output – Year 2003 and beyond. International Building Exhibition Seminar, Accra, Ghana.

Angel, S. (2000). *Housing policy matters*. Oxford: Oxford University Press.

Arimah, B.C. (1992). Hedonic prices and the demand for housing attributes in a Third World city: The case of Ibadan, Nigeria. *Urban studies*, 29:639–651.

Bank of Ghana (2007). The housing industry in Ghana: Prospects and challenges. Policy brief. Available from: www.bog.gov.gh/privatecontent/File/Research/PolicyBrief/pbrief-housing-new1.pdf (accessed 30 July 2011).

Bell, S. (1996). *Learning with information systems: Learning cycles in information systems development*. 1st edn. New York: Routledge.

Benjamin, C. (2007). A brief history of housing in Ghana. Available from: www.thestatesmanonline.com (accessed 20 August 2010).

Berry, L. (1995). *Ghana. A country study*. Area handbook series. Lanham, MD: Bernan.

Bruce, J. (1998). *Review of tenure terminology*. Tenure brief no. 1, Land Tenure Center. Madison: University of Wisconsin.

Chambers, R. (1995). Poverty and livelihoods: Whose reality counts? *Environment and urbanization*, 7(1):173–204.

Decardi-Nelson, I. and Solomon-Ayeh, B. (2009). Provision of affordable housing in Ghana: The realities. In E. Atiemo, E. Osei-Tutu, B. Solomon-Ayeh, I. Decardi-Nelson & P.K. Amankwah (eds) *Proceedings of National Housing Conference*, 7–8 October at STEPRI, pp. 34–44.

De Soto, H. (2000). *The mystery of capital*. London: Bantam.

Farzana, F. (2004). Shortages of middle-income owner-occupied housing in Dhaka – Failures of government or market? Available from: http://scholarbank.nus.edu.sg/handle/10635/14687 (accessed 9 July 2011).

Ferguson, B. (2001). Housing policy in the new millennium conference. Conference proceedings of the US Department of Housing and Urban Development, Washington, DC.

Ghana Statistical Service (2017). 2010 population and housing census. Available from: www.statsghana.gov.gh/ (accessed 5 March 2017).

Government of Ghana (2005). *Draft national housing policy*. Ministry of Water Resources, Works and Housing. Accra, Ghana: Government of Ghana.

Government of Ghana (2010). The coordinated programme of economic and social development policies, 2010–2016. Available from: https://new-ndpc-static.s3.amazonaws.com/pubication/Coordinated+Programme+2010-2016.pdf (accessed 1 May 2018).

- Since Ghana's independence, provision of housing has remained cen all development agendas of the various governments as evident fro review of the housing policy from the pre- to post-colonial eras.
- Various governmental administrations and institutions have soug address issues such as land-ownership, land-title regulation, and the prc of affordable housing units to the working and non-working populatio
- From the above analysis of the history and development of housing in Ghana, the literature revealed that the main housing policy direct Ghana have been in the direct supply of quite a small number of dw and a number of measures to influence demand.
- The NSS and the Ghana Vision 2020 are the country's current direc urban housing policy in Ghana with United Nations' assistance, w formulated by the MoWH. However, subsequent governments re-m the strategies and the vision to suit their own various manifest purposes.
- There was a shift from the formal national ideology in Ghanaian l when the economy was liberalized, resulting in the re-orientation approach to housing delivery. Housing is now currently seen economic commodity in Ghana, which is produced and sold for prc
- The constitution of Ghana does not contain justifiable socio-ec rights that enshrine everyone's right to access adequate housing.
- Also revealed from this chapter of the book is that the fundamental phies underpinning housing development vision in Ghana are th political manifestos of the various governments that have ruled Ghan
- Current government intervention in housing is at the level of prov enabling environment for the various stakeholders to help amelio housing backlog.

Summary

This chapter revealed that the government of Ghana has a detailed trac of a holistic national support for the provision of housing to its p However, with the recent general development plan for the Ghanaian e the government has distanced itself from the old practice of housing pro supporting housing delivery by other stakeholders. Another fundamenta from this chapter is that the constitution of Ghana does not explicitly justifiable socio-economic rights that enshrine everyone's right to ac quate housing despite being signatories to international treaties that this right. The next chapter discusses the housing policy evolution ar opment in Nigeria.

References

Agyemang, K.K. (2001). *The political economy of housing and urban development Ghana's experience from colonial times to 1998*. Westport, CT: Praeger Publishe

Graham, T. & Korboe, D. (1998). *Housing policy in Ghana: Towards a supply-oriented future. Habitat international*, 22(3):245–257.

Ibem, E.O., Anosike, M.N. & Azuh, D.E. (2011). Challenges in public housing provision in the post-independence era in Nigeria. *International journal of human sciences*, 8(2):421–443.

Koenigsberger, O. (1986). Third world housing policies since the 1950s. *Habitat international*, 10(3):27–32.

Kwofie, T.E., Adinyira, E. & Botchway, E. (2011). Historical overview of housing provision in pre- and post-independence Ghana. In S. Laryea, R. Leiringer & W. Hughes (eds) *Proceedings of West Africa Built Environment Research (WABER) Conference*, Accra, Ghana, pp. 541–557. Available from: http://centaur.reading.ac.uk/20829/1/WABER_2011_conference_proceedings.pdf (accessed 1 May 2018).

Mahama, C.A. (2004). *Institutional and legal arrangements for land development in Ghana*. Cambridge: University of Cambridge Press.

Malpezzi, S. (1990). Urban housing and financial markets: Some international comparisons. *Urban studies*, 27(6):971–1022.

Olotuah, A.O. (2006). Housing quality in suburban areas: An empirical study of Oba-Ile, Nigeria. *DIMENSI (Jurnal Teknik Arsitektur)*, 34(2):133–137.

Republic of Ghana (2011). Ghana at a glance. Available from: www.ghana.gov.gh/index.php/about-ghana/ghana-at-a-glance (accessed 1 May 2018).

Skinner, J. (1989). Housing wealth and aggregate saving. *Regional science and urban economics*, 19(2):305–324.

Tibaijuka, A.K. (2005). *Report of the fact-finding mission to Zimbabwe to assess the scope and impact of Operation Murambatsvina by the UN special envoy on human settlement issues in Zimbabwe*. New York: United Nations, pp. 1–100.

UN-Habitat (2010). The state of African cities 2010: Governance, inequality and urban land markets. Nairobi: United Nations Human Settlements Programme.

United Nations (1995). *World urbanization prospects: The 1994 revision: Estimates and projections of urban and rural populations and of urban agglomerations*. ST/ESA/SER.A/150. New York: United Nations.

Wiredu, G.O. (2000). An assessment of the post-commercialisation performance of the State Housing Company Limited (SHC Ltd) in the solution of housing problems in Ghana: Focus on Kumasi. Unpublished material.

5 Housing development in Nigeria

Introduction

This chapter looks into housing in Nigeria. The policies and agencies supporting housing delivering in Nigeria, such as the government, the private sector and others are presented. An evaluation of past policies and government-intervention programmes are also presented. The philosophical basis for housing provision in Nigeria is discussed. Also explored in this chapter are the challenges facing provision and the needs, demand and supply of housing in Nigeria.

Background

Nigeria, a former British colony, became an independent nation on 1 October 1960 and a republic in 1963. According to the country comparison by the Central Intelligence Agency (2017), Nigeria's population is currently estimated at 186,053,386, with conservative estimates concluding that more than 20% of the world's black population lives in Nigeria. Nigeria's population is projected to grow from more than 186 million people in 2016 to 392 million in 2050, becoming the world's fourth most populous country. The rate of urban population growth is thought to be 5.5% annually, roughly twice the national population growth rate of 2.9%. More than seven Nigerian cities have populations that exceed one million, and over 5,000 towns and cities of various sizes have populations of between 20,000 and 500,000. Greater Lagos, the former national capital, has grown from 1.4 million in 1963 to 3.5 million in 1975. It is currently over 13 million strong, and is projected to reach 24 million by 2020 (Nwaka, 2005). Furthermore, Nigeria has the greatest diversity of cultures, ways of life, cities and terrain. With the current annual population growth rate of 2.9%, which is nearly the same as the annual GDP growth rate (3.5%), the Nigerian population is set to double in the next 25 years.

Up until 1989 the country's capital was Lagos, with a population of about 2,500,000, but the government has since moved the capital to Abuja. The country's governmental structure was increased to 12 states in 1967, then to 19 states in 1976, with Abuja as the new federal capital. Nigeria is located in western Africa on the Gulf of Guinea with a land and water total area of

923,768km^2 making it the world's 32nd-largest country (following Tanzania). Nigeria has a varied landscape. From the Obudu Hills in the southeast through to the beaches in the south, the rainforest, the Lagos estuary and savannah in the middle and southwest of the country and the Sahel to the encroaching Sahara in the extreme north. The highest point in Nigeria is Chapel Wadi at 2,419 m (7,936 ft). According to the United Nations, Nigeria has been undergoing explosive population growth and has one of the highest growth and fertility rates in the world. By the United Nations' projections, Nigeria will be one of the countries in the world that will account for most of the world's total population increase by 2050. According to current data, one out of every four Africans is a Nigerian. Presently, Nigeria is the most populous country in Africa, the seventh most populous country in the world, of which the majority of the population is black. The economy of Nigeria is one of the fastest growing in the world, with the International Monetary Fund projecting a growth of 8% growth in the Nigerian economy in 2011.

Nigeria has become progressively more urbanized in the last five decades; the proportion of the population living in urban areas rose from 15% in 1950, to 23.4% in 1975 and to 43.3% in 2000. Projections indicate that more than 60% of Nigerians will live in urban centres by 2025, and a substantial percentage of these is likely to live in slums if urgent action is not taken. Over time, one of Nigeria's greatest challenges is providing adequate housing for its growing population. The problem of inadequate housing for the teeming population of approximately 186 million is getting even more complicated. As of 1991, Nigeria was said to have a housing deficit of 7 million units. Twenty-four years down the line, the deficit had skyrocketed by about 250% according to statistics. The housing deficit at the moment is put at 17 million units. The World Bank has also estimated the cost of bridging Nigeria's 17-million-unit housing deficit at N59.5 trillion ($29.5 million). This is not too far from the estimation of the Federal Mortgage Bank of Nigeria (FMBN) that had put it at about N56 trillion ($26 million) to be able to adequately meet the housing needs of Nigerians.

Housing in Nigeria

Housing in Nigeria is a highly contentious and politicized issue that is of great concern to administrators, scholars and the Nigerian general public. The influx of people into the urban areas, the natural population increase and insufficient responses by the government have contributed to the deterioration of the housing situation in Nigeria over time. The extent of this situation is such that the economic development and the welfare of the citizens are adversely affected. The housing problem in Nigeria is more critical in the cities, where a huge housing supply deficit exists, which is coupled with dilapidated housing conditions and the high cost of housing construction, as well as the proliferation of urban slums and squatter settlements that are the norm. As such, a large majority of urban residents, particularly the low-income earners who constitute about 50% of Nigeria's 186 million people, is forced to live in conditions that constitute an affront to human dignity. In acknowledgement of the fact that neither the public nor the private sectors are able to address this problem individually, current efforts in addressing the housing situation in Nigeria are mostly based on collaborative efforts (Mabogunje, 2003); public–private partnerships (PPPs) are among the most collective forms of such collaborative efforts (Ibem, 2010).

Thus, the provision of affordable housing for its citizens has remained the principal focus of every successive government in Nigeria. This is because of the pivotal roles played by housing in national development and growth, on the one hand, and its being a necessity in the life of the people, on the other. Since Nigeria's independence, affordable housing has been the major policy concern of relevant housing and mortgage institutions. However, critics are of the view that, despite the policy efforts, only the needs of the middle- and high-income classes are met, which defiles the generally acknowledged fact that the right to housing is one of the most important basic human rights recognized in many international human rights treaties (Bret, 2002) because housing is a basic human need of all citizens.

In Nigeria, a home of one's own represents a precious refuge. For instance, in the traditional African setting and in most developing nations, housing is one of the greatly cherished material properties. This is because of the other functions that a house performs in the traditional society, which includes the protection of family cohesion and values, taking care of the aged through the extended-family system, and the protection of the ancestral values, among others. Indeed, the debate on housing in Nigeria often shows that housing ranks above education and health services as a priority. Thus, households in Nigeria value home-ownership more than households in advanced industrialized countries. In fact, in most developing nations like Nigeria, when a family does not have a house they can call their own, that family is regarded as the poorest of the poor. Thus, the importance of providing adequate housing (housing that meets the needs and expectations of the people, ranging from the supplied quantity to the quality, thus assuring the quality of life of the people) in Nigeria cannot be over-emphasized. However, acquiring access to a house and to the components that comprise housing such as land and property rights, building materials, basic services, regulations, subsidies and credit are extraordinarily difficult for most people in Nigeria. This is because of the poor land records, tenure rights with dysfunctional legal systems and regulatory bodies typically cloud ownership rights for a large number of households.

However, the efforts of the government aimed at providing shelter especially for the low-income groups have not yielded expected positive results compared to the level of effort. This is because it has been apprehended more as the product of a politically motivated official intervention in the housing crisis, usually at urban level, than a genuine concern to shelter the poor and needy. For instance, housing schemes designed for the citizens especially the low-income groups have been forcefully taken over by the high- and medium-income earners. It been previously reported that most chairmen (persons) of the allocation committees of these housing schemes are politicians who allocated the houses to party members who neither had the need for them nor could be classified as low-income earners (Shyllon, 1999). Also, the housing corporations that are supposed to provide shelter for the public (low-income earners and disadvantaged groups) only catered for the high-income groups who can afford or meet up with their stringent terms and pre-qualification conditions. Furthermore, frantic efforts by the low-income earners for owner-occupier houses are thwarted by their inability to mobilize adequate funds to execute the project (Jolaoso, Musa & Oriola, 2008). As a result, the Nigerian housing question is primarily that of a crisis situation, manifesting and expressing itself in qualitative and quantitative forms. As a matter of fact, past Nigeria governments cannot be said to have ignored housing in the process of national development. The emphasis and implementation may be weak, but past governments have shown some commitment to housing matters as reported by various scholars (Adeyemo & Dekolo, 2000; Aigbavboa & Thwala, 2009, 2011; Federal Government of Nigeria, 2004).

In spite of the efforts of various stakeholders that have been involved in the provision of housing, there are still numerous challenges affecting these efforts as highlighted: the limited use of co-operative housing approaches is one of the challenges facing delivery of adequate housing for the majority of people needing housing (Onukwugha, 2000). The high cost of building materials, inadequate housing statistics for proper planning, institutional challenges and low housing investment are some of the factors responsible for inadequate housing in Nigeria (Jinadu, 2004). Furthermore, difficulties in land acquisition, inability to access long-term mortgage finance and the high cost of building materials are other factors responsible for inadequate housing delivery (Ademiluyi & Raji, 2008). Another issue is that a disproportionate number of professional builders (less than 2,000) relative to the population of Nigeria (more than 186 million) contributes indirectly to the inadequate delivery of housing (Jimoh & Olayiwola, 2008). Aigbavboa and Thwala (2009) established the following factors as being responsible for the inadequate housing delivery experienced in Nigeria:

- legislation;
- contracts enforcement;
- inadequate infrastructure;
- unstable macroeconomic environment; and
- lacklustre implementation of the NHP.

In addition to the above challenges, high interest rates charged by banks for mortgage loans and the concentration of primary mortgage institutions in urban centres such as Lagos and Abuja are also responsible for the slow pace of affordable housing delivery for the low-income group.

The present housing difficulty in Nigeria does not necessarily arise from poverty, but because of the absence of an effective administrative arm to mobilize and organize the country's natural, human and industrial resources among others for housing and urban development (Jolaoso, Musa & Oriola, 2008). However, the problem of poor co-ordination and ineffectiveness of some public housing agencies in Nigeria is in most cases responsible for the failure of certain laudable housing policies and programmes. Some of the agencies with adequate knowledge have refused to perform their duty of seeing to it that the beneficiaries of the housing schemes fulfil their obligations and hence this has constituted a threat to the successful execution of the housing scheme for the low-income groups (Shu'aibu, 2007).

Philosophical basis for housing development in Nigeria

The fundamental philosophy underpinning housing development vision in Nigeria is the existing Nigerian Constitution of 1999. Chapter II of the Nigerian Constitution popularly referred to as the 'fundamental objectives and directive principles of state policy', states that the security and welfare of the people shall be the primary purpose of government. The constitution further expresses that the government is entrusted with the responsibility to harness the resources of the nation to serve the common good of all and to promote national prosperity based on an efficient, dynamic and self-reliant economy (Eboh, 2010). Also, it states that government should manage the economy so as to secure the maximum welfare, freedom and happiness of every citizen. Furthermore, it specifically requires that the state shall ensure that suitable and adequate shelter is provided for the citizens (Federal Republic of Nigeria, 1999). In effect, this national philosophy (which was also enunciated in previous constitutions) has been the generic basis for housing development and planning since Nigeria gained independence. Despite this background, the Nigerian Constitution does not employ the expression 'adequate housing', but it provides in Section 16(1) (d), under the chapter dealing with the 'fundamental objectives and directive principles of state policy', that the state shall ensure that 'suitable and adequate shelter' is provided to all citizens. Section 13 of the constitution further states that, 'it shall be the duty and responsibility of all organs of government, and of all authorities and persons, exercising legislative, executive or judicial powers, to conform to, observe and apply the Fundamental Objectives and Directive Principles'. However, Section 6(6) (c) diminishes the impact of Section 13 by expressly stipulating that it does not establish enforceable rights. This contrasts with the constitutional provisions on fundamental rights, which though enforceable do not include access to adequate housing or shelter. Thus, the Nigeria Constitution does not explicitly contain justifiable socio-economic rights and does not directly enshrine everyone's right to have access to suitable and adequate housing, but it indirectly informs of the support for everyone to have access to 'suitable and adequate shelter'. This indirect support has been a major hindrance in the effort to adequately house the poor and the low-income groups.

The history of housing policy in Nigeria

Before the arrival of the colonial rule at the beginning of the twentieth century, a communal system of housing delivery was practised in most Nigerian communities. Houses were built through communal efforts by peer groups. Members of all ages and different groupings and other social organizations would turn out as a group on an appointed day to assist the builder in whatever task of the project. In return, the builder would provide meals while the project lasted. This system continued up to 1928, and still remains in some communities to date despite the disruption of people's 'communitarian' values by 'Westernization' and urbanization. Housing issues in colonial Nigeria were based on the politics of 'separate areas' (Adisa, Agunbiade & Akanmu, 2008). During the early years of colonial administration, the Nigerian government was involved in the construction of official residences for expatriates and senior indigenous staff (in the public services, such as the police and railway personnel) in specially zoned Government Reserved Areas through the Public Works Department. Also, the then three regional governments, through the colonial housing policy in place, catered exclusively for the housing needs of the top echelons of the civil service. When Nigeria became an independent state in 1960, the colonial politics of discriminatory housing changed somewhat. After the attainment of independence and the immediate period after achievement of sovereignty, public housing was limited, elitist and largely in the form of middle-class housing estates for government officials. The exit of the colonial masters afforded Nigerians the opportunity to move into residential areas hitherto reserved for the European workers. Despite the removal of the discriminatory housing format operated under colonialism with the advent of the Nigerian independence, housing in Nigeria has remained a contentious issue. Regardless of the laws and all attempts made to date, Nigeria still faces a severe housing shortage with much of the population living in sub-standard housing. However, evidence clearly shows that public housing provision in Nigeria has not recorded any impressive results in matching housing production to housing demand, as there are huge housing supply deficits.

Furthermore, the outbreak of bubonic plague in Lagos, the then capital city of Nigeria in the 1920s, led to the first slum clearance and settlement upgrading policy programme by the Lagos Executive Development Board (LEDB) (Aribigbola, 2008). Between 1973 and 1995 about 36 other cases of slum clearance were reported in urban areas in Nigeria, including the widely publicized demolition of Maroko, Lagos in 1990 (Agbola & Jinadu, 1997), which was regarded as a violation of the housing rights of the occupants. Although the aim of the slum clearance was to upgrade blighted areas in the cities, the approach failed to provide decent and affordable housing to Nigerians. This is due to the non-availability of land in locations that were acceptable to the displaced persons, as well as the lack of adequate funds to resettle them: however, the vacant land was sold at high prices to the rich in the society (Agbola & Jinadu, 1997; Umeh, 2004; Nwaka, 2005).

In 1958, the defunct regional governments, that is, Western, Eastern, Northern and Mid-Western regions, established housing corporations to construct and manage housing estates, as well as to grant 'soft' loans to individuals wishing to build their own houses. Unfortunately, the established agencies were unable to extend their services to the low-income group due to the lack of commitment to low-cost housing (Federal Republic of Nigeria, 1991; Ibem, 2010). The first National Development Plan (NDP) (1962–1968), which spilt into the 1970s, brought about the establishment of the Federal Housing Authority (FHA), the Federal Ministry of Housing, Urban Development and Environment, the Federal Ministry of Works and Housing (FMWH), state housing corporations and the FMGN. At this stage, Nigeria was set to witness massive government involvement in housing construction, which was supposed to have extended to the low-income group. The first government-assisted self-help housing programme took off in the then newly created states of Bauchi, Benue, Gongola, Imo, Niger, Ogun and Ondo, as well as in Lagos State, in the mid-1970s (Ibem, 2010). With assistance from the World Bank, the scheme succeeded in providing serviced plots, soft loans and technical assistance for some in the low-income groups towards owning houses in the eight states' capitals, but it could not be extended to other states because of logistics and funding constraints on the part of the government. Conversely, the plan made provision for the erection of at least 59,000 dwelling units, 15,000 for Lagos and 4,000 for each of the then 11 states. However, the success rate was only 12% (Okpala, 1986). Its spread was wide and even but was skewed in favour of low-income workers, who constituted 60% of the workforce. The middle-income group constituted 30%, while the upper-income group made up the remaining 10%. The second NDP of 1970–1974, with the launch of the National Low-Cost Housing Scheme in 1975 committed a total of NGN53.35 million ($380,000) to the building of new houses and upgrading of the old ones.

In the third NDP (1975–1980), both the federal and the state governments attempted, for the first time, direct construction of housing units to be let out at subsidized rates. Similarly, the FMBN, a latter-day convert of the Nigerian Building Society (Adisa, Agunbiade & Akanmu, 2008), was established primarily to grant loans to mortgage institutions in order to facilitate housing delivery. About NGN2.6 billion ($130 million) was earmarked for the construction of 202,000 housing units across the country. With the proposal of 202,000 units during this planned period, Lagos State, the then national capital, was allocated 46,000 units and the remaining 156,000 were to be built in the different parts of the country. The dismal performance of the public sector's direct involvement in housing is shown by the fact that only 18% of the intended dwelling units (8,500) were built in Lagos, while only 13% (20,000 units) of the proposed units were constructed in the rest of the country by the end of the planned period (Ogu & Ogbuozobe, 2001). In all, about 24% of the 202,000 housing units were constructed at the expiration of that development plan, while many of the uncompleted housing units were abandoned. As a result, the dream of home-ownership of many Nigerians could not be realized through that scheme

(Onibokun, 1985). The targets were not met and it necessitated the incorporation of another housing plan in the fourth NDP.

The fourth NDP period (1981–1985) witnessed the launching and implementation of the third National Housing Programme by a civilian administration. During this period, only 20% of the planned 1600,000 dwelling units were constructed. The fourth Development Housing Programme was frustrated by fraud and politicization of these projects, lack of supervisory technical staff at building sites and lack of service infrastructure (Ogu & Ogbuozobe, 2001). Likewise, the plan earmarked 600 million dollars for housing development but, from 1984, the military administration abandoned direct intervention in the housing market and embarked on demonstration projects. Table 5.1 below shows a summary of the planned and constructed number of housing units in the different public housing programmes, initiated between 1962 and 2014. An analysis of Table 5.1 reveals that an aggregate of 618,498 housing units were intended for construction in the various public housing schemes across the country. The total of 85,812 housing units actually constructed represents around 14% of the intended housing units. This achievement level clearly shows that many of the public housing programmes initiated by governments within that period failed to meet the targeted number of housing units (Ibem, Anosike & Azuh, 2011). The cumulative effect of this failure is that an estimated 75% of Nigeria's 60 million urban population lives in slums, and not less than 700,000 housing units are required annually to improve on this appalling housing situation across the country (Federal Republic of Nigeria, 1991; Olotuah, 2010). This denotes that suitable measures need to be urgently put in place to combat the challenge of low productivity in public-sector housing in the country.

Furthermore, the failure of the National Low-Cost Housing Scheme led to the initiation of the National Site-and-Services Programme. The National Site-and-Services Programme was proposed to make serviced plots available to housing developers without many inconveniences (Onibokun, 1985). Under the guidance of the FMWH, the FHA and other related housing provision agencies, the programme recorded initial success in seven states, namely, Lagos, Kano, Imo, Kwara, Ondo, Rivers and Imo, as well as in Federal Capital Territory (FCT). The majority of beneficiaries for this scheme were the middle- and high-income groups who could afford the high cost of transfer fees and who met the requirements for allocation of the serviced plots. Regardless of the obvious poor performance of the public housing schemes, among others, the number of produced housing units fell far below the intended housing units. Hence, this led to the launch of a new public housing scheme in 1994 by the military administration. Thirteen months after the inauguration of the housing scheme, a review committee set up by the FMWH admitted that the new housing scheme had failed to meet its objective. The units produced were too expensive for the low-income groups to afford, even when the cost of infrastructure and land were waived.

Table 5.1 Performance of public housing in Nigeria (1960–2014)

Period	*Programme target*	*Achievement level*
First National Development Plan (1962–1968)	– Planned construction of 61,000 housing units.	– Only 500 units less than 1% of the planned units were constructed. The political chaos and the resulting civil war (1966–1970) contributed to the marginal progress recorded during this period.
Second National Development Plan (1971–1974)	– Establishment of National Council of housing (in 1972) to advise the government on housing matters and the FHA in 1973 to co-ordinate public housing provisions – Plan direct construction of 59,000 'low-cost' housing units across the Federation.	– 7,080 housing units representing 12% of planned houses were actually built.
Third National Development Plan (1975–1980)	– Creation of the Federal Ministry of Housing, Urban Development and Environment and conversion of Nigerian Building Society to FMBN. – Promulgation of the Land Use Decree (1978). – Planned construction of 202,000 low-cost housing units nationwide.	– 30,000 housing units representing less than 15% of planned houses were completed.
Fourth National Development Plan (1981–1985)	– National Housing Programme launched for the first time in 1980. Earmarked NGN1.9 billion for the construction of 160,000 housing units, for low-income groups. – The second phase of the housing programme set out to construct 20,000 housing units across the country.	– A total of 47,234 housing units representing about 23.6% of planned housing units were constructed in the first phase. The second phase was cut short by the military coup of 1983.
Military government (1986–1999)		– 5,500 housing units (less than 5%) of planned houses were actually constructed.

	– National Housing programme planned 121,000 houses with National Site-and-Services Housing Programme between 1993 and 1995–1988. – NHP launched to provide Nigerians access to quality housing and basic infrastructure. – 1991, NHP was launched with the goal of granting all Nigerians access to decent housing by 2000 in response to the slogan 'housing for all by the year 2000' of the United Nations.	– Provision of rural infrastructure through the Directorate of Food, Roads and Rural Infrastructure.
Civilian governments (1999–2014)	– The new National Housing and Urban Development Policy launched in 2002 with the goal of ensuring that 'all Nigerians own or have access to decent housing through private-sector-led initiatives'. – Planned construction of about 10,271 housing units through the PPP arrangements in different PPP housing schemes across the country. – Planned construction of 500 housing units in the Presidential Mandate Housing Scheme in all 36 state capitals and Abuja. – Government planned pilot projects involving the construction of 40,000 housing units per annum nationwide.	– 2,000 serviced plots through PPP site and service in Ikorodu, Lagos. – 4,440 housing units completed in Abuja, Port Harcourt, Akure and Abeokuta through PPP. – The Presidential Mandate Housing Scheme did not take off in many states. In Ogun State about 100 housing units representing 20% of the planned units were constructed. – Records of the achievement level of the pilot projects are not yet available.

Sources: Omole (2001), Ajanlekoko (2001); UN-Habitat (2006); Olotuah (2010).

In the last few decades, the Nigerian housing agencies have delivered an insufficient number of low-quality but expensive housing units for some middle- and high-income earners (Awotona, 1990; Ogu, 2002; Ogu & Ogbuozobe, 2001) thus creating a huge backlog for the low-income group in the country. The problem of poor funding, bureaucracy, the politicization of housing programmes and the absence of proper organization and transparency in the management of housing programmes all account for the minimal successes recorded by the housing schemes. However, the UN-Habitat II conference held in Istanbul, Turkey in June 1996 heralded a renewed advocacy of an initiative in housing delivery in Nigeria. At this time, people started subscribing to the National Housing Fund, which was established by Decree 3 of 1992. Conversely, the subscribers were disappointed by the upward review of the agreed amounts. Since then, many Nigerians have been suffering from problems of housing but they are forced to pay higher rent in spite of the existence of the State Rent Control and Recovery of Residential Premises Edict of 1997.

Housing policy in Nigeria

In an attempt to meet the housing challenges of the Nigerian populace, a number of programmes and policies has been articulated and introduced. The first explicitly formulated NHP was launched in 1991 by the federal government of Nigeria with the set goal of providing housing accommodation for all Nigerians by the year 2000. This policy came about because of Agenda 21 of the Global Shelter Strategy, aimed at achieving sustainable human settlement development., which was in response to the exploding population and urban growth rate. There was also an acceptance, for the first time, that government alone was incapable of addressing the alarming gap in the housing needs of all Nigerians (Aigbavboa & Thwala, 2011). The failure of the set goals for the first housing policy necessitated the adoption of a new policy in 2002 aimed at providing necessary solutions to the previously intractable housing crisis in Nigeria (Aribigbola, 2008).

The federal government of Nigeria revised the NHUDP in 2002, in line with the new democratic dispensation, which required the promotion of sustainable urban development and social order in the country, centred on citizen participation in decision-making and programme implementation, monitoring and evaluation (Aribigbola, 2008). The resultant 2002 NHP was directed towards all Nigerians owning or having access to decent, safe and sanitary housing accommodation at affordable cost with secure tenure through private-sector initiative with government encouragement and involvement. The 2002 policy introduced some new measures and innovations that were considered suitable to making housing accessible to all Nigerians in line with global thinking and action.

The adopted 2002 housing policy, which was a review of the 1991 policy, has again been reviewed in 2004 with the ultimate goal of ensuring that all

Nigerians own or have access to decent, safe and healthy housing accommodation at an affordable rate (Federal Republic of Nigeria, 2006). The most significant differences between the new policy and the previous ones are, first, that housing was now seen in the context of overall national development in contrast to when housing was regarded as a social service and a natural fall-out of the national economic development. Second, the policy identified the fact that different people both within and between income groups tend to have different demands for housing, moving away from the one-size-fits all syndrome. This is evident from the ultimate goal of the housing policy, which is to ensure that all Nigerians own or have access to decent housing accommodation at affordable cost. Third, the current focus is on removing all barriers to the supply of housing and provision of incentives to all parties involved in the housing delivery system. Previous policies have always been formulated with good intentions, but the formulators of the policies neither spell out the direction, nor do they take into consideration the amount of involvement required from the would-be beneficiaries. A typical shortcoming of the previous policies was that they usually carried the slogan of 'housing for all Nigerians'. This statement ordinarily assumed that all families in Nigeria would be provided with adequate housing regardless of who needed one and with no contribution or participation being expected from the beneficiaries.

In Nigeria, the major policy steps taken, so far, towards solving the housing crisis in the country can be summarized as shown below in Table 5.2. Others are the formulation of the NHP in 1984, the establishment of the Infrastructural Development Fund in 1985, and the Urban Development Bank in 1992 (Federal Republic of Nigeria, 1997). In addition to the above, all the introduced NDPs from 1962 to 1985 and the National Rolling Plans from 1990 to date plainly recognize the importance of providing affordable housing in the country as a tool for stimulating the national economy (Ademiluyi, 2010; Gbolagade, 2005), but little has been done to bring about an actualization of the policy intentions.

Challenges facing the provision of housing in Nigeria

Housing provision in Nigeria faces major challenges coupled with the limitations imposed by the income levels of Nigerian citizens. In the face of a daunting deficit put at about 17 million houses and the level of achievement over the past 57 years of the government programmes and policies, the Nigerian government is faced with the difficult task of overcoming this backlog and delivering homes to the low-, medium- and high-income groups, respectively. There are several challenges facing the provision of housing in Nigeria, with particular emphasis on the low-income groups. This is unlike the case of South Africa, where the government provide houses free of charge to the low-income groups or the disadvantaged poor through the South African National Housing Subsidy schemes, which ensures the beginning of economic independence and freedom.

Table 5.2 Major housing policy steps in Nigeria (1928–2010)

Policies to date	*Reason for policy formation*
Formation of the LEDB – 1928	The LEDB was authorized to carry out slum clearance, land reclamation and the development of residential and industrial estates.
The setting up of Nigerian Building Society – 1956	Provision of housing loans to both civil servants and the Nigerian public.
Establishment of housing corporations – 1964	The regional housing corporations were mandated to develop estates and at the same time provide mortgages for people to build houses and pay back over many years.
Establishment of the FHA, established under Decree No. 40 of 1973 and amended by CAP 136 LFN of 1990–1973	Its role was to make proposals to the government for housing and ancillary infrastructural services and implementing those approved by government.
The creation of the National Site-and-Services Programme – 1986	Formed to provide land for government housing with essential infrastructural facilities for housing developments in well-planned environments. Also, to provide well-laid-out serviced plots in each of the 36 state capitals of the federation, including FCT Abuja.
The formation of the National Prototype Housing Program by the FMWH	To complement the objectives of the National Site-and-Services Programme. The project was embarked upon to demonstrate the feasibility of constructing functional, effective and affordable housing units through imaginative designs, judicious specification of materials and efficient management of construction.
The setting up of the SHC	To provide housing to the populace at affordable prices.
The creation of the FMBN – 1977	To finance housing loans to prospective housing developers at minimal interest rates.
The setting up of the National Housing Programme in 1991 and the National Housing Fund scheme by Decree No. 3 of 1992	To provide self-loans to potential housing developers and also monitor developments in the housing sector.
The deconsolidation of the FMBN through the establishment of the Federal Mortgage Finance Limited	To take over retail mortgage portfolios previously handled by the bank and also to facilitate effective management of the National Housing Fund scheme.
The setting up of a Housing Policy Council	To monitor development in the housing sector and also to set up the machinery for the review

(*Continued*)

Table 5.2 (Continued)

Policies to date	*Reason for policy formation*
	of the 1978 Land Use Decree in order to make more land available for large-scale land developers.
The creation of the Ministry of Housing and Urban Development – June 2003	Charged with the responsibility of ensuring adequate and sustainable housing delivery and maintenance of a conducive living environment that meets the needs and aspirations of Nigerians.
The review of the mandate given to the FHA to include provisions of the national social housing as part of the strategy towards meeting the Millennium Development Goals.	The FHA also plans to facilitate the provision of two million housing units before 2015, which is not a realistic goal with the way housing issues are still being treated in the country.

Sources: Adisa, Agunbiade and Akanmu (2008); Ajanlekoko (2001); Aribigbola (2008); Ogu and Ogbuozobe (2001); Olotuah (2010); Omole (2001).

The problems associated with the attainment of affordable housing in Nigeria, include corruption, compromises during implementation and lack of political sensitivity among others. Any compromises made during implementation that sought to alter basic policy goals are normally detrimental to the successful execution of a housing policy. Though policy implementation is a tedious process that requires a great deal of analysis before starting it, the reality of basic housing can only be realized if there is proper implementation of policies. Further problems include a lack of adequate data relating to the magnitude of the problem, which is as a result of the absence of a national data bank for housing; inconsistency in policies and programmes, including regular changes of policies with changes of government without proper assessment of the existing ones; lack of efficient and sustainable credit delivery to the housing sector; the income levels of those needing houses, which are relatively low in comparison with house market prices, resulting in an affordability problem; the high cost of building materials; and the rapid annual growth rate of the Nigerian population, which was estimated at 3.3% on the basis of an annual birth rate of 49.3 per 1,000. All these issues are coupled with rapid urbanization and the problem of increasing poverty levels among citizens, as well as a lack of effective co-ordination among housing agencies. While all the three tiers of the government are involved in one way or the other in housing matters, their activities are hardly co-ordinated.

Programmes supporting housing delivery in Nigeria

Nigeria's efforts towards sustainable housing development since 1986 are marked by policy formulation and the establishment of agencies for implementation.

One such 'effort' is the establishment of the Family Support Programme (FSP) initiated by the then First Lady of the Federal Republic of Nigeria, Her Excellency, the late Mrs Maryam Babaginda. The FSP recognizes that one of the most important needs for the survival of any family and healthy living is the provision of decent and affordable housing, as most low-income families in cities do not own houses because they cannot afford them. The FSP also recognizes that women are handicapped in their access to land and property in the country. This seriously affects their role since they need a secure place to live and to carry out their subsistence farming and generate income. Widows and single women are worse off as they are denied rights to inherit landed property. In this regard, the FSP sets out, among others, the above objectives to ensure adequate housing for the less privileged in society.

Furthermore, the federal government through the FHA started the National Housing Programme in 1994. The objective was to produce 121,000 housing units for low-, medium- and high-income earners. Records show that as of 2010 about 5% of the target was achieved. Further efforts on direct construction of houses continue to be made through the National Prototype Housing Programme aimed at demonstrating the feasibility of constructing functional, cost-effective and affordable housing units. As of the end of 2010, 600 housing units had been completed in Lagos, Kaduna, Port-Harcourt and other areas. Also, the National Housing Fund was established in 1992 to solve the problem of finance for housing development. All workers (both public and private sector) earning NGN3,000 and above per annum contribute 2.5% of their income to the fund. The funds are disbursed as mortgage loans through primary mortgage institutions to the subscribers of the fund (UN-Habitat, 2008). Currently, the Nigerian Urban Renewal Programme is directed at improving existing slums in the core of cities. The programme has been implemented in 18 cities across the nation. A total of about NGN20 million has been spent on the programme since 1992. The federal government also provided over 15,000 plots at subsidized rates to the public through the National Sites and Services Programme; and over NGN250 million was committed to the programme in the last six years, as reported by the UN-Habitat in 2007. Moreover, the ongoing federal housing schemes will, according to plans, make possible the provision of adequate housing for all government workers in Nigeria so that at retirement they and their families will have a place to live.

Further to the achievement of the goal of improving urban management, the country is now participating in the Sustainable Cities Programme (SCP) under the Urban Management Programme of the United Nations Centre for Human Settlement/World Bank/United Nations Development Programme (UNDP). Through this programme, the Sustainable Ibadan Project was implemented. Also, through this initiative, local governments, NGOs, community-based organizations and private individuals were encouraged to participate and contribute to urban improvement and management. Presently, the process of replicating the SCP in other cities has already begun. Two other cities, Kano and Enugu, have commenced their projects. The Sustainable Kano Project has already prepared the Kano Environment Profile Study forming the basis for consultative actions on the management of Metropolitan Kano. The SCP emphasizes a two-way relationship between development and environment, which promotes better awareness and understanding of the priority issues to be addressed in urban environment and development, a consideration of modern urban and environmental management methods, and the most effective and lasting impact (UN-Habitat, 2008).

In addition, because of the determination of the government to replicate the success of the objectives of programmes under the Infrastructure Development Fund Programme, the Urban Basic Services Programme is being undertaken in the country to promote the integrated provision of environmental infrastructure, water, sanitation, drainage and solid waste management. The project involves the identification of core areas in some Nigerian cities and the packaging of improvement programmes targeted at women and children. Also, the Nigerian government is currently working on developing future programmes aimed at improving the human settlement development and management sectors. These sectors include: poverty alleviation programmes in collaboration with the World Bank and the UNDP; a programme support document for governance in collaboration with the UNDP; a national strategy for the replication of the SCP in other Nigerian cities; and replication of the Urban Basic Services Programme in collaboration with the United Nations Children's Fund. The government intends to concentrate efforts in the near future on the following areas: capacity building for improved management; institutional and policy reforms; social reorientation; increased participation of NGOs and the private sector; and promotion of appropriate technologies (UN-Habitat, 2008). These future plans are aimed at achieving a state of environmentally sound human settlements, free of slum conditions, in which every disadvantaged and poor Nigerian will have access to adequate and affordable shelter, as well as efficient infrastructure and services, which will foster sustainable economic growth and an improved standard of living and well-being.

Housing in Nigeria – need, demand and supply

Housing needs are considerable in Nigeria, the deficit is currently estimated at over 17 to 20 million units; if put in monetary terms, it will amount to four times the annual national budget of Nigeria. The rate of urbanization in Nigeria has witnessed tremendous increase in the last two decades. Census in the early 1950s showed that there were about 56 cities in the country and about 10.6% of the total population lived in these cities. This rose dramatically to 19.1% in 1963 and 24.5% in 1985 and, according to the country comparison report by the Central Intelligence Agency (2011), Nigeria's population is currently estimated at 186 million with the urban population constituting approximately 60%. The rapid growth rate of the urban population in Nigeria since the early 1970s is mainly due to migration promoted by the concentration of the gain from the oil sector in urban areas. While the United Nations estimates that Nigeria's population could reach 289 million by 2050, the United States Census Bureau projects that the population of Nigeria will reach 264 million by 2050, while the Central Intelligence Agency projects the population to reach 392 million by 2050. The rapid growth in population will create demand for shelter and efficient supply and distribution of basic utilities and services for city dwellers. The effect of the explosion from the population growth will manifest in overcrowding in housing. Nigeria, being one of the fastest urbanizing countries on the African continent, faces a huge challenge of adequately providing affordable housing to its citizenry. As more and more Nigerians make towns and cities their homes, the resulting social, economic, environmental and housing needs should be urgently addressed. A study of the housing situation in Nigeria put existing housing stock at 23 units per 1,000 inhabitants while housing deficit is put at 17 million units, and about NGN56 trillion will be required to finance this deficit.

As at the beginning of 1999, housing development had been so neglected by successive governments, which for years did not regard housing as a priority and which on many occasions made no annual budgetary provision for housing, that this brought about a 'no-housing' situation in Nigeria. According to the Federal Republic of Nigeria (2006) about 60% of Nigerians are said to be homeless. If this is represented by the current population of the country as represented by the Central Intelligence Agency report, which put the Nigeria population at 186 million people, it means that more than 100 million Nigerians are 'homeless'. In the context of the six people per household recommendation of the United Nations, it thus confirms that Nigeria has a housing backlog of 17 million units. Nigeria is in dire need of a minimum of 36 million houses if it must meet the minimal housing demands of its citizens based on the United Nations standard. The House of Representatives Committee also estimated that Nigeria currently has about 6.3 million houses and to maintain the United Nations standard of six persons per house for its population, Nigeria actually needs about 36 million houses in addition to the 6.3 million that already exist today. There is no doubt that the housing needs of Nigerians are as of yet unmet judging by the high demand and the limited supply of residential accommodations in Nigeria.

While virtually all governments in Nigeria since independence have highlighted housing as a major priority, Nigeria is yet to develop a vibrant housing market, and housing continues to be provided through traditional methods of buying land and building over some years, which could mean an individual's entire life. The problem of housing in Nigeria has been a concern for both the government and individuals. In acknowledging these challenges, both public- and private-sector developers make an effort through various activities to bridge the gap between housing supply and demand, but the cost of building materials, deficiency in housing finance arrangement, stringent loan conditions from mortgage banks and government policies among other problems have significantly affected the rate of housing delivery in Nigeria (Raji, 2008). For instance, the FHA has targeted to deliver 100,000 housing units yearly. Despite the relevance of the initiative, housing development should not be centred on office holders, but a matter of national interest and a goal to adequately house those needing housing (FHA, 2011). The proposed housing units according to the FHA will be achieved through the following Sustainable Mass Housing Delivery Framework and as typified in Figure 5.1:

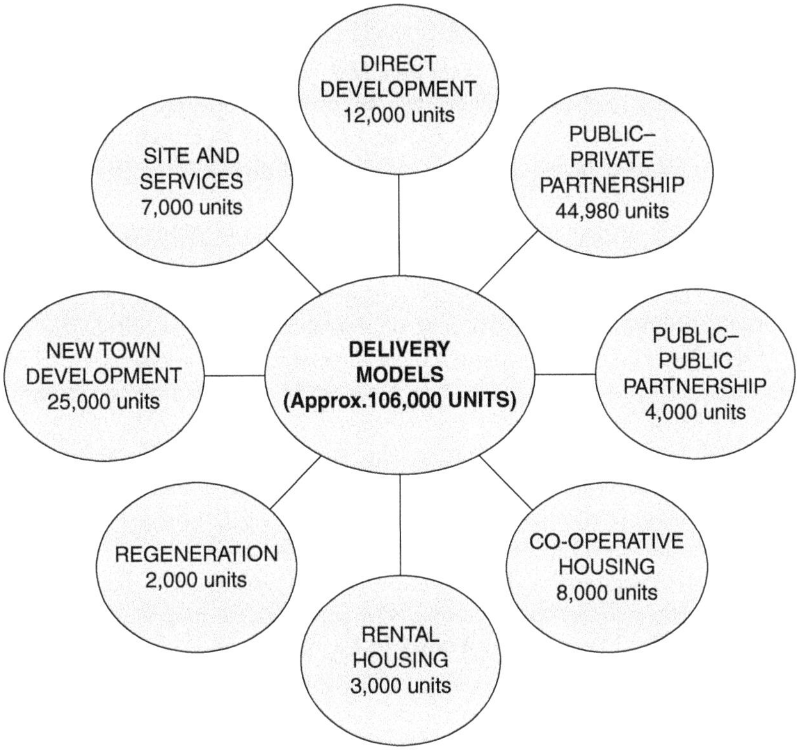

Figure 5.1 Sustainable mass housing delivery framework
Source: FHA (2011).

- Direct development – This will be done by utilizing internally generated resources and institutional financing of projects to be executed by the FHA. A total of 12,000 housing units are to be built through this delivery model.
- PPP – The key objective of the present model is to foster partnerships, which are profitable and cost-effective, leveraging on the strength of the private-sector partners in project financing, financial prudence and

effective management. About 14,000 housing units are to be built through PPPs.

- Public–public partnership – This is a newly introduced housing procurement system in Nigeria, which is a partnership between the FHA, with other tiers of government also involved, and military and para-military organizations to facilitate housing delivery that meets the needs of their staff. A total of 4,000 housing units are targeted for delivery through public–public partnership.
- Co-operative housing – The FHA is set to partner with housing co-operatives to facilitate housing delivery for the needs of their members. About 8,000 housing units are targeted for delivery through this model.
- Site-and-Services will be made available within estates to be developed. Additionally, Site-and-Services will be provided on parcels of land to be acquired to create serviced plots that will be sold to citizens who desire to build their own houses. About 7,000 serviced plots will be provided under the Site-and-Services Programme.
- New towns development – The FHA also wants to promote the development of new towns across the nation in key cities starting with Abuja, FCT. The new towns will reduce pressure on the existing cities by providing additional accommodation at affordable rates. For example, the Bwari Area Council has been identified for development of a new town in FCT, Abuja, Nigeria. A total of 25,000 housing units are targeted under the FCT, Abuja New Town.
- Rental housing – Additional to the development of housing units for outright sale to the public, the FHA has proposed to provide rental housing for low-income dwellers in the cities. About 3,000 housing units will be provided for rental in the period under consideration.
- Estate regeneration – Regeneration of old estates will be pursued in partnership with private investors. The estates being proposed for regeneration include: Maitama, Asokoro and Lugbe estates in Abuja, and Festac Town Estate in Lagos.

The Nigerian government needs to make available supportive mechanisms to provide its citizens with decent and affordable housing because housing constitutes an essential need to complement other social assets of human beings if they are to lead a productive life. It is of higher importance than food, education and medical care because of its intrinsic connection to security, which is paramount to human survival. Without adequate security, preservation of life is difficult and without shelter, people are exposed to the vagaries of weather and predatory animals (Akintokunbo, 2008). Despite these initiatives, the implementation of a subsidized low-cost housing scheme in Nigeria is still in its developmental stage whereas in South Africa it has been through the developmental threshold and hence is properly implemented. In most developing nations, 90% of the houses are built by private individuals in an informal market, which is highly unreachable for the low-income to access.

Lessons learnt from Nigerian housing studies

The following are the lessons learnt from the review of literature on the housing situation in Nigeria:

- The provision of affordable housing for its inhabitants has remained the principal focus of every successive government in Nigeria. This is because of the pivotal role played by housing in national development and growth on the one hand and it being a necessity in the life of the people, on the other.
- Housing in Nigeria is a highly contentious and politicized issue that is of great concern to stakeholders such as administrators, scholars and the Nigerian general public.
- Likewise, the difficulties in land acquisition, inability to access long-term mortgage finance and the high cost of building materials are some of the factors responsible for inadequate housing delivery in Nigeria.
- Housing problems in Nigeria are more critical in the cities, where a huge housing supply deficit, coupled with the dilapidated housing conditions, the high cost of housing construction, as well as proliferation of urban slums and squatter settlements, is the norm.
- Households in Nigeria value home-ownership more than households in advanced industrialized countries, as the literature reveals that housing ranks above education and health services as a priority.
- The federal government of Nigeria should not engage in direct housing construction, because such effort yields poor results. Studies have shown that individuals build better and cheaper houses and at a faster rate than government agencies.
- The government should place more emphasis on the use of local materials for building construction so as to reduce building costs.
- The government must promote alternative strategies for housing construction, such as provision of services and sites with basic infrastructure before making them available for sale to individuals who need them.
- The present housing difficulty in Nigeria arises not necessarily out of poverty, but because of the absence of an effective administrative arm to mobilize and organize the country's natural, human and industrial resources, among others for housing and urban development.
- Also revealed is that the fundamental philosophy underpinning housing development vision in Nigeria stems from the existing Nigerian Constitution of 1999.
- The constitution of Nigeria does not contains a justifiable socio-economic right that enshrines everyone's right to have access to adequate housing.
- Current governmental intervention in housing is at a level of providing an enabling environment for the various stakeholders to help ameliorate the housing backlog.

Summary

From the discussions in this chapter, it is evident that there have been challenges in the quantitatively and qualitatively adequate provision of affordable housing by the public sector in Nigeria since independence in 1960. Some of these challenges are contextual and are primarily due to the external social, economic and political environment in which public housing schemes were conceived, designed and implemented while others are organizational challenges within public housing agencies. The current study is primarily concerned with the causes of, and possible solutions to, these challenges. Also, the chapter revealed that the Nigerian government has been very influential in the provision of housing to its citizens, but the problem is that the low-income earners and the disadvantaged groups for whom the housing programmes are designed, do not benefit from the programmes because the processes are politicized. The Nigerian government has embarked on the provision of housing for its citizens with a good housing policy framework to fight the huge housing backlog. However, the problem with management and implementation of housing policy by the agencies given the responsibility has made these laudable policies ineffective. Also, it was found that the present housing difficulty in Nigeria arises not necessarily from poverty, but because of the absence of effective administrative machinery to mobilize and organize the country's natural, human and industrial resources, among others, for housing and urban development. To date, there is no government housing subsidy programme in place to help provide houses for the low-income groups. Nevertheless, a fundamental finding from the chapter is that the Nigeria Constitution does not explicitly contain justifiable socio-economic rights that enshrine everyone's right to have access to adequate housing despite being signatories to international treaties that advance the right to adequate housing. The next chapter extensively discusses housing development in South Africa.

References

Ademiluyi, A.I. & Raji, B.A. (2008). Public and private developers as agents in urban housing delivery in sub-Saharan Africa: The situation in Lagos state. *Humanity & social sciences journal*, 3(2):143–150.

Ademiluyi, I.A. (2010). Public housing delivery strategies in Nigeria: A historical perspective of policies and programmes. *Journal of sustainable development in Africa*, 12(6):153–161.

Adeyemo, J. & Dekolo, T. (2000). Housing situation of the poor in Lagos metropolis. *The professional builder*, June/July:20–30.

Adisa, A.L., Agunbiade, O.M. & Akanmu, O.E. (2008). House ownership as a well-being index among retirees in Osun state, Nigeria. *Journal of international social research*, 1(5):30–46.

Agbola, T. & Jinadu, A.M. (1997). Forced eviction and forced relocation in Nigeria: The experience of those evicted from Maroko in 1990. *Environment and urbanization*, 9(2):271–288.

Aigbavboa, C.O. & Thwala, W.D. (2009). Problems facing the implementation of low cost housing schemes in Nigeria: Sixth Post-graduate Conference on Construction Industry Development, Midrand: Johannesburg, pp. 1–16.

Aigbavboa, C.O. & Thwala, W.D. (2011). An overview of human settlement in Nigeria: A ray of hope for the slum dwellers? In S. Laryea, R. Leiringer & W. Hughes (eds) *Proceedings of West Africa Built Environment Research (WABER) Conference*, 19–21 July. Accra, Ghana, pp. 167–179.

Ajanlekoko, J.S. (2001). Sustainable housing development in Nigeria – The financial and infrastructural implication. International conference on spatial information for sustainable development, 2–5 October, Nairobi, Kenya.

Akintokunbo, A.A. (2008). Social housing in Nigeria – An imminent mass housing revolution. Available from: http://nigeriavillagesquare.com/forum/threads/social-housing-in-nigeria-an-imminent-mass-housing-revolution.26359/ (accessed 1 May 2018).

Aribigbola, A. (2008). Housing policy formulation in developing countries: Evidence of programme implementation from Akure, Ondo State, Nigeria. *Journal of human ecology*, 23(2):125–134.

Awotona, A. (1990). Nigerian government participation in housing: 1970–1980. *Habitat international*, 14(10):17–40.

Bret, T.J. (2002). The human right to adequate housing: Tool for promoting and protecting individual and community health. *American journal of public health*, 92(5):712–715.

Central Intelligence Agency (2011). *World factbook*. Available from: www.cia.gov/library/publications/resources/the-world-factbook/ (accessed 21 July 2011).

Central Intelligence Agency (2017). *World factbook*. Available from: www.cia.gov/library/publications/resources/the-world-factbook/ (accessed 21 March 2018).

Eboh, E. (2010). MDGs-based planning in Africa: Lesson, experiences and challenges: A case study of Nigeria: Economic commission for Africa, MDGs/LDCs section, EDND case studies. Available from: http://invenio.unidep.org/invenio//record/18816/files/Mdgs_Nigeria.pdf (accessed 1 May 2018).

Federal Republic of Nigeria (1991). *National housing policy*. Lagos: Federal Ministry of Works and Housing.

Federal Republic of Nigeria (1999). *Economic policy direction for Nigeria, 1999–2003*. Abuja: Federal Ministry of Information.

Federal Republic of Nigeria (2004). *Draft national housing policy*. Abuja: Chebychev Ventures Ltd.

Federal Republic of Nigeria (2006). *National housing policy*. Abuja: Chebychev Ventures Ltd.

FHA (2011). Delivery models and targets in Nigeria. Available from: www.fha.gov.ng/housing (accessed 1 May 2018).

Gbolagade, M.O. (2005). An appraisal of maintenance of privately owned and publicly owned multi-tenanted estate in Lagos metropolis. Unpublished material.

Ibem, E.O. (2010). An assessment of the role of government agencies in public–private partnerships in housing delivery in Nigeria. *Journal of construction in developing countries*, 15(2):23–48.

Ibem, E.O., Anosike, M.N. & Azuh, D.E. (2011). Challenges in public housing provision in the post-independence era in Nigeria. *International journal of human sciences*, 8(2):421–443.

Jimoh, R.A. & Olayiwola, S.J. (2008). Managing safety on construction sites. *Environmental technology & science journal*, 3(1):29-34.

Jinadu, A.M. (2004). *Understanding the basics of housing: A book of study notes for students in tertiary institutions*. Minna, Nigeria: King James Publishers.

Jolaoso, B.A., Musa N.A. & Oriola, O.A. (2008). Self-help contribution: A viable source of financing low-income housing. The third Built Environment Conference, Cape Town, South Africa.

Mabogunje, A.L. (2003). The new mass housing and urban development policy: Social and economic impact. Unpublished material.

Nwaka, G.I. (2005). The urban informal sector in Nigeria: Towards economic development, environmental health and social harmony. *Global urban development magazine*, 1(1):1–11.

Ogu, V.I. (2002). Urban residential satisfaction and the planning implications in a developing world context: The example of Benin City, Nigeria. *International planning studies*, 7(1):37–53.

Ogu, V.I. & Ogbuozobe, J.E. (2001). Housing policy in Nigeria: Towards enablement of private housing development. *Habitat international*, 25(4):473–492.

Okpala, D. (1986). Aspects of urban housing and human settlements policies and strategies in Africa. *Habitat international*, 10(3):203–223.

Olotuah, A.O. (2010). Housing development and environmental degeneration in Nigeria. *The built & human environment review*, 3:42–48.

Omole, F.K. (2001). *Basic issues in housing development*. Ondo, Nigeria: FemoBless Publishers.

Onibokun, A.G. (1985). *Housing in Nigeria*. Ibadan: Nigerian Institute for Social and Economic Research (NISER).

Onukwugha, V.C. (2000). Agricultural – Villages: A pragmatic co-operative approach to poverty alleviation housing schemes in Nigeria. Fourth International Conference on Housing, Abuja, Nigeria.

Raji, O. (2008). Public and private developers as agents in urban housing delivery in Sub-Saharan Africa. The situation in Lagos State. *Humanity of social sciences journal*, 3(2):143–150.

Shu'aibu, M.U. (2007). Housing policy implementation problems in Nigeria. *Daily triumph* (newspaper).

Shyllon, Y. (1999). National housing policy in perspective, a building. Manufacturer's view point. *The Professional builders* (magazine), Lagos, June/July, pp. 21–24.

Umeh, L.C. (2004). Towards improving degraded urban neighbourhoods in Nigeria: Prospects for residential participation. In H.C. Mba, S.N. Uchegbu, C.A. Udeh & L.N. Muoghalu (eds) *Management of environmental problems and hazards in Nigeria*. Aldershot: Ashgate Publishing Ltd, pp. 285–297.

UN-Habitat (2006). *Shelter for all: The potential of housing policy in the implementation of the habitat agenda*. HS/488/97E. New York: United Nations/Earthscan.

United Nations Human Settlements Programme (2008). *Un-Habitat and the Kenya slum upgrading programme strategy document*. May, HS/1010/08E. New York: United Nations.

6 Housing development in South Africa

Introduction

This chapter of the book provides an outline of housing legislation and jurisprudence, policy and implementation in South Africa since 1994. It outlines the housing legislative and policy framework in South Africa; examining the constitution with specific reference to the Bill of Rights and the Right to Housing, the NHC and the National Housing Programmes categorized therein with a specific focus on state-subsidized housing (Housing Subsidy Scheme). This chapter also provides an overview of the developments in housing policy since 1994, including a summary of the negotiations at the National Housing Forum (NHF) held between 1992 and 1994. The chapter further examines the supreme policy framework contained in the 1994 White Paper on Housing, and the problems associated with the Reconstruction and Development Programme (RDP) (subsidized) houses built after 1994. The chapter also discusses the 2004 Breaking New Ground (BNG) Policy Amendment, among others. Lastly, a summary of the lessons learnt to date from the housing delivery process is presented.

Housing policy development in South Africa

The housing environment in South Africa is complex, in large part due to the deliberate policy and legislative framework of socio-economic and spatial exclusion and marginalization created during the Apartheid era. Also, the complexity of the housing process in South Africa is due to many failures and a full understanding of the problems by the Apartheid government and the inability of the post-Apartheid state government to satisfactorily redress these problems since 1994. However, it must be genuinely acknowledged that the post-Apartheid state government has been actively involved in trying to create a level playing field for the previously disadvantage and also trying to repair the disadvantaged conditions created by almost 42 years of the Apartheid government. Simply put, it is easier to destroy than to create – so much so that the post-Apartheid government has been faced with a situation that is not irreparable but manageable, a situation that needs patience and a little firmness to address. Hence, as with other socio-economic rights, the legislative and policy framework created by the national government around housing is progressive in addressing the situation on the ground. However, implementation to date has been skewed and unable to address the land, housing and basic services needs of millions of poor South Africans, who still lack adequate housing and access to water, sanitation and electricity (Tissington, 2011). While the urban and rural spatial divide still remains pronounced in respect of access to socio-economic goods and services, the phenomenon of the inadequately housed urban poor is increasing. Redressing the inherited inequalities of the Apartheid state has established a complex and challenging context for meeting basic needs in contemporary South Africa. Given the physical and political segregation of Apartheid, meeting the demand for housing has been a central development challenge since 1994 (Pottie, 2003). However, Apartheid alone cannot be held responsible for the housing conditions in South Africa but equally no account of housing policy and conditions can be credible if it does not take into account the history of South Africa and the colonial legacy of the African continent (Goodlad, 1996).

Much of the debate in respect of the South African housing policy has been centred on the politico-economic background of the policy itself. The policy has been described by some as an extension of World Bank neo-liberalism, while others have labelled it as economically conservative (Pottie, 2003). However, the South African housing policy is rather the result of a mixed bag of international influences and local creativity – mostly due to the policy of spatial segregation in the Apartheid state, which contributed to a policy that is defined in terms of the 'scan globally, reinvent locally' principle according to Gilbert (2004). Clearly seen, a number of World Bank policy elements comprise an integral part of the South African policy, for example, the emphasis on incremental housing, economic conservatism, the one-off subsidy element and the instrumental role of formal ownership (Marais, 2007). However, it should also be acknowledged that two important differences are discernible in the South African policy. First, the South African policy suggests that only housing structures should be subsidized while the World Bank policy suggests that only site-and-services should be subsidized. Second, as the South African policy has developed, an increasing emphasis has been placed on housing size – a factor that does not comprise part of the World Bank policy (Marais, 2007).

Although it can be contended that the current South African housing policy was founded on the RDP's basic needs approach, which emphasizes providing the poor with basic shelter, public services and addressing the social unequal nature of the Apartheid state, the South African housing agenda has objectives that go beyond this. For instance, an important aim in the policy is that housing should contribute to the national economy. Also, in line with the World Bank's view of the 1990s, the South African housing policy aims to enable the housing markets to work. Hence, the housing programmes are expected to contribute to the development of urban citizenship with the creation of new communities of home-owners helping to develop a democratic and integrated society.

However, certain key dimensions of the current policy framework cannot be fully grasped in isolation from an understanding of the legacy bequeathed by

South Africa's peculiar history (Wilkinson, 1998). In a very direct sense, the problems of the past have profoundly shaped the situation to which the present policy seeks to respond. The next section of this chapter discusses an historic development of the evolution of housing policy in South Africa.

The evolution of housing policy in South Africa

Housing policy is an element of the trend of all modern states in the twentieth century to intervene extensively in the societies over which they exercise power (Wilkinson, 1998). The moment South Africa first emerged as a recognizable policy arena in the early 1920s, housing policy was greatly involved in the state's efforts to establish and maintain a particular social order, sometimes referred to as 'racial capitalism' (Saul & Gelb, 1981; Wilkinson, 1998). The housing policy in South Africa has generally been a contentious issue since 1910. Housing in South Africa is described as both an emotional and a very personal issue (De Loor, 1992).

When the then Union government was established in 1910, it developed several strategies in form of orders (decrees) to control the movement of blacks, especially in areas referred to as white urban areas. Since 1910 to the end of the segregation rule, various approaches were used to advance the inhumane idea of restricting blacks. Most significantly was the drafting of the Segregation Policy, which was advanced at both the national and provincial level of government. Foremost in the acts that were promulgated was the Natives Land Act 27 of 1913. This Act was concerned with land issues and, since land and housing issues are inextricably linked, this also affected the provision of housing for the blacks and other groups (Phago, 2010). The enactment of the Natives Land Act 27 of 1913 in South Africa cemented housing policy issues in the Apartheid era, which created the divide in housing issues up to date. This meant that houses could only be built where the land had been made available through proper government approval. As such, the Natives Land Act 27 of 1913 had direct implications on the housing situation in the country since it specified the territorial separation of the 'black and white races' (Morris, 1981; Reader's Digest, 1989).

Following the establishment of the Natives Land Act 27 of 1913, the then Central Housing Board (CHB) introduced the first housing policy documents in 1920, called the Housing Act 35 of 1920. The purpose of the CHB through the drafting of the Housing Act was to have control over the development of houses in local authorities, with a special control on the mechanisms of financing, which had a sinister motive to deprive the blacks and other groups of any assistance to receive housing (Morris, 1981; De Loor, 1992). Hence, during the first two decades of the CHB's existence, expenditure was allocated to alleviating the housing plight of poor whites only without any extension to the blacks and other groups. Nonetheless, a broader evaluation of the Housing Act by Rodgers (1980) indicates that the Housing Act only strengthened the policy of separate development. Besides, although these policies were introduced with good intentions such as developing communities based on their ethnic locations, it was later more evident that housing became an instrument for the implementation of the policy of separate development.

Following the Land Act 27 of 1913 and the Housing Act 35 of 1920, the Natives Act of 1923 was also enacted. This Act lasted for more than 60 years, until its desertion in 1986 on attempts to enforce 'influx control' on African urbanization. The key provisions of this legislation remained at the core of efforts to be achieved: during the 1930s, 'total segregation' and, after the then National Party Government came to power in 1948, 'Grand Apartheid'. The 'Stallard Principle', also known as the Natives Act of 1923, itself held that the right of municipal 'enfranchisement' should be denied to African urban residents only if they are given right to permanent residence in those areas (Wilkinson, 1998). This policy directly withdrew the rights of the Africans to freehold tenure of urban land. Consequently, a 'native' was permitted to enter the 'white' cities and towns only to attend to the needs of the white man and then had to return to the 'Reserves'. Thus, blacks were considered as 'temporary citizens' in all areas outside of their homelands. As a result of this, South Africa continued to develop housing backlogs, which still continue to date. Inherent in all the enacted decrees was the policy of separate development propagated by the Apartheid government to deceive the world into accepting Apartheid policies as another developmental approach with no racial degradation pertinent to South Africans (Phago, 2010).

However, a considerable number of Africans were already long established in the major urban centres, with some already having acquired freehold on properties. The implementation of the Stallardist doctrine required that a comprehensive system of social control be established (Wilkinson, 1998). Hence, the first element of this system eventually became a massive accretion, of truly Kafkaesque complexity, of 'pass laws' and labour bureaus, which, apart from their primary task of regulating the supply of African labour to the various sectors of the economy, could be used to control the movement of Africans to the 'white' urban areas. The second element of the system was the institutionalization of the form of residential segregation known successively as the 'location' or 'township'. The fundamental purpose underlying the prolonged and often ferociously contested efforts to segregate the African urban population into separate residential areas was to regulate the degree of permanence with which the African population could establish itself there (Wilkinson, 1998). Thus, it is in relation to this strategy of 'containing' African urbanization through a cruel but highly developed racial oppression that the evolution of South African housing policy must be understood (Wilkinson, 1998).

Prior to 1920, the only efforts to regulate or improve the generally very poor housing conditions of Africans living in the urban areas in South Africa were irregular ventures by the larger local authorities to clear so-called 'plague spots' and a few half-hearted efforts to establish municipal 'native locations', invariably far removed from the rest of the city or town. In contrast to this, the provision of barracks and compounds to house single and domestic workers, usually migrants, was already well established. However, Africans and, in general, the poorer sections of the population as a whole, were left to cater largely for themselves, with many ending up in squalid, overcrowded and very unhealthy slum tenements or 'yards' (Wilkinson, 1998). However, during this period, blacks in the rural areas were accustomed to building their own traditional dwellings (Morris, 1981). This approach to housing provision has attracted considerable interest from the post-1994 government as this form of development (building of traditional dwellings) has contributed to the fact that proper and quality housing in South Africa is an integral part of government policy to the provision of housing.

Furthermore, the formation of the very first CHB in terms of the 1920 Housing Act was a direct consequence of public concern about the impact of the devastating influenza epidemic of 1918. The formation seems also to have reflected a growing unease, which subsequently underpinned the codification of the 'Stallard Principle' in the 1923 Natives (Urban Areas) legislation about the accelerated influx of Africans into the urban and industrial heartland during the First World War. The CHB provided the somewhat limited means to enable black access to adequate housing, while the Natives (Urban Areas) Act had as its objective a programme of residential segregation of the African population that gradually unfolded during the 1920s and 1930s in the larger centres. For the most part, the initiation of 'slum clearance' schemes and the building of municipal 'locations' were hindered during the period between the World Wars by the continuing unwillingness and the limited capacity of the local authorities, on the one hand, to bear the costs involved in fulfilling their statutory obligations (Wilkinson, 1998). The central government, on the other hand, prevented any extension of its financial responsibilities for executing residential segregation in the urban areas, which devolved essentially to making subsidies available for the provision of very basic 'sub-economic' houses by the local authorities (Wilkinson, 1998).

In the beginning, the newly installed nationalist government directed its attention primarily to choke off what had become an only partially controlled flow of Africans to the cities. By the end of 1950, Hendrik Verwoerd – the key ideologue of Apartheid – was brought into the Cabinet as Minister of Native Affairs and, with the assistance of Dr W.M. Eiselen as his Departmental Secretary, he moved with a single-minded determination to resolve the 'Bantu housing problem' to truly accord with the commitment of the National Party's 1948 election manifesto, which was the 'ideal of total Apartheid'. The policy of separate development was further reinforced in spite of media reports condemning it and despite the international stance towards South Africa. One aspect of the proposed resolution of the 'Bantu housing problem' involved an effort to eliminate the apparently uncontrollable areas 'held in Native ownership'. The instant target was undoubtedly the various so-called 'black spots' on the perimeters of some of the larger centres, which generally had their origins in irregular sales of land to Africans during a slump in the property market after the South African War at the turn of the century (Wilkinson, 1998). However, the fundamental attack was on the right of Africans to possess or acquire freehold land tenure in 'white' areas. In retrospect, all efforts to address the other aspects, such as the 'provision of adequate housing in properly planned Native townships', can now be seen to have produced a material legacy that came to lie at the centre of subsequent attempts to restructure the South African housing policy (Wilkinson, 1998).

The period between 1978 and 1986 was evidently a resistance period through the perpetuation of violence in townships and mass industrial actions (De Loor, 1992). Accordingly, through such pressures, the then National Party government introduced reform measures to address the economic and political crises, such as poverty and political unrest during that period. One of the most important victories for blacks was the acceptance by the then Apartheid government of the permanence of black settlements in non-homeland cities and towns, as well as the introduction of new institutions to accommodate regional labour markets. Furthermore, the release of political prisoners and the subsequent commencement of the democratic negotiations during 1990 brought about a new direction in the housing policy, especially through the appointment of the De Loor Commission of Inquiry in 1991. The Commission was tasked to investigate the status quo regarding housing matters and to advise on the new housing policy and strategy. The new housing policy and strategy, generally viewed as the housing vision, was intended to encompass principles such as adequate shelter for all, security of tenure, equitable access to potable water, sanitary facilities and refuse removal as well as access to energy sources, including electricity (De Loor, 1992).

Housing statutory and policy framework in South Africa

It is imperative to note at this very point that the details of the current housing policy in South Africa remain somewhat fluid and that the overall policy framework has yet to be cast in its final statutory form. This ongoing fluidity is undoubtedly due, for the most part, to the significant political changes that the country has undergone in the last few years, since the installation of South Africans' first fully democratic government in mid-1994 and the initial adoption of the RDP presented by the African National Congress (ANC) in 1994. This is an overarching framework for the formulation and implementation of policy in a wide range of social and economic policy arenas in South Africa including housing.

The current South African housing policy is rooted in the 1994 Housing White Paper. The fundamental policy and development principles introduced by the Housing White Paper remain relevant and guide all developments in respect of housing policy and implementation. The fundamental policy framework of the South African housing policy established in the White Paper, which was published in December 1994, contains the fundamental principles of the government's housing policy to achieve the housing vision. The housing vision is underpinned by principles of sustainability, viability, integration, equality, reconstruction, holistic development and good governance. According to the

Department of Human Settlement (DHS), the South African housing policy and strategy must contribute to a non-racial, non-sexist, democratically integrated society. The goal is to improve the quality of living of all South Africans with an emphasis on the poor and those who cannot independently satisfy their basic housing needs. Furthermore, the government's human settlement development mandate emanates from the South African Constitution of 1996. Based on the provisions of the constitution, it is the government's duty to work progressively towards ensuring that all South Africans have access to secure tenure, housing, basic services, materials, facilities and infrastructure on a progressive basis. The government is therefore required to apply legislative, administrative, financial, educational and social measures to fulfil its housing obligations. The following is a list of some of the primary and secondary legislation relating to various regulatory, financial, technical, environmental, institutional and developmental aspects of housing in South Africa enacted within the past 27 years:

Primary legislations:

- Constitution of the Republic of South Africa, 1996 (Constitution);
- Prevention of Illegal Eviction from and Unlawful Occupation of Land Act 19 of 1998 (PIE Act);
- Housing Act 107 of 1997 (Housing Act);
- Housing Consumers Protection Measures Act 95 of 1998;
- Housing Amendment Act 28 of 1999;
- Rental Housing Act 50 of 1999 (Rental Housing Act);
- Housing Second Amendment Act 60 of 1999;
- Local Government: Municipal Systems Act 32 of 2000 (Municipal Systems Act);
- Housing Amendment Act 4 of 2001;
- Rental Housing Amendment Act 43 of 2007;
- National Norms and Standards for the Construction of Stand Alone Residential;
- Dwellings Financed through National Housing Programmes (2007) (National Norms and Standards);
- Social Housing Act 16 of 2008 (Social Housing Act);
- Housing Development Agency Act 23 of 2008;
- Housing Amendment Bill 2009;
- Rental Housing Bill;
- Social Housing Bill;
- Housing Consumers Protection Measures Amendment Bill, 2009;
- Sectional Titles Schemes Management Bill, 2009; and
- Community Scheme Ombud Service Bill, 2009; and PIE Amendment Bill.

Secondary legislations:

- Expropriation Act 63 of 1975;

- National Building Regulations and Building;
- Standards Act 103 of 1977 (NBRA);
- Sectional Titles Act 95 of 1986 (amended by Acts 24 and 29 of 2003);
- Environment Conservation Act 73 of 1989 (amended by Act 79 of 1992);
- Land Titles Adjustment Act 111 of 1993 (LTA);
- Development Facilitation Act 67 of 1995 (DFA);
- Land Reform (Labour Tenants) Act 3 of 1996;
- Interim Protection of Informal Land Rights Act 31 of 1996;
- Extension of Security of Tenure Act 62 of 1997 (ESTA);
- Water Services Act 108 of 1997;
- National Environmental Management Act 107 of 1998 (NEMA);
- Public Finance Management Act 1 of 1999 (PFMA);
- Home Loan and Mortgage Disclosure Act 63 of 2000;
- Division of Revenue Act 7 of 2003 (DORA);
- Municipal Finance Management Act 56 of 2003 (MFMA);
- Intergovernmental Relations Framework Act 13 of 2005 (IRFA); and
- Co-operatives Act 14 of 2005.

In the following sections highlights of the important information contained in the Constitution of the Republic of South Africa, 1996 and key housing-related policy and legislation, including the Housing Act 107 of 1997 (amended by Acts 28 and 60 of 1999; Act 4 of 2001) (Housing Act), will be discussed.

Constitution of the Republic of South Africa (1996)

The fundamental philosophy underpinning housing development goals in South Africa is the existing South African Constitution of 1996. The Constitution of the Republic of South Africa of 1996 is the supreme law of the country. It is the basis of all activity in the Republic of South Africa. This means that any law or conduct that is inconsistent with the constitution is invalid, and that the obligations that it imposes must be fulfilled. Everything done must conform to what is contained within the constitution. In the context of post-Apartheid South Africa, it is significant that on the basis of the constitution, the NHP as contained within the Housing White Paper and the Housing Codes applies equally to the total geographic area of the Republic of South Africa. At a most basic level, the constitution defines the fundamental values, such as equality, human dignity and freedom of movement and residence, to which the housing policy subscribes. These notions are also contained broadly in the Bill of Rights, in Chapter 2 of the constitution. Two components of the constitution especially relevant to housing – the specific right to have access to adequate housing, as enshrined in Section 26 of the constitution; and the powers of national, provincial and local governments with respect to housing activities – are framed by the concept of 'concurrent competence' and developmental local government.

The constitution also contains justifiable socio-economic rights and enshrines everyone's right to access to adequate housing. For instance, in the Bill of Rights in Chapter 2 of the constitution, Section 26(1–3) outlines: 'Everyone has the right to have access to adequate housing. The state must take reasonable legislative and other measures, within its available resources, to achieve the progressive realisation of this right . . .' The Bill of Rights also includes a number of other rights, which relate either directly or indirectly to the enjoyment of the right to housing. These include, among others:

- Everyone has inherent dignity and the right to have their dignity respected and protected (Section 10).
- No one may be deprived of property except in terms of the law of general application, and no law may permit arbitrary deprivation of property (Section 25(1)).
- Everyone has the right to sufficient water (Section 27[b]) (The Water Services Act 108 of 1997).
- Every child has the right to basic shelter (Section 28[c]).

Section 26(1) of the constitution enshrines that everyone has the right to access to adequate housing and that it is the government's responsibility to take reasonable legislative and other measures, within its available resources, to achieve the progressive realization of this right. When defining the concept of adequate housing, the wording of the housing right provision corresponds with the International Covenant on Economic, Social and Cultural Rights of 1966. However, as has been discussed in Chapter 2 of this book, the concept of 'adequate housing' is not easy to define as it depends on the exact context and circumstances of households and individuals, together with their needs and priorities (Tissington, 2011). Similarly, the right to housing is also bound to the rights of other socio-economic goods and amenities including rights to land, water, sanitation, electricity, livelihood, transport, clinics and hospitals, schools, universities and other cultural and recreational amenities, such as parks, libraries, public spaces, swimming pools, sports fields etc. In addition, the right to housing is also fundamentally bound to a number of other cross-cutting rights, including rights to public participation, equality, human dignity, just administrative action, freedom of expression, access to information and access to justice among others (Tissington, 2011). This inter-relatedness and 'interdependency of rights' is acknowledged by the international human rights law as the principle of interdependency of rights, which means that socio-economic rights and civil and political rights are interrelated, and that the enjoyment of one right (or group of rights) requires enjoyment of others (which may or may not be in the same group).

In terms of Section 26 of the South African Constitution, the government should endeavour to ensure that all people living in South Africa are able to satisfy all the requirements with regard to access to adequate housing as engraved in the constitution. In responding to the constitutional right to 'access to adequate housing' for all South Africans, the government is under an obligation to not only pass enabling legislation, but also to apply other measures of an administrative, a financial, educational or a social nature to fulfil its housing obligations. This commitment would characterize the move to transformation, equality and socio-economic well-being for all citizens including non-citizens (Tissington, 2011). Since the foundation to housing provision is enshrined in the new South African Constitution, individuals unable to access housing through the 'normal' residential market are assisted with new schemes that make that right a realization. Thus, state prioritization should be people-centred, so as to ensure their access to livelihoods as contained in the constitution.

The Housing Act (1997)

Apart from the South African Constitution that contains justifiable socio-economic rights and enshrines everyone's right to have access to adequate housing, the Housing Act of 1997 is the primary piece of housing legislation in South Africa. It legally entrenched the housing policy principles outlined in the 1994 White Paper on Housing. The South African housing vision is confirmed in the Housing Act (No. 107 of 1997). Within the Housing Act 1(vi), 'housing development' is defined as:

> [T]he establishment and maintenance of habitable, stable and sustainable public and private residential environments to ensure viable households and communities in areas allowing convenient access to economic opportunities, and to health, educational and social amenities in which all citizens and permanent residents of the Republic will, on a progressive basis, have access to:
>
> - permanent residential structures with secure tenure, ensuring internal and external privacy and providing adequate protection against the elements; and
> - potable water, adequate sanitary facilities and domestic energy supply.

The housing goals are further reiterated in both the Urban and Rural Development Frameworks. In each of these documents, the environment within which a house is situated is recognized as being equally as important as the house itself in satisfying the needs and requirements of the occupants (Republic of South Africa, 1997). The ultimate goal of the Housing Act is that the housing process must make a positive contribution to a non-racial, non-sexist, democratic and integrated society. The goal of the housing vision for both urban and rural areas is to improve the quality of life of all South Africans with a special emphasis on the poor and those who have been previously disadvantaged.

The Housing Act further provides for a sustainable housing development process, laying down general principles for housing development in all spheres of government. It defines the functions of national, provincial and local governments in respect of housing development, and it lays the basis for financing

National Housing Programmes. In Section 2(1) the Act states that 'all spheres of government must give priority to the needs of the poor in respect of housing development, and consult meaningfully with individuals and communities affected by housing development'. This forms the basis for housing participation in South Africa, which is the major subject discussed in the development of a conceptual framework for low-income housing satisfaction in South Africa as discussed in the latter chapters of this book. The government must ensure that housing development provides: as wide a choice of housing and tenure options as is reasonably possible; is economically, fiscally, socially and financially affordable and sustainable; is based on integrated development planning; is administered in a transparent, accountable and equitable manner; and upholds the practice of good governance in all sectors. In addition, Section 2(1)[e] of the Act states that all spheres of government must promote inter alia the following:

- a process of racial, social, economic and physical integration in urban and rural areas;
- measures to prohibit unfair discrimination on the ground of gender and other forms of unfair discrimination by all actors in the housing development process;
- higher density in respect of housing development to ensure the economical utilization of land and services;
- the meeting of special housing needs including the needs of the disabled;
- the provision of community and recreational facilities in residential areas; and
- the housing needs of marginalized women and other groups disadvantaged by unfair discrimination.

However, amendment was made to the principal Act in 1999 and 2001, respectively. Section 4 of the Housing Act requires the minister to publish a code that includes the NHP and procedural guidelines for the implementation of the policy.

National Housing Code (2000, revised in 2009)

The NHC, first published in 2000 in accordance with the Housing Act, set out the underlying policy principles, guidelines, norms and standards that apply to the National Housing Programmes. The NHC 2009 sets the same underlying policy principles, guidelines, norms and standards that apply to government's various housing assistance programmes introduced since 1994. Some of the initially created programmes have been updated or removed, and new programmes included, after the adoption of BNG in 2004. The NHC is binding on provincial and local spheres of government. The Housing Code includes the national housing vision, housing goal, basic points of departure and the fundamental principles of the housing policy. The NHC set the tone for the understanding of existing policies and the development of new ones. It is the basis for all housing activities in South Africa. The NHC 2000 has been substantially revised. The revised NHC of 2009 is aimed at simplifying the implementation of housing projects by being less prescriptive while providing clear guidelines, as against the initial provision of the 2000 NHC.

The NHC set out the NHP of South Africa collectively with practical guidelines for its effective implementation through the inclusion of the National Housing Programmes. The Code's vision for housing in South Africa echoes the definition of 'housing development', as outlined in the Housing Act. The initial 2000 Code states that the government's housing goal is, subject to fiscal affordability, to increase housing delivery on a sustainable basis to a peak level of 350,000 units per annum until the housing backlog is overcome. In 2004, the BNG policy made provision for a new NHC to be published, with the intention to align and cohere with the policy so that its goals and aims can be implemented. The new Housing Code is meant to accommodate any changes made since 2000 and to convert the National Housing Programmes into flexible provisions and guidelines (Tissington, 2011). Further to the BNG provision, the revised NHC was adopted and published in February 2009. A few old programmes have been removed from the new Code such as the Project Linked Subsidy Programme, Relocation Assistance Programme, Blocked Projects Programme and Rectification of RDP Stock 1994–2002 Programme. However, it is important to note that in respect to all programmes that are not contained in the Housing Code 2009, the rules of the NHC 2000 still apply whenever they are initiated. The NHC is proposed to be revised on an annual basis in order to ensure that it keeps up to date with legislative or policy changes. However, this has not been done since the last revision of 2009. The revised NHC is all-embracing and addresses a variety of housing programmes mentioned in BNG.

National Housing Programmes

The government's primary housing objective since the dawn of the new administrative government is to undertake housing development, which Section 1 of the Housing Act No. 107 of 1997 (Housing Act) defines as the establishment and maintenance of habitable, stable and sustainable public and private residential environments to ensure viable households and communities in areas allowing convenient access to economic opportunities, and to health, educational and social amenities in which all citizens and permanent residents of the Republic will, on a progressive basis, have access to 'permanent residential structures with secure tenure, ensuring internal and external privacy, and providing adequate protection against the elements, and potable water, adequate sanitary facilities and domestic energy supply'.

The past and existing National Housing Programmes have been based on this objective and the principles embodied therein. However, in response to the South Africa constitutional imperative, the government has, in terms of the Housing Act (107 of 1997), introduced a variety of programmes that provide the poor households access to adequate housing. Thus, the policy principles set out in the White Paper on Housing aims to provide poor households with houses, as well as basic services such as potable water and sanitation on an equitable basis. The limited resources available from the 'fiscus', however, necessitate the provision of housing, security and comfort to all over time. The National Housing Programmes are categorized into different 'Intervention Categories' as follows:

Financial Programmes:

- individual housing subsidies;
- Enhanced Extended Discount Benefit Scheme;
- social and economic facilities;
- accreditation of municipalities;
- Operational Capital Budget;
- housing chapters of Integrated Development Plans (IDPs); and
- rectification of pre-1994 housing stock.

Incremental Housing Programmes:

- Integrated Residential Development Programme (IRDP);
- Enhanced People's Housing Process (ePHP);
- Upgrading Informal Settlements Programme (UISP);
- consolidation subsidies; and
- emergency housing assistance.

Social and Rental Housing Programmes

- institutional subsidies;
- Social Housing Programme (SHP); and
- community residential units.

Rural Housing Programmes:

- rural subsidy: informal land rights; and
- Farm Residents Housing Assistance Programme.

From the above list, the DHS has identified three programmes as core programmes for future housing delivery: the IRDP, UISP and Social/Rental Housing Programme. The following section of this chapter will provide a detailed review of the IRDP and the SHPs. Also, it should be noted that there is a set of generic qualifying criteria that must be fulfilled by those applying for state housing subsidies under the National Housing Subsidy Scheme (NHSS) for the National Housing Programmes. However, there are also specific rules that apply to each subsidy programme and, in some cases, there are specific eligibility criteria that apply over and above the generic criteria. The specific criteria are likewise discussed in the chapter.

Integrated Residential Development Programme

One of the key lessons learnt in the review of the outcomes of housing programmes since 1994 is that, owing to an array of reasons, the initially developed low-income settlements continued to be located on the urban periphery without the provision and consideration for social and economic amenities, as in the Apartheid Era. Hence, this necessitated the introduction of the IRDP, which replaces the previous Project Linked Subsidy Programme, in order to facilitate the development of all-inclusive human settlements in well-located areas that provide convenient access to urban amenities, including places of employment. As stated in the IRDP document, IRDP provides a tool to plan and develop integrated settlements that include all the necessary land uses and housing types and price categories to become a truly integrated community.

The programme is also aimed at creating social cohesion. The IRDP provides for the acquisition of land, servicing of stands for a variety of land uses including commercial, recreational, educational and medical, as well as residential stands for low-, middle- and high-income groups. The land use and income group mix is based on local planning and needs assessment. This is because if the concept of needs assessment is prioritized, the end product will eventually satisfy the need of the occupants as they will be aware of what they will receive when the houses are allocated to them. The IRDP provides for phased area-wide planning and development of integrated housing projects in situations where:

- a project is undertaken in an area where unoccupied vacant land is developed; or
- a project is undertaken in an existing township where an undeveloped parcel of land is utilized for development purposes.

However, the IRDP moves away from the requirements found in the previous Project Linked Subsidy Programme version, which required the identification of subsidized housing beneficiaries up front and provided for both subsidized, as well as finance-linked (Misselhorn, 2008), housing that only catered for households earning between R3,500 and R7,000 a month. The IRDP further provides for social and rental housing, commercial, institutional and other land uses to be developed.

In the plans of the IRDP, a municipality assumes the role of the developer (where they lack financial, technical and managerial capacity, a provincial department can take on this role), undertaking all planning and project activities. As developers, the municipality appoints construction industry professionals (who design and establish the township, design and monitor the installation of services, and design the houses) and contractors (who construct the services and housing) to assist with the housing development process. Municipalities apply for funding from the provincial department of the DHS that approves project applications, reserves and distributes funds, as well as assesses and adjudicates various aspects of the project process. The plans for projects undertaken within the scope of the IRDP are only based on approved housing chapters of the IDP. An IDP is a single, inclusive strategic plan for the development of a municipality. It incorporates, integrates and organizes plans and take into account proposals for the development of the municipality (Tissington, 2011). It aligns resources and capacity of the municipality with the implementation of the plan, complies with the requirements of the Municipal Systems Act and is compatible with national and provincial development plans and planning requirements binding on the municipality in terms of legislation. Hence beneficiaries are able to obtain non-residential stands in the development.

Most provinces and municipalities used the Turnkey Contracting Strategy in the past, which transfers all the development duties to a private-sector contractor, including the administration of beneficiaries (Tissington, 2011). This model encountered numerous problems and gaps in policy and process of beneficiary registration and allocation. In the present IRDP model, the developer must ensure that identified beneficiaries complete and sign the application form for the grant of an IRDP Individual Subsidy, which is submitted to the principal municipal department. The identification of beneficiaries to receive housing construction subsidies is undertaken before the design and housing construction planning phase commences, which enable beneficiaries' needs assessments to be conducted shifting away from the one-size-fits-all system of the past. This ultimately will guarantee housing satisfaction as the variation between what they receive will be in-line to what they expect.

Phase 1 of the IRDP involves planning, land acquisition, township establishment and the provision of serviced residential and other land use issues to ensure a sustainable integrated community. Phase 2 consists of the house construction phase for qualifying housing subsidy beneficiaries and the sale of stands to non-qualifying beneficiaries and for commercial interest. During Phase 1's execution, non-residential stands are allocated, for instance institutional stands such as police stations, clinics and public-sector use among others; business and commercial stands; serviced stands for use by not-for-profit community service providers such as churches, crèches/pre-school/nursery schools and old age residential homes among others; and public uses such as parks, recreation areas, informal trading areas and taxi ranks among others. Conversely, there are rules as to how these stands are allocated. However, the allocation of the stands and the submission of application forms for housing subsidies and applications to buy the stands are undertaken and finalized before the approval of the housing construction project phase, which enables the houses to be constructed for those needing them, as against the previous patterns where houses are constructed for the sake of construction. Once the provincial department has received and approved a subsidy application, within three months it records the name and identity number of the applicant (and their spouse plus dependants, if applicable) on the National Housing Subsidy Database to prevent the duplication of an applicant.

Table 6.1 IRDP housing subsidy guideline amounts for the 2009/2010 financial year

Income category	*Top structure funding*	*Own contribution*	*Product price*
R0 to R1,500	R55,706	None	R55,706
R1,501 to R3,500	R53,227	R2,479	R55,706
Indigent: Aged, disabled and health stricken R0 to R3,500	R55,706	None	R55,706

Source: DHS (2010)

At present the subsidy quantum for the IRDP is R55,706 for the construction of the top structure only. Those earning between R1,501 to R3,500 per month must contribute R2,479 (Table 6.1). The cost for the provision of internal municipal engineering services is financed from alternative sources and the use of the housing subsidy allocation for the financing of internal services is only approved as an option of last resort. If the latter is the case, a subsidy amount of R22,162 is available for the preparation of a serviced stand. This programme currently benefit persons who satisfy the generic housing qualifying criteria, as outlined in the revised NHC of 2009.

Social Housing Programme

Security of tenure remains one of the fundamental ideologies of the South African housing policy because of the disadvantaged nature of the past policies against a majority of the citizens. Where most of the created policy programmes provide freehold tenure to households, there has been an increasing need for affordable rental units, which provide security of tenure to households who prefer the mobility provided by rental accommodation (DHS, 2010).

The Social Housing Policy for South Africa was approved in June 2005 and the Implementation Guidelines published in November 2006. The Policy has been included in the new NHC of 2009, as the SHP. The Social Housing Act provides the legal framework for the implementation of the Social Housing Policy. Social housing is defined as follows: a rental or co-operative housing option for low-income persons at a level of scale and built form, which requires institutionalized management and which is provided by accredited social housing institutions or in accredited social housing projects in designated restructuring zones. The SHP applies only to 'restructuring zones', which are identified by municipalities as areas of economic opportunity and where urban renewal/restructuring impacts can best be achieved (DHS, 2010). Designated restructuring zones are geographic areas identified by local authorities and supported by provincial government for targeted and focused investment. Restructuring zones were approved (as of 2006) in the following areas: Ekurhuleni Metropolitan Municipality, City of Cape Town, City of Johannesburg, eThekwini

Metropolitan Municipality (Durban), Nelson Mandela Bay Municipality (Port Elizabeth), City of Tshwane (Pretoria), Buffalo City Municipality (East London), Mangaung Local Municipality (Bloemfontein), Msunduzi Local Municipality (Pietermaritzburg), Polokwane, Potchefstroom, Kimberley and Nelspruit. The Programme is also aimed at developing affordable rental in areas where bulk infrastructure (sanitation, water, transport) may be under-utilized, therefore improving urban efficiency. There is a significant capital contribution from government for the development of social housing in these defined localities as part of a broader goal of social restructuring in South Africa. Social housing in restructuring zones, according to the guiding principles, takes the form of medium-density multi-unit complexes requiring institutionalized management. This includes townhouses, row housing, multi-storey units and walk-ups among others, but they all come in detached housing units.

The SHP adheres to the general principles laid down in the Housing Act (107 of 1997) Part 1, Section 2, as well as in relevant sections of subsequent legislation such as the Rental Act (50 of 1999). In addition, the policy is read in conjunction with the White Paper on Housing (1994), the Urban Development Framework of 1997 and with the NHC. Thus, it is important to note that the Department of Housing's 'Comprehensive plan for the development of sustainable human settlements' of 2004 provides direction in matters of the principle guiding SHP. The fundamental principles underpinning SHP include (DHS, 2010):

- promoting urban restructuring through the social, physical and economic integration of housing development into existing areas, likely to be urban or inner-city areas;
- promoting the establishment of well-managed, quality rental housing options for the poor;
- responding to local housing demand; delivering housing for a range of income groups (including, inter alia, middle income, emerging middle class, working class and the poor) in such a way as to allow social integration and financial cross subsidization;
- supporting the economic development of low-income communities in various ways, which is done by ensuring that projects are located close to job opportunities, markets and transport, and by stimulating job opportunities to emerging entrepreneurs in the housing services and construction industries;
- fostering the creation of quality living environments for low-income persons;
- promoting a safe, harmonious and socially responsible environment both internal to the project and in the immediate urban environment;
- promoting the creation of sustainable and viable projects;
- encouraging the involvement of the private sector where possible;
- facilitating the involvement of residents in the project and/or key stakeholders in the broader environment through defined meaningful consultation, information sharing, education, training and skills transfer;

- ensuring secure tenure for the residents of projects, on the basis of the general provisions for the relationship between residents and landlords as defined in the Housing Act (107 of 1997) and the Rental Act (50 of 1999 – Chapter 3, Section 4 (1) to (5)).
- supporting mutual acceptance of roles and responsibilities of tenants and social landlords, on the basis of the general provisions for the relationship between residents and landlords as defined in the Rental Act (50 of 1999 – Chapter 3, Sections 4 and 5), in the Co-operatives Act (91 of 1981), as well as in the envisaged Social Housing Act;
- ensuring transparency, accountability and efficiency in the administration and management of social housing stock; and
- promoting the use of public funds in such a manner that stimulates and/or facilitates private-sector investment and participation in the social housing sector.

A fundamental constraint to the ability of social housing to assist poor individuals and households to access affordable and well-located rental housing is that Social Housing Institutes (SHIs) have tended to look 'up-market' (above the eligibility cut-off point) in order to survive and very little has been done to increase the range of options available to those in the lower bands of the subsidy range, also known as the 'deep-down market'. The Social Housing Policy acknowledges that there is a perception that social housing is for a small, relatively privileged elite and does little to contribute to the housing challenge in South Africa (DHS, 2010; Tissington, 2011). While the SHP aims to tackle these challenges, it admits that the primary policy objective of the SHP is restructuring, not mass delivery (Charlton & Kihato, 2006). Despite the fact that South Africa has made great progress in the past 20 years since the election of its first democratic government, a number of structural constraints in accomplishing vital changes remain a cause for concern. Though political constraints have largely been removed, obstacles arising from the economic structure and spatial patterning of South African society have proven stubborn and persistent (DHS, 2010). For instance, some post-Apartheid programmes have even unconsciously reinforced Apartheid inequities. Thus, there is therefore a need to ensure that the links between processes of social restructuring and housing policies and instruments are brought into closer orientation. Hence, social housing is a useful key instrument in this regard, and can contribute strongly towards the achievement of urban restructuring and urban renewal through urban integration and impacting positively on urban economies. Specifically, the involvement of social housing to such restructuring objectives comprises of three dimensions, which are spatial, economic and social. While the SHP aims to maximize 'deep-down reach' and target those earning R1,500 a month (and less if possible), it aims for mixed-income projects and requires participants to demonstrate a regular income, which is able to sustain the monthly rental, and the payment of a deposit equal to three months' rent (Charlton & Kihato, 2006).

Currently, the SHP has moved away from the earlier individual subsidy-based approach to a project-based approach. It is predicted that appropriate targeting will be addressed in the project approval process and that it will be a pre-condition for the awarding of a project grant or subsidy. Respective projects will specify a range of housing products targeted at income groups appropriate to the area and context, based on tested demand and in line with the broader restructuring aims of the Social Housing Policy (DHS, 2010). The DHS states that the difference between rental revenues and the cost of providing the units will be subsidized by way of a grant from the government. This grant will be calculated with reference to the project as a whole rather than with reference to particular unit types. However, the units meant for the very poor will attract proportionately more subsidy than units meant for those low-income groups with more substantial incomes.

The mechanism and funding for the SHP is through a dedicated capital fund at national level, which the DHS (or the Social Housing Regulatory Authority) disburses to accredited local authorities and provinces (who apply for social housing development in restructuring zones). There are two ways of accessing this grant. The first is through a standard/fixed component of the social housing grant by way of the capital restructuring component, which is allocated by the national government. In order to qualify for the capital grant on every unit, a social housing project must have at least 30% of units contributing to 'deep-down market reach' and maximum rentals not higher than R2,500 (implying an income of R7,500 per month, within the top of the income band) according to Charlton and Kihato (2006) and DHS (2010). A major constraint in the provision of social housing for the very poor is the ongoing management and operations and management associated costs. The unwillingness of private SHIs to share the risks associated with very low-income rental housing provision is a major concern and should necessitate a policy rethink by the DHS with regard to this aspect.

Qualifying criteria for Housing Subsidy Programmes

The set of generic qualifying criteria as outlined in the revised NHC of 2009 for consideration in the National Housing Programmes is summarized as follows:

- Citizenship: All applicants must be citizens of the Republic of South Africa, or be in the possession of a Permanent Resident Permit.
- Competent to contract: Applicant must be legally competent to contract (i.e. over 18 years of age and of sound mind).
- Not yet benefited from government funding: The applicant or their spouse may not have received previous housing benefits from the government. In the event of a divorce involving a person who previously derived benefits, the terms of the divorce order will determine such person's eligibility for further benefits.

- First-time property owner: The applicant or their spouse may not have owned and/or currently own a residential property. Exceptional cases may include: disabled persons; persons who own a vacant stand that was obtained through the Land Restitution Programme; and those who have acquired a residential property for the first time without government assistance and where the house/dwelling on the property, if any, does not comply with the National Norms and Standards in respect of permanent residential structures.
- Married or financial dependants: The applicant must be married or constantly be living together with a spouse. A single person with proven financial dependants (such as parents or parents-in-law, grandparents or grandparents-in-law, children, grandchildren, adopted children or foster children) may also apply.
- Monthly household income: The applicant's gross monthly household income must not exceed R3,500. Adequate proof of income must be submitted.
- Beneficiaries of the Land Restitution Programme: Should they satisfy the other qualification criteria, may apply for housing subsidies.
- Persons classified as military veterans as confirmed by the South African National Defence Force: Military veterans who are single without financial dependants may also apply for housing subsidies.
- Persons classified as aged: Aged persons who are single without financial dependants may also apply for housing subsidies. Aged persons are classified as male and female persons who have attained the minimum age applicable to government's old age social grant scheme.
- Persons classified as disabled: Persons who are classified as disabled, whether single, married, cohabiting or single with financial dependants, may apply for housing subsidies. If a person who has already received state funding for housing and/or who already owns or owned a house, is or becomes disabled, or if his or her dependant(s) is or becomes disabled, such a person may receive an additional variation on the subsidy amount to finance special additions to provide independent living conditions.

Housing policy progress in South Africa (1994–2010)

In the past 22 years, there have been several shifts in South African housing policy, which corroborates the socio-economic significance and political imperative of housing provision in the country. The housing policy shifts that have occurred since 1994 were most often responses to flaws in policy execution or were compelled by other agendas, such as political pressure or internal departmental politics (Charlton & Kihato, 2006). Besides, housing policy shifts in South Africa are not explicitly rooted in a rigorous interrogation of the needs of the poor, such as the impact of housing programmes on livelihoods and economic activity of the poor beneficiaries. Much of this had to do with the movement of personalities and senior housing officials out of the policy and research division of the housing department, and a lack of continuity and institutional memory to carry the policy development forwards strongly and decisively.

While the South African housing policy may have been moderately reformed, urban policy, IDP processes and land availability, which are crucial elements for successful housing provision, have lagged behind. The IDP is a single, inclusive strategic plan for the development of a municipality. It links, integrates and co-ordinates plans and takes into account proposals for the development of the municipality. It aligns resources and capacity of the municipality with the implementation of the plan, complies with the requirements of the Municipal Systems Act and is compatible with national and provincial development plans and planning requirements binding the municipality in terms of legislation.

Also, the contentious issue of well-located land for housing was never adequately addressed and almost all housing scholars and practitioners have affirmed that this has to do with the reluctance of the urban elite to grapple with an issue in which they themselves may hold a significant stake (Charlton & Kihato, 2006). This section of the chapter provides an overview of housing policy development since 1994. It briefly examines the NHF, a process which preceded the development of a NHP and moves to an analysis of the guiding NHP; the White Paper on Housing; as well as the BNG policy and a discussion of the Human Settlement Vision 2030.

National Housing Forum (1992–1994)

It is useful to briefly recount the debates that dominated the NHF, which was a multi-party non-governmental negotiating forum that met between 1992 and 1994 to discuss the post-Apartheid housing situation. The formulation of South Africa's housing policy commenced prior to the democratic elections, with the formation of the NHF. The multi-party non-governmental negotiating body comprising 19 members from business, the community, government, development organizations and political parties outside the government at the time. At these negotiations, the foundation for the new government's housing policy were developed and agreed. This culminated in the achievement of the broad housing sector convention also referred to as the Housing Accord that concluded with the White Paper on Housing in 1994. The Government of National Unity in 1994 made use of these negotiations and investigations when it formulated South Africa's NHP.

The objective of the NHF was to formulate a consensus around a new non-racial housing policy, which centred around two main debates. First among these was whether housing should be provided by the state or the market; and, second, whether the housing standard should be a completed four-room house or a 'progressive' (incremental) house (Tomlinson, 1999). The NHF set the tone for the first democratic NHP in 1994. Despite a holistic number of stakeholders that participated in the NHF, criticisms still emerged about the dominance of the private sector and big business at the negotiations, and the implications of this on the final housing policy that emerged. Furthermore, the impact of international experience affected the outcome, as well as the need for pragmatism around operational implementation and the heightened sense of urgency of the need to demonstrate delivery (Charlton & Kihato, 2006).

The NHF debate was centred on who would provide the housing and how it would be provided. The constituencies on the 'left' and the private construction sector argued, for different reasons, that the government should provide mass rental housing. The 'left', also referred to as the Mass Democratic Movement (consisting of the ANC, COSATU and the civic movement) argued that this would immediately entail a high standard of provision. The private sector held a similar standard with the caveat that the private sector should be employed as contractors and not developers so as to limit their financial risk. However, the opposition to this view was centred on a concern that the proven financial and organizational burdens of this approach would be too onerous for a fledgling government (Tomlinson, 1999). Besides, critics argued that local authorities were keen to rid themselves of the responsibility of managing rental housing because of difficulties in collecting rent, maintaining stock and applying qualifying criteria to tenants (Tomlinson, 1999). Those in favour of a mass state rental programme were challenged to explain how the state would finance and manage it; conversely, they were unable to persuasively do so and hence a more practical approach was pursued relating to the Mass Democratic Movement idea, which at the current time is not sustainable.

In October 1994, the newly-elected government hosted a National Housing Summit in Botshabelo, where it was able to secure formal support from a broad range of key stakeholders for the new housing policy and strategy in what is known as the Botshabelo Housing Accord. The National Housing Accord was signed by a range of stakeholders representing the homeless, the government, communities and civil society, the financial sector, emerging contractors, the established construction industry, building material suppliers, employers, developers and the international community. This accord set down the beginning of the common vision that forms the core of South Africa's NHP. Primarily, it comprised an agreement that all of these stakeholders would work together to achieve the vision summarized in the accord. As such, the National Housing Accord was soon followed by the Housing White Paper, which was promulgated in December 1994.

In terms of the debate around the role of the state versus the market in driving housing delivery, it was decided that the government would provide the context for housing provision and facilitate delivery, while the private sector would apply for subsidies on behalf of communities, identify and service land, and construct structures where possible. This approach was heavily criticized by many who believed that it would not address endemic flaws in the South African housing market and would simply perpetuate them; thus, this was rightly predicted as the policies initially formulated had been revised to adequately cater for the needs of the larger disadvantaged members of the society. However, the approach was a consensual one and related to the 'pacted' nature of the

South African transition, in which the private sector had a powerful leverage over both the National Party and incoming ANC governments (Huchzermeyer, 2004). The debate about what type of housing would be delivered concerned the cost of addressing the housing backlog and different estimates of budgets, time-frames and standards. It was agreed that a one-off capital subsidy scheme would be adopted to benefit households with an income of less than R3,500 per month and hence the government launched the NHSS. The subsidy was linked to individual ownership (as opposed to rental) and households effectively 'bought' a housing option with their subsidy (Tomlinson, 1999). This was to enable housing delivery opportunities and options to as many previously disadvantaged and deprived South Africans as quickly as possible.

Eventually, the White Paper on Housing emerged from the NHF process and the Housing Accord, which was influenced by the broad principles and targets of the ANC's RDP in 1994. However, the RDP cabinet was disbanded and replaced with the Growth, Employment and Redistribution macro-economic policy framework that favoured a market-oriented approach and relied heavily on the private sector for housing delivery. This latter strategy focused on meeting basic needs and was heavily concerned with delivery (Charlton & Kihato, 2006).

White Paper on Housing (1994)

The ANC government adopted the White Paper on Housing after the historic 1994 democratic elections, with the aim of creating viable, integrated settlements, where households could access opportunities, infrastructure and services, within which all South Africa's people will have access on a progressive basis to: a permanent residential structure with secure tenure, ensuring privacy and providing adequate protection against the elements; and potable water, adequate sanitary facilities, including waste disposal and domestic electricity supply.

The White Paper marked the end of the NHF process. From its inception in 1992, the NHF played a seminal role in creating the conditions necessary for a National Housing Accord, most visibly evident at the National Housing Summit in Botshabelo on 27 October 1994. Out of the accord, South Africa earned the task of harnessing the skills, resources and energy that the nation has in abundance, and directing them to the task at hand, which was to adequately house all South Africans. The White Paper also marked the beginning of a process. This is because for the first time in its history, South Africa now had a policy framework that would cater for all of its citizens. The approach adopted by the White Paper was the search for the creation of an enabling environment, and not for the publication of a new set of rules. It aimed to contribute to the certainty required by the market, as well as to give the provincial and local governments their capacity to fulfil their constitutional obligations. Throughout the document, a partnership between the various tiers of government, the private sector and the communities was envisaged. This is seen as a fundamental prerequisite for the sustained delivery of housing at a level unprecedented in the history of the country as the community can be truly for the citizens, if they participate in developmental decision that affects them. It also required all parties not only to argue for their rights, but also to accept their respective responsibilities.

The objective of the policy was to increase the national budget allocation of housing to 5% and to increase housing delivery on a sustainable basis to a peak level of 338,000 units each year and to reach the government's target of one million houses in five years (a target that has since been met). The White Paper outlined seven key strategies it would pursue in order to achieve its objectives, which are:

- stabilizing the housing environment in order to ensure maximal benefit of state housing expenditure and mobilizing private-sector investment;
- facilitating the establishment or directly establishing a range of institutional, technical and logistical housing support mechanisms to enable communities to, on a continuous basis, improve their housing circumstances (supporting the People's Housing Process);
- mobilizing private savings (whether by individuals or collectively) and housing credit at scale, on a sustainable basis and simultaneously ensuring adequate protection for consumers;
- providing subsidy assistance to disadvantaged individuals to assist them in gaining access to housing (through the NHSS and National Housing Programmes);
- rationalizing institutional capacities in the housing sector within a sustainable long-term institutional framework;
- facilitating the speedy release and servicing of land (utilizing the Development Facilitation Act and the Housing Development Act); and
- co-ordinating and integrating public-sector investment and intervention on a multifunctional basis.

On adoption of the White Paper in 1994, the government's intention was to deliver a 'starter house' (sometimes consisting of building materials, where the subsidy only covered land and servicing costs), which beneficiaries would add to and consolidate over time (Charlton & Kihato, 2006). This incremental approach of achieving the right to housing was related to a key assumption in the policy that beneficiaries would be able to access loan finance to be spent on improving the house, which never materialized. However, by the late 1990s, the nature of the houses being delivered shifted from the open-ended concept of a 'starter house' to a minimum 30 square metre housing unit with a defined specification, which has since been adjusted, but without the consent or any participatory involvement of the beneficiaries.

Nevertheless, in 1999 the National Norms and Standards for the Construction of Stand Alone Residential Dwellings were introduced by the Minister of Housing in terms of Section 3(2) (a) of the Housing Act. The National Norms and Standards placed an increasing focus on the size and quality of the top structure or house and stipulated minimum standards. As stipulated on the National Norms and Standards, each house must have: a minimum gross floor area of 40 square metres; two bedrooms; separate bathroom with a toilet, a shower and hand basin; combined living area and kitchen with wash basin; and ready board electrical installation, if electricity is available in the project area (DHS, 2009). However, this norm was never followed in most developments, which has brought about complaints and other social issues with the houses developed to date. Thus, beneficiaries' quality of life is not better enhanced with the provided housing, as the quality of these buildings is unappealing and as such they are even a burden with the further problems of having to carry out repairs and upgrade the newly constructed housing units.

In addition, an undesired effect of this new policy, according to Charlton and Kihato (2006), was that service standards relating to sanitation, water and roads were often dropped in order to deliver houses in greater numbers and of greater size. Thus, substandard latrines, communal standpipes and gravel roads were accepted as adequate, reinforcing the trend towards development on peripheral land as housing projects were built in areas where lower service levels were more acceptable. This policy adjustment, driven by a political need to deliver acceptable houses, was not rooted in a deeper understanding of the consequences of the service levels/location/top-structure trade-off on beneficiaries. Rather, it was an irritable move related to the historic rejection of the notion of 'incrementalism' – the gradual consolidation of a starter house over time by the end-user – and may again, in fact, have further contributed to the spatial marginalization of the poor. Nevertheless, the NHSS was used to finance the construction of over 1.5 million housing units across South Africa between 1994 and 2003. In March 2007, the Department of Housing announced that a total of 3,043,900 subsidies had been approved and 2,355,913 houses built since 1994. While this achievement has been greatly applauded, the government often notes that the backlog is increasing due to rapid urbanization, among other factors. The DHS currently estimates the housing backlog at around 2.2 million units.

Breaking New Ground (2004)

From its inception, the Housing Policy and Strategy of 1994 focused on stabilizing the environment to transform the extremely fragmented, complex and racially-based financial and institutional framework inherited from the previous government, while simultaneously establishing new systems to ensure delivery to address the housing backlog (BNG, 2004). The policy has come with significant achievements, which have been recognized both nationally and internationally with significant socio-economic, demographic and policy shifts occurring within the first ten years of the New South African government. While the government believed that the fundamentals of the 1994 policy remained relevant and sound, a new plan was required to redirect and enhance existing mechanisms to move towards more responsive and effective delivery. This brought about the formulation of a new human settlements plan referred to as the Comprehensive Plan for the Development of Sustainable Human Settlements, also known as BNG. BNG reinforces the vision of the then Department of Housing, to promote the achievement of a non-racial, integrated society through the development of sustainable human settlements and quality housing.

As of 2002–2003, the Department of Housing carried out a comprehensive appraisal of its housing programme after identifying a number of 'unintended consequences' of the existing programme. These unexpected problems included peripheral location of residential development; poor-quality products and settlements; the lack of community participation; the limited secondary low-income housing market; corruption and maladministration; a slowdown in delivery; underspent budgets; limited or decreasing public-sector participation; the increasing housing backlog; and the continued growth of informal settlements. The review process aimed at providing a new policy direction and to establish a research agenda to inform and support policy decision-making within the housing programme, particularly to counter the dispersal of knowledge and intellectual capacity that had occurred over the previous decade (Tissington, 2011).

BNG comprises nine elements or programmatic interventions, and seven objectives as shown in Table 6.2. The elements and objectives of BNG are a mix of substance and procedure as well as outcomes, outputs and inputs. Nevertheless, BNG can be understood to set out the ends to be achieved, the means to achieve them and the instruments to be used in the process of achieving the defined policy goals (Rust, 2006). With the review, BNG shifted away from a focus on the quantity of houses delivered to quality, with better size and workmanship of housing product, settlement design, alternative technology among others and a choice on tenure type and better locations. BNG implementation has increased the rate of delivery of well-located housing of satisfactory quality through a range of innovative and demand-driven housing programmes and projects. It also sought to place increased emphasis on the process of housing delivery, which is the planning, engagement and the long-term sustainability of the housing environment. Its key objective was to eradicate all informal settlements by 2014 (National Treasury, 2009).

BNG policy recognized the change in the dynamics of the housing demand, the increasing average annual population growth, the drop in average household size, significant regional differences, increasing urbanization, skewed growth of the residential property market, growth in unemployment and a growing housing backlog despite substantial delivery in the first decade of the initiated housing policy. Also, it recognized that the lack of affordable, well-located land for low-cost housing had led to development on the periphery of existing urban areas, achieving limited integration. Thus, the Department of Housing in 2008 stated that the dominant production of single houses on single plots in distant locations with initially weak socio-economic infrastructure was inflexible to local dynamics and changes in demand. Hence, the 2004 human settlements plan moves away from the commoditized focus of housing delivery towards more responsive mechanisms, which address the multi-dimensional needs of sustainable human settlements.

In addition, BNG recognized that the initially constructed subsidized houses had not become the valuable assets envisioned in earlier policy. Besides,

Table 6.2 BNG elements and objectives

BNG elements	*BNG objectives*
1 Supporting the entire residential property market	Accelerate the delivery of housing as a key strategy for poverty alleviation
2 Moving from housing to sustainable human settlements	Utilize the provision of housing as a major job-creation strategy
3 Using existing and new housing instruments	Ensure that property can be accessed by all as an asset for wealth creation and empowerment
4 Adjusting institutional arrangements within government	Leverage growth in the economy
5 Building institutions and capacity	Combat crime, promote social cohesion and improve quality of life for the poor
6 Defining financial arrangements	Support the functioning of the entire single residential property market to reduce duality within the sector, by breaking the barriers between the first economy residential property boom and the second economic slump
7 Creating jobs and housing	Utilize housing as an instrument for the development of sustainable human settlements, in support of spatial restructuring
8 Building information, communication and awareness	
9 Establishing systems for monitoring and evaluation	

Source: Rust (2006).

beneficiaries' inability to pay for municipal services and taxes revealed that municipalities viewed such housing projects as liabilities, and were not particularly responsive to the national department's more progressive intentions around housing. The BNG document frames housing delivery more clearly as a catalyst for achieving a set of broad socio-economic goals. Hence, the key intention of BNG was to move away from a supply-centred model to a demand-centred model driven by the needs of the beneficiaries, which is considered a tangible way to guarantee a lasting satisfaction with the produced houses from the beneficiaries.

Furthermore, BNG introduces an expanded role for municipalities. That is, in shifting away from a supply-driven framework towards a more demand-driven process, it places an increased emphasis on the role of the state in determining the location and nature of housing, as part of a plan to link the demand for and supply of housing. In so doing, the problems of placing housing in the urban boundary will be done away with – however, BNG has not succeeded in doing this since the endorsement. Thus, this approach has only enabled municipalities to assume overall responsibility for housing programmes in their areas of jurisdiction, through a greater devolution of responsibility and resources to them. However, BNG defines four primary ends (BNG, 2004; Rust, 2006), which are the basis of its acceptance:

1 Sustainable human settlements: Well-managed entities in which economic growth and social development are in balance with the carrying capacity of the natural systems on which they depend for their existence and result in sustainable development, wealth creation, poverty alleviation and equity.
2 Integration: The shift from housing units, to sustainable human settlements in BNG largely captures the integration end. Spatial restructuring is also critical and sustainable human settlements are seen to support spatial restructuring. BNG utilizes housing as an instrument for the development of sustainable human settlements, in support of spatial restructuring. There is also an institutional dimension as integration is both intra-governmental (within a sphere of government) and inter-governmental, requiring integrated planning and co-ordinated investment.
3 Housing assets: Ensuring property can be accessed by all as an asset for wealth creation and empowerment and supporting the functioning of the entire residential property market to reduce duality.
4 Upgraded informal settlements: Progressive eradication of informal settlements and urban inclusion.

The means to achieve the above-mentioned primary responsibilities, as defined in the policy includes:

- Municipal accreditation: To reduce transaction costs and unnecessary administration, funds will flow directly from national government to accredited municipalities.
- Effective inter-governmental relations: Co-ordination and alignment is essential to ensure the effective and efficient flow of resources. This will be achieved through the enhanced planning framework; bilateral co-operation between the Department of Housing, the Social Cluster Partner Departments and the other spheres of government, particularly municipalities, the Department of Housing and the metros working together to achieve the required alignment.
- Delivery defined by demand: Demand responsiveness cuts across many BNG proposals and the notion of demand definition underpins the rationale for an expanded role for municipalities.
- Effectively functioning housing markets: BNG develops a strategy around supporting the entire residential property market, which includes: assisting lower–middle income groups (expanding the scope upwards); a more flexible approach to accommodate demand responsiveness and shift from product uniformity; enhancing the role of the private sector; and creating linkages between the primary and secondary residential property markets.

Already, the cities of Johannesburg, Ekurhuleni, eThekweni, Tshwane and other metropolitan cities have all redrafted their housing strategies in line with BNG. While their policies are in line with the budgetary allocations and inherent conditionalities defined at national level for BNG, the local implementations are thus, giving expression to the intentions of BNG.

Human Settlement Vision 2030

The DHS has taken progressive steps towards achieving the vision of the NDP of transforming human settlements and the spatial economy to create more functionally integrated, balanced and vibrant urban settlements. More specifically, the DHS planned to implement the human settlements reforms before 2019. The reforms aim to ensure that poor households have adequate housing in better living environments, to support the development of a functional and equitable residential property market, and to improve institutional capacity and co-ordination for better spatial targeting. In this regard, provinces, municipalities and the department's public entities will be implementing agents of national policy directives as they are defined. They will be responsible for delivering housing opportunities, funded by transfers from the DHS.

The Human Settlements Vision 2030, tagged on the road to 2050 aims to provide houses and services in rural and urban areas simultaneously. The vision is also referred to as Each-One-Settle-One. The Each-One-Settle-One Campaign was launched by the then Minister of Human Settlements, Mr Tokyo Sexwale, in 2012 at the Johannesburg Stock Exchange in partnership with the top 200 companies. The vision is focused on the total eradication of backlogs of more than 2.1 million housing units, which translates to about 12.5 million people. The campaign motivates stakeholders, private-sector institutions, donor agencies and ordinary citizens to help the department to reduce the housing backlog. The inefficiencies and inequalities in South Africa's settlement patterns are deeply entrenched; townships were developed and are still being developed on the periphery of the cities and town far from places of work, shopping and social facilities.

Under Vision 2030's framework, it is planned that most South Africans will have affordable access to services and a quality environment; instead of living in isolation on the periphery of cities. The key highlights of the Vision 2030's framework is to:

- respond systematically to entrenched spatial patterns across all geographic scales that exacerbate social inequality and economic inefficiency;
- to consider the unique needs and potentials of different rural and urban areas in the context of emerging development corridors in the southern African sub-region;
- the state will review its housing policies to better realize constitutional housing rights, ensure that the delivery of housing is to be used to restructure towns and cities, and strengthen the livelihood prospects of households;

- active citizenship in the field of spatial development will be supported and incentivized through a range of interventions including properly funded, citizen-led neighbourhood vision and planning processes and the introduction of social compacts from neighbourhood to city level;
- planning in South Africa will be guided by a set of normative principles to create spaces that are liveable, equitable, sustainable, resilient and efficient, and support economic opportunities and social cohesion; and
- South Africa will develop a national spatial framework and resolve the current deficiencies with the local system of integrated development planning and progressively develop the governance and administrative capability to undertake planning at all scales.

Housing delivery and backlogs

In 2009, the DHS admitted that the data it relies on to estimate the housing backlog in South Africa are most likely unpredictable, and that a state-subsidized house that is delivered may remain inadequate because of lack of access to basic services. Consequently, in terms of eliminating the housing backlog and delivering adequate housing to the low-income groups especially, the department is not really clear where it stands (Tissington, 2011). Hence, the DHS indicated that in relation to its statistics collection and verification, it is hoping that the 2011 census will be able to give it a better sense of the accuracy of the data needed to measure backlogs and access delivery. However, there are various reasons for unreliability of data such as poor provincial and municipal record-keeping in many parts of the country, as well as incomplete data on house construction among others. The South African National Treasury states that detailed records of spending on subsidy instruments per municipality are not readily available on a national basis, and that these data weaknesses are a problem for the sector and the situation reflects the ongoing co-ordination problems being experienced by the municipalities. Thus, this severely undermines any detailed analysis, oversight and accountability. As such, this section of the book provides review on housing delivery since 1994, as well as on the current and growing housing backlogs in the country.

Housing delivery since 1994

The Department of Housing states that from 1994 to 2004, about R29.5 billion was spent on state-assisted housing investment generating 1.6 million housing opportunities and providing 500,000 families with the opportunity to secure titles of old public housing stock (Department of Housing, 2003). Also, the Department of Housing (2007) states that the government had made good progress in eradicating backlogs and providing adequate housing. It further reported that over 3 million subsidies had been approved, benefiting over 13.5 million poor people in terms of housing. Cumulatively, the government stated it had spent R40 billion on housing developments since the inception of the housing programme, contributing to 2.4 million houses being constructed including those still in the process as of 2007. However, while approximately 3.3 million subsidies were approved as of 2009, actual delivery of subsidized housing units had been much slower (National Treasury, 2009). However, between 2001/2002 and 2007/2008 delivery was said to have declined in most provinces, while the allocation from the Integrated Housing and Human Settlement Development (IHHSD) grant increased (National Treasury, 2009). The National Treasury further reported that between 1995 and mid-2008 the IHHSD grant disbursed approximately R49 billion, which provided a total of 2.6 million housing opportunities at a gross average cost of R18,850 per unit and an average annual delivery rate of 200,000 units a year. According to the then Department of Housing, although accurate data are not readily available, the bulk of this spending occurs through project-linked subsidies (now IRDP), where developers implemented housing projects at scale and a qualifying household obtained ownership of a complete residential unit.

In 2010, the Minister of Human Settlements stated that since 1994 more than 3 million housing units have been made available for nearly 13.5 million people. To date, the DHS has delivered 4.3 million houses and housing opportunities since the dawn of democracy. These opportunities include over 2.8 million fully-subsidized houses, 121,784 social/rental houses, 6,329 Financial Linked Individual Subsidy Programme houses and 986,608 serviced sites. This historic milestone has provided suitable shelter for more than 20 million people. As impressive as the delivery statistics, they becomes less so when stacked up against the housing backlog. This amounted to 1.5 million units in 1994, was put at 2.7 million units in 2012, and now stands at some 2.1 million units. This last figure is based on the number of people with their names on the national housing waiting list. The reasons for these differences lie partly in the fact that backlog statistics are neither systematically compiled nor located in a single place, which leaves them open to varying interpretations. Hence, South Africa nevertheless sits today with a housing backlog of 2.1 million units despite spending about R125 billion, in 2010 prices, over 20 years, delivering more than 4.3 million units. In addition, in 1993 there were an estimated 300 informal settlements across the country, whereas by the 2009/2010 financial year the number had risen to some 2,700, an increase of almost 800%. More recent figures provided by the DHS put the total number of informal settlements at 2,225, of which some 1,260 are located in KwaZulu-Natal, Gauteng and the Western Cape (Tomlinson, 1999).

This large increase in the number of informal settlements since 1994 shows that seemingly impressive delivery figures have in fact been insufficient either to clear the backlog or to keep up with new family formation. Today's backlog numbers are thus more likely the result of how policy has in practice been interpreted over the past two decades, rather than how it was intended to be implemented. One key issue is that the housing policy adopted in 1994 has no 'grandfather' clause limiting the provision of housing to those who lived and suffered under Apartheid (Tomlinson, 1999). There is also no time limit to the constitutional clause (Section 26) stating that 'everyone has the right to have access to adequate housing'. South Africans born both before, as well as after, the end of Apartheid thus take the view that 'they have a right to a free house' if their monthly income is below R3,500 per month. Accordingly, households continually break themselves up into smaller units in the expectation that each new unit will become entitled to a housing subsidy. National, provincial and local government housing officials all refer to this as the growth of an 'entitlement syndrome' and say it has made the goal of eliminating the housing backlog simply unattainable.

Over time, the housing subsidy has thus grown from its original R12,500 per household to R160,500 per household in 2014, an overall increase of over 1,200%. Today, moreover, this increased housing subsidy is intended to cover only the construction of a house, with land and service costs coming out of provincial and local government budgets. In 1994 government spending on housing and community amenities accounted for 1% of GDP. In 2015/2016, according to the current budget, expenditure in these spheres will have risen to 3.7% of GDP, making for an overall increase of 270%. This is a faster rise even than expenditure on social grants and other forms of social protection, which is expected to rise from 2.8% of GDP in 1994/1995 to 3.8% of GDP in 2015/2016, an increase of 36%. Already, annual spending on housing and community amenities consumes 11.4% of government expenditure, which is almost as much as health (Tomlinson, 1999).

Housing delivery in South Africa

The delivery of housing in post-Apartheid South Africa is characterized by three streams of provision and allocation that run parallel and often overlap to some extent. These three housing streams are: public-sector built; private-sector provided; and self-provided. However, public-sector built housing is only delivered through the housing subsidy schemes, hence the name state-subsidized housing. In this section of the chapter, the concept of state-subsidized housing in South Africa is discussed, with a particular emphasis on the delivery mechanism and the problems associated with the housing delivered to date.

State-subsidized housing in South Africa

State-subsidized housing in South Africa is a form of housing delivery system in which the properties and associated infrastructure are financed by the government and transferred to qualifying low-income families, elderly and handicapped individuals with little or no contribution coming from them. However, it hasn't proved easy to help the poor through housing subsidies, particularly in developing countries (Gilbert, 2004) such as South Africa with numerous social-economic issues and racial divides. Today, very few governments are prepared to offer housing subsidies to the poor unless they are delivered as up-front or targeted capital subsidies. Also, the lack of resources has forced most governments into making difficult decisions about the size and the number of subsidies to be offered.

In order to address the housing shortage and the urban and rural housing backlog in the post-Apartheid South African state, the government instituted a number of programmes and mechanisms to assist lower-income households. Foremost among these included the housing subsidy system, as well as other innovative mechanisms to encourage the increase of affordable housing to the poor (Landman & Napier, 2010). Also dependent on these decisions, has come a series of implementation problems relating to the quality of construction, the location of the new housing solutions, the use of credit and how to allocate subsidies between so many beneficiaries. While there have certainly been positive experiences from the South African housing delivery mechanism, there is also a very long list of failures particularly with the process of delivery and the product that was and is still being delivered. However, housing delivery for the low-income groups in South Africa is reliant on the housing subsidy process. The subsidy scheme facilitates the provision of a range of housing types. Prominent among this is the RDP housing (named after the Reconstruction and Development Programme initiated to promote delivery in 1994), which was developed by government and allocated to beneficiaries with a household income of less than R3,500. Beneficiaries of the housing subsidy scheme receive a one-off grant. The housing subsidy grant is a grant by government to qualifying beneficiaries for housing purposes. The qualifying criteria have been discussed above. The grant is not paid in cash to beneficiaries; it is either paid to a developer, or in new housing developments for the provision of a house. The grant is used to construct a house (top structure as approved) that complies with the minimum technical and environmental norms and standards, as well as the land for the house and the basic services (water and sanitation), which is then transferred to the qualifying beneficiary after completion.

Despite the impressive delivery of houses, the housing backlog has increased from 1.5 million in 1994 and has continued to grow and is currently estimated at between 2.1 million and 2.5 million. This, according to the DHS, translates into approximately 20 million people still needing houses in the country. South Africa has spent billions of rand to provide housing to the poor, but the government's 2015 General Household Survey showed that 14.4% of South African households were living in 'RDP' or state-subsidized dwellings. The percentage of households that received a government housing subsidy increased from 5.5% in 2002 to 14.4% in 2015, while female-headed households were more likely to have received housing subsidies (18%) than male-headed households in 2015 (12%). This is in line with government policies that give preference to households headed by individuals from vulnerable groups, including females, and individuals with disabilities. Also, in 2015, more than three-quarters (78.1%) of South African households lived in formal dwellings, followed by 14.1% who lived in informal dwellings, and 6.9% in traditional dwellings. Despite spending about R125 billion, in 2010 prices, over 20 years, delivering more than 4.3 million units, the authorities still regularly battle protests in shantytowns by destitute black residents angered by rampant joblessness and poor amenities such as water, toilets and electricity. However, some housing scholars argue that there may be many more people still needing housing, as the number of those living in informal settlements are not adequately captured and the number most times does not include foreign nationals. However, the housing subsidy scheme is in line with the government housing strategy as contained in the NHP Framework, which is to provide subsidy assistance to the low-income groups, thus enabling them to become home-owners and to improve their quality of life.

Though delivery through social housing has significantly increased since then, it still constitutes a small percentage of the overall housing supply in the country. Other forms of state-provided housing include public housing at a local level. Government-subsidized homes, or 'RDP' housing, usually provides a stand-alone house of about 30–40m^2 on a 250m^2 plot. However, lately, developers and designers have started to experiment with alternative housing types where RDP units are semi-detached and located on smaller sites to accommodate densification. These are evident in projects, such as the Alexandra Urban Renewal Programme and the Pennyville Development in the City of Johannesburg (Landman & Napier, 2010). For instance, in Pennyville the developers have also experimented with semi-detached RDP units on two levels such as the semi-detached simplexes, while in another project in the Nelson Mandela Metropolitan Municipality in the Eastern Cape Province, namely Sakhasonke, semi-detached duplexes have also been built. These newly experimental houses are significantly larger (46 square metres) than the previous models of 40 square metres. This shows some flexibility being adopted regarding the implementation of subsidy housing for ownership in South Africa. Currently, there is very little supply of housing for households earning between R3,500 and R8,000. These households do not qualify for a housing subsidy as recommended by the Housing Policy Framework, yet are unable to afford housing in the market. This gap in the housing market is known as Gap Housing (Rust, 2006). In attempting to address part of this gap, housing institutions are also making use of institutional subsidies to co-fund the development of social housing units for the more affordable housing market sector, thus addressing the gap market. This current initiative is supposed to sufficiently address the Gap Housing as government has committed resources to it. For example, the Brickfields and Carr Gardens projects developed in the inner city of Johannesburg and the Amalinda Housing Project in the Buffalo City Municipality are pilot projects of this initiative. Cross (2008) states that the majority of government-delivered dwelling units are concentrated in the urban sector, while the rural sector is not being given considerable attention. The integration of the rural consideration is what the Human Settlement Vision 2030 specifically speaks to.

Despite the efforts of the NHSS to deliver housing to all, there have been problems with both the quantity and quality of housing delivered since 1994. Prime among these, as noted by the Department of Housing more recently, are that housing delivery has had a limited impact on poverty alleviation and that houses have not become the financial, social and economic assets as envisioned in the early 1990s and as stated in the Housing White Paper.

This was supported in a 2010 study by Aigbavboa on the housing subsidy post-occupancy evaluation, which found that a majority of the beneficiaries do not consider their houses an asset for wealth creation. This is because most of the houses built via the project-linked subsidies for large-scale housing developments (now IRDP) were often located on the periphery of existing townships, land previously acquired or zoned for township development under Apartheid (Charlton & Kihato, 2006). This system maintains the marginalization of the poor and does not contribute to the compaction, integration and restructuring of the Apartheid city (Charlton & Kihato, 2006). This trend has thus reinforced the spatial segregation of cities, which isolates the poor from livelihood opportunities and social services, as well as the tendency towards urban sprawl. This problem has often been exacerbated by the fact that there has also been little co-ordination between government departments to ensure that public transport, schools, clinics, libraries and police stations are provided for the new community. However, with the modification and enhancement of the NHP and with particular emphasis on the SHP design to bring about restructuring of the urban divide, this has greatly been attended to through the IRDP scheme.

Because of the numerous problems associated with the RDP houses over the years, Tissington (2011) asserts that they have become residential dormitories, thus many beneficiaries choose to trade their houses and move back to informal settlements or other informal housing to be closer to work. Also, since 2005, approximately 11% of all RDP houses were unofficially traded by owners who were barred from selling their houses due to the mandatory lock-in period of eight years set for all state-subsidized housing in the country (Urban LandMark, 2010). Over half of the unofficially traded transactions were between R5,750 and R17,000 in 2010. Eight years is a long time as this duration makes it incredibly difficult for an RDP house to be used as a financial asset to acquire lending against it (Wessels, 2010; Rust, 2006). Also, because the location of the constructed houses often fails to match beneficiaries' needs, financial institutions are reluctant to lend using the houses as collateral security (Tissington et al., 2010). As a result, the low-income groups accept the RDP houses but rent them out to generate income, while they choose to live in an informal settlement or backyard shack in a township to be closer to jobs and livelihood opportunities. Also, only about 34% of the beneficiaries who were originally allocated state-subsidies are actually occupying the housing units.

Another problem that concerns the RDP houses is the delays in the transferal of title deeds and the protracted length of township establishment has meant many beneficiaries do not have their title deeds or proof of ownership. Also of late, the Minister of Human Settlements announced that the government would be using R1.3 billion, or 10% of the department's budget, to demolish and rectify badly constructed RDP houses (Prinsloo, 2010). The Minister of the DHS since coming to office has focused greatly on the issue of the quality of RDP houses previously built and those being constructed, as well as corruption in housing projects through his national audit task team. There have been several problems with this model including corruption in the allocation of subsidized housing units as well as in construction tenders, the latter resulting in construction short cuts being taken and poor-quality houses being built.

Statistics South Africa, through its 2015 General Household Survey (GHS) across the country, states that about 14.2% of households living in RDP or state-subsidized dwellings felt that the walls of their dwellings were weak/very weak, while 13.8% felt that their roof was weak/very weak. Furthermore, the GHS report states that there was a considerable variation between provinces in perceptions about housing quality. For instance, in the Western Cape and Eastern Cape, nearly a third of all households reported that they have a problem with their walls and roofs. While in the Northern Cape, 17% of households had problems with their walls and 18% had problems with their roofs. Also in KwaZulu-Natal, 14.9% of households had problems with their walls. Hence the DHS claims that approximately R359 million would be needed to demolish and rectify approximately 20,000 shoddy RDP houses in the Eastern Cape. However, towards the end of 2009, about 3,000 RDP houses identified in the Eastern Cape and KwaZulu-Natal provinces were demolished because of inferior workmanship. These houses had been built in the 18 months prior to their identification as intolerably poor structures.

Furthermore, in delivering state-subsidized RDP housing, the government has overlooked a key principle of the RDP policy, which is to promote integrated development. However, this is currently being addressed through the IRDP scheme, which is aimed at creating social cohesion in the developed settlements.

Lessons learnt from South African housing studies

The following are the lessons learnt on the study of the South African housing situation:

- The housing environment in South Africa is complex, in large part due to the deliberate policy and legislative framework of socio-economic and spatial exclusion and marginalization created during the Apartheid era.
- The post-Apartheid state government has been actively involved in trying to create a level playing field for the previously disadvantaged and also in trying to repair the disadvantaged condition created by the almost 42 years of the Apartheid government.
- The implementation of the South African housing policy to date has been skewed and unable to address the land, housing and basic services needs of millions of poor South Africans who still lack adequate housing and access to water, sanitation and electricity.
- The South African housing policy is the result of a mixed bag of international influences and local creativity – mostly due to the policy of spatial segregation in the Apartheid state, which contributed to a policy that is defined in terms of the 'scan globally, reinvent locally' principle.

- The South African housing agenda objectives go beyond simply providing housing structures, but that housing construction should contribute to the national economy, demonstrating delivery, contributing to the economic performance and assisting with poverty alleviation.
- The enactment of the Natives Land Act 27 of 1913 cemented housing policy issues in the Apartheid era, creating a divide in housing issues, which exists to date, thus ascertaining that the housing backlog and current problems date back to the 1913 Native Land Act.
- The first effort to adequately assist local authorities in their task of meeting the housing needs in their areas of jurisdiction was through the adoption of the first South African Housing Code in 1964.
- The fundamental principles of the South African housing policy and developmental framework were established in the Housing White Paper, which was published in December 1994.
- The fundamental policy and development principles introduced by the Housing White Paper remain relevant and guide all developments in respect of housing policy and implementation in South Africa.
- The fundamental philosophy underpinning housing development goals in South Africa is the existing South African Constitution of 1996.
- The constitution contains justifiable socio-economic rights and enshrines everyone's right to have access to adequate housing.
- The South African Housing Act of 1997 is the primary piece of housing legislation in South Africa. It legally entrenched housing policy principles outlined in the 1994 White Paper on Housing.
- The Housing Act provides for a sustainable housing development process, laying down general principles for housing development in all spheres of government; it defines the functions of national, provincial and local governments in respect of housing development; and it lays the basis for financing National Housing Programmes.
- The NHC, which was first published in 2000 in accordance with the Housing Act, set out the underlying policy principles, guidelines and norms and standards that apply to the National Housing Programmes.
- Housing policy shifts in South Africa are not, however, explicitly rooted in a rigorous interrogation of the needs of the poor, such as the impact of housing programmes on livelihoods and economic activity of the poor beneficiaries.
- There is a lack of continuity and institutional memory to carry the policy development forwards strongly and decisively, as housing department personnels change over time.
- Housing delivery for the low-income groups in South Africa is reliant on the housing subsidy process. The subsidy scheme facilitates the provision of a range of housing types. Prominent among this is the RDP housing, which was developed by government and allocates properties to beneficiaries with a household income of less than R3,500.

Summary

This chapter provided an outline of housing legislative and policy framework in South Africa, examining the constitution with specific reference to the Bill of Rights and the Right to Housing, the NHC and the National Housing Programmes categorized therein with a specific focus on state-subsidized housing (housing subsidy scheme). Also, an evolution of housing policy in South Africa was discussed. Further, an overview of the developments in housing policy since 1994 was illustrated, including a summary of the negotiations at the NHF held between 1992 and 1994. The section further examined the supreme policy framework contained in the 1994 White Paper on Housing, and the problems associated with the RDP houses built after 1994.

In many ways, despite the 'miracle' of the negotiated settlement, which established a fully democratic order without the liberation of a full-scale revolution, the new South African state remains a hostage of its past, as evident from the history of its housing policy down to the development and amendments made to the policies after 1994. Precisely, the legacy of Apartheid in the form of profound social polarization, extreme economic inequalities and spatially divided cities massively complicate the task of building a new society informed by the constitutional right that all South Africans should have access to adequate housing. Though Apartheid alone cannot be held responsible for the housing conditions in South Africa, equally no account of housing policy and conditions can be credible if it does not take into account the country's history.

This chapter revealed that housing policy in South Africa appears to remain wedded to the sort of supply-side approach that, for the most part, can deliver only a fairly standardized product or range of products. The degree to which the present housing policy and the supporting programmes will overcome certain of the major problems inherited from the past, even if the obstacles to more rapid delivery at scale can be overcome, remains questionable. In particular, the current policy framework has clear limits in terms of addressing the fundamental social and spatial divisions that characterize the country's cities. Also, the failure to clearly and steadily integrate housing policy into a coherent strategy of urban restructuring in South Africa was the former housing framework's deficiency. This deficiency has now been addressed through the SHP framework that applies to 'restructuring zones', which are identified by municipalities as areas of economic opportunity and where urban renewal/restructuring impacts can best be achieved.

Despite the numerous challenges that have come with the delivery of housing in the new South African state, over 4.3 million subsidies had been approved, helping over 20 million poor people with housing. The most important point to stress in conclusion is that the vital objective of housing policy framework must be to stimulate the environments that give dignity to people's lives: it is not simply the provision of shelter. Against this criterion, the record of housing policy and implementation in South Africa in recent decades has been average, albeit alleviating the suffering of the disadvantaged groups. In order for the money spent not to be wasted, there is a need to evaluate the residential satisfaction of the housing occupants so that errors made can be corrected for future developments. A narrow focus on the individual housing unit and the provision of shelter, which is the prevalent disposition, gives rise to a particular mind-set and approach, which ensures the generation of poorly-performing, sterile environments. Significant improvement demands a paradigm shift, a shift that places not the individual unit but collective spaces, institutions and facilities at the centre of housing research, which is beneficiary-driven. The last part of this book will be focused on this second central aim, which provides the readers with ideas on residential satisfaction theories and their formation in a low-income housing setting.

References

BNG (2004). Breaking New Ground. A comprehensive plan for the development of sustainable human settlements. Available from: www.thehda.co.za/uploads/files/BREAKING_NEW_GROUND_DOC_copy-2_1.pdf (accessed 12 June 2015).

Charlton, S. & Kihato, C. (2006). Reaching the poor: An analysis of the influences on the evolution of South Africa's housing programme. In U. Pillay, R. Tomlinson & J. du Toit (eds) *Democracy and delivery: Urban policy in South Africa*. Cape Town, South Africa: HSRC Press, p. 263.

Cross, C. (2008). Profiling housing demand: Settlement typology and survey results. Report prepared for the demonstrator Toolkit for Integrated Planning, for the Department of Science and Technology. CSIR Report No. CSIR/BE/PSS/ER/2008/0048/B.

De Loor, J.H. (1992). *Housing in South Africa: Report by the task group on national housing strategy*. Pretoria: Department of Housing.

Department of Housing (2003). *ABC of housing statistics*. Pretoria: Department of Housing.

Department of Housing (2007). *Framework for an inclusionary housing policy in South Africa*. Pretoria: Department of Housing.

DHS (2009). *Technical and general guidelines: Part A of Part 3, Vol. 2 of the National Housing Code (2009) 21*. Pretoria: Department of Human Settlement.

DHS (2010). Subsidy quantum – Incremental interventions. Available from: http://policyresearch.limpopo.gov.za/bitstream/handle/123456789/1084/National%2520Housing%2520Policy%2520and%2520Subsidy%2520Programmes.pdf?sequence=1 (accessed 12 March 2017).

Gilbert, A. (2004). Helping the poor through housing subsidies: Lessons from Chile, Colombia and South Africa. *Habitat international*, 28(1):13–40.

Goodlad, R. (1996). The housing challenge in South Africa. *Urban studies*, 33(9):1629–1645.

Huchzermeyer, M. (2004). *Unlawful occupation: Informal settlements and urban policy in South Africa and Brazil*. Trenton, NJ: Africa World Press.

Landman, K. & Napier, M. (2010). Waiting for a house or building your own? Reconsidering state provision, aided and unaided self-help in South Africa. *Habitat international*, 34 (3):299–305.

Marais, L. (2007). Does housing size matter? The politics and realities of housing size. *Town and regional planning*, 51:75–81.

Misselhorn, M. (2008). Draft position paper on informal settlements upgrading: part of a strategy for the second economy. Compiled for Urban LandMark. Available from:

www.pptrust.org.za/wp-content/uploads/delightful-downloads/informal-settlement-paper.pdf (accessed 7 April 2018).

Morris, P. (1981). *A history of black housing in South Africa*. Johannesburg: South African Foundation.

National Treasury (2009). Chapter 6: Human settlements' in provincial budgets and expenditure review 2005/06–2011/12. Available from: www.treasury.gov.za/publications/igfr/2009/prov/06.%20Chapter%206%20-%20Human%20Settlements.pdf (accessed 3 September 2011).

Phago, K.G. (2010). Effects of the development and implementation of the National Public Housing Policy in South Africa with specific reference to the Gauteng province. Doctoral paper. Pretoria: University of South Africa.

Pottie, D. (2003). Challenges to local government in low-income housing delivery. In P. Thring & F. Kahn (eds) *Housing policy and practice in post-Apartheid South Africa*. Sandown, SA: Heinemann.

Prinsloo, L. (2010). NHBRC to crack down on unregistered home builders: engineering news. Available from: www.engineeringnews.co.za/article/nhbrc-to-crackdown-on-unregistered-home-builders-2010-05-12 (accessed 10 September 2011).

Reader's Digest (1989). *The building blocks of segregation: Reader's Digest illustrated history of South Africa*. Cape Town: Reader's Digest.

Republic of South Africa (1997). *Housing code*. Available from: www.thehda.co.za/uploads/files/Housing_Act_107_of_1997.pdf (accessed 12 December 2016).

Rodgers, B. (1980). *Divide and rule: South Africa's Bantustans*. London: International Defence and Aid Fund.

Rust, K. (2006). *Analysis of South Africa's housing sector performance*. Johannesburg: FinMark Trust.

Saul, J. & Gelb, S. (1981). *The crisis in South Africa: class defence, class revolution*. New York: Monthly Review Press.

Tissington, K. (2011). *A resource guide to housing in South Africa 1994–2010 legislation, policy, programmes and practice*. Johannesburg: Socio-Economic Rights Institute of South Africa (SERI).

Tissington, K., Rust, K., Mcgaffin, R., Napier, M. and Charlton, S. (2010). Let's see the real value in RDP houses. Available from: www.businessday.co.za/articles/Content.aspx?id=119621 (accessed 10 September 2011).

Tomlinson, R. (1999). *Urbanization in a post-Apartheid South Africa*. London: Unwin Hyman.

Urban LandMark & Social Housing Foundation (2010). Small-scale private rental: a strategy for increasing supply in South Africa. Available from: www.urbanlandmark.org.za/downloads/small_scale_rental_booklet_2010.pdf (accessed 3 September 2011).

Wessels, L. (2010). Black market highlights RDP cracks. Available from: www.fin24.com/Business/Black-market-highlights-RDP-cracks-20100331 (accessed 10 September 2011).

Wilkinson, P. (1998). Housing policy in South Africa. *Habitat international*, 22(3):215–229.

Part IV

Residential satisfaction theories and research

Part IV of this book discusses the theoretical and conceptual perspectives of residential satisfaction studies, thus addressing the second focus of the book that explores the theories underpinning residential satisfaction and the formation of residential satisfaction through the development of a conceptual framework in low-income housing typology. This part contains two chapters:

- Chapter 7 – Residential satisfaction theories; and
- Chapter 8 – Conceptual perspective of residential satisfaction formation.

7 Residential satisfaction theories

Introduction

The failure of many housing projects is the result of a lack of knowledge and understanding of the determinants of the residential satisfaction concept. The success of housing programmes does not only depend on the mere provision of housing units, but also on other factors that should be considered during the housing developmental process. The achievement of government housing programmes does not only depend on bulk quantitative delivery of housing units, but also on the understanding of the factors that influence the needs of residents and the eventual satisfaction they derive from the housing product. Hence, residential satisfaction deals with housing occupants' satisfaction with housing products, with the aim of informing housing policy and planning intervention (Yiping, 2005). Residential satisfaction has been credited as one of the most significant concepts that should be considered in design and planning processes for different nations' housing policies. Nevertheless, residential satisfaction is a subjective concept because of its multifaceted nature (Ge & Hokao, 2006). Research in residential satisfaction is a valid way to assess the overall performance of the housing system (Francescato, Weidemann & Anderson, 1987). Therefore, this chapter of the book is focused on the review of theoretical and conceptual perspectives of residential satisfaction research. Also discussed are previous residential satisfaction models and theories, residential satisfaction research (conceptual issues on residential satisfaction) such as the appropriate ways of measuring residential satisfaction, followed by a discussion on the determinants of residential satisfaction. The problems raised to date in residential satisfaction research are also reviewed in this chapter of the book.

The theories of satisfaction

The foundation for satisfaction lies in 'mankind's ability to learn' from previous experiences (Peyton, Pitts & Kamery, 2003: 41). Likewise, users' preferences are constantly being updated by way of the learning process. Learning theory posits that

> a given response is strengthened either positively or negatively to the extent that it is followed by a reward. Reward, in turn, leads to an evaluation that

> the purchase or achievement was satisfactory . . . and hence it can exert an effect on product beliefs and attitude. The probability of engaging in a similar buying act or continuance in a housing scheme will be increased if there are positive consequences in the act of purchase [use of the unit and vice versa].
>
> (Engel, Kollat & Blackwell, 1968: 532)

The word satisfaction first appeared in English in the thirteenth century. The word itself is derived from the Latin word *satis* (meaning 'enough') and the Latin ending *-faction* (from the Latin *facere* 'to do/make'). Early usage of the word satisfaction focused on satisfaction being some sort of release from wrongdoing. Later citations emphasized satisfaction as a freedom from uncertainty (The Oxford Library of Words and Phrases, 1993: 1258). Modern usage of the word has tended to be much broader, and satisfaction is clearly related to other words such as satisfactory (adequate), satisfy (make pleased or contented) and satiation (enough). The study on satisfaction has grown rapidly over time with more than 1 million studies carried out on the concept to date. However, despite the overwhelming quantity of literature surrounding the concept, certain key issues have either gone unresolved or have recently been brought into question with regards to a comprehensive understanding of the attributes that determine satisfaction in a typical user environment (Anderson & Fornell, 1994).

Satisfaction is a concept that has appeared in many fields, such as evaluation and employee satisfaction, patient satisfaction and visitor satisfaction of sites, among others. However, the idea has been fundamental to the marketing concept for over five decades as the most extensive use of satisfaction has been in literature concerned with customer satisfaction. Several models of satisfaction have emerged over time in this field (customer relations) and in others. The models developed to date all view satisfaction as a consumer attitude in relation to the consumer's belief and evaluation about merchandise and buying behaviour (Wilton & Nicosia, 1986; Kim, 1997). The broad use of behaviour demonstrates the appealing validity of the concept and its utility in explaining the success of a range of phenomena (Parker & Mathews, 2001).

While everyone knows broadly what satisfaction means, it clearly does not mean the same thing to everyone (Day, 1980). Initial conceptualization of user satisfaction views it as a 'single variable which involves a single evaluative reaction from the users' (Peyton, Pitts & Kamery, 2003: 42), which may or may not be related to pre-evaluation concepts. Further conceptualization of satisfaction notes that

> satisfaction is a kind of stepping away from an experience and evaluating it . . . One could have a pleasurable experience that caused dissatisfaction because even though it was pleasurable, it was not as pleasurable as it was supposed to be; so satisfaction is not an emotion, it is the evaluation of the emotion.
>
> (Hunt, 1977: 39)

The most generally acknowledged conceptualization of the user satisfaction concept is the Expectancy Disconfirmation Theory (McQuitty, Finn & Wiley, 2000). Expectancy Disconfirmation Theory was developed by Oliver (1980a), who proposed that a user's satisfaction level is a result of the difference between expected and perceived product performance, and expectations as predictions of future performance. The inclusion of expectations suggests that products satisfying high expectations are predicted to generate greater user satisfaction than products that meet low expectations. Other researchers employ perceived performance as an additional predictor of satisfaction (Churchill & Surprenant 1982; Tse & Wilton 1988). On the one hand, satisfaction (positive disconfirmation) is known to occur when a product or service is better than expected. On the other hand, a performance worse than the expected results is labelled as dissatisfaction (negative disconfirmation). In this theory, expectations originate from beliefs about the level of performance that a product/service will provide, which is the predictive meaning of the expectations concept. In comparison, satisfaction is also a person's feeling of pleasure or disappointment resulting from comparing a product's perceived performance (or outcome) in relation to his or her expectations (Kotler, 2000). Satisfaction can also be associated with the feelings of acceptance, happiness, relief, excitement and delight (Hoyer & MacInnis, 2001). Similarly, Hansemark and Albinsson (2004) established that satisfaction is an overall customer attitude towards a service provider, or an emotional reaction to the difference between what users anticipate and what they receive, regarding the fulfilment of some need, goal or desire. While in the case of a state-subsidized housing scheme for the poor and the low-income groups where the government is responsible for provision of the houses, it would mean the overall beneficiaries' emotional reactions towards the government provided houses. This is in comparison to the difference between what they had anticipated and what they later received.

The vast majority of satisfaction studies have used some variation of the Expectancy Disconfirmation Model. A variety of scholars' definitions of satisfaction are consistent with the Expectancy Disconfirmation Model; it is generally agreed that satisfaction can be defined as 'the evaluation of the perceived discrepancy between prior expectation' and 'the actual performance of the product; thus concurring with the belief that satisfaction is a function of the discrepancy between a users' (beneficiaries') prior expectation and the perception regarding the product, for instance, an allocated subsidised housing unit' (Churchill & Surprenant, 1982; Oliver, 1993; Iacobucci & Oston, 1995; Tse & Wilton, 1988). From the above, it is clear that the study of satisfaction both in academic spheres and in the real world is to understand the determinants and process of users' (beneficiaries') evaluations. This is with a view to ensure that the beneficiaries of the state-subsidized housing schemes, for instance, are satisfied with the product and that it will enhance their well-being.

Nonetheless, satisfaction is further defined as a process of evaluation between what was received and what was expected, which is the most widely adopted description of satisfaction in most current literature (Parker & Mathews, 2001).

Satisfaction can also be viewed as an outcome of a consumption activity or experience, which is also referred to as a process. Currently, there are two principal clarifications of satisfaction, which are satisfaction as a process and satisfaction as an outcome. However, these are complementary classifications as often one depends on the other. When satisfaction is viewed as a process, the definition concentrates on the 'antecedents to satisfaction' rather than satisfaction itself. When viewed as an outcome, it is perceived as a consumption activity or experience, which is moderated by different variables (Parker & Mathew, 2001). This book conforms to the later conceptualization, as the satisfaction of residents in low-income housing in South Africa, for instance, is said to be moderated by different variables, which exacts influences on the occupants.

Approaches to the study of satisfaction

The theory of satisfaction has its origins in the Discrepancy Theory (Porter, 1961) and other scholars have over the years used some form of comparison to model satisfaction (Parker & Matthews, 2001). A number of theoretical approaches has been developed to explain the relationship between satisfaction or positive disconfirmation and dissatisfaction or negative disconfirmation. These approaches can be seen as variants of the consistency theories and focus primarily on the nature of the user's post-usage evaluation process (Oliver, 1980a). Consistency Theory conceptualizes that when expectations and the actual product performance do not match, the consumer will feel some degree of dissatisfaction (Peyton, Pitts & Kamery, 2003). In order to discharge this dissatisfaction the user will make adjustments either in expectations or in the perceptions of the product's actual performance. This theory informed the Morris and Winter's Mobility Theory of residential satisfaction of 1978.

Over the years, a number of frameworks has been used to model satisfaction. Some theoretical approaches that have been advanced, among others, include: Assimilation Theory, Contrast Theory, Assimilation–Contrast Theory and Negativity Theory. The next sections of this work will be devoted to the discussion of the various approaches that have been used to model satisfaction.

Assimilation Theory

Kurt Lewin (1890–1947) originally formulated the Theory of Cognitive Dissonance (Cognitive Dissonance Theory), further developed and refined by Festinger (1957), which formed the basis of the Assimilation Theory (Smith, 2001). The Cognitive Dissonance Theory posits that the users of a particular product make some kind of cognitive comparison between expectations about the product and the perceived product performance. Hence, if there is a discrepancy between expectations and perceived product performance then dissonance or negative disconfirmation arises. This view of user post-usage evaluation was introduced into the satisfaction literature in the form of

Assimilation Theory by Anderson in 1973. In his work on consumer dissatisfaction, the effect of disconfirmed expectancy on perceived product performance was extrapolated, explaining that consumers seek to avoid dissatisfaction by adjusting perceptions about a given product to bring it more in line with expectations. Consumers can also reduce the dissatisfaction resulting from a discrepancy between expectations and product performance either by altering expectations so that they coincide with perceived product performance or by raising the level of satisfaction by minimizing the relative importance of the dissatisfaction experienced (Anderson, 1973; Olson & Dover, 1979).

However, the Assimilation Theory has a number of weaknesses. First, the approach postulates that there is a relationship between expectation and satisfaction but does not specify how disconfirmation of an expectation leads to either satisfaction or dissatisfaction. Next, the theory also postulates that users are inspired enough to adjust either their expectations or their perceptions about the performance of the product (Forman, 1986), meaning that if the user adjusts either expectations or perceptions about product performance then dissatisfaction would not be an outcome of the post-usage evaluation process (Peyton, Pitts & Kamery, 2003). Controlling actual product performance can lead to a positive relationship between expectation and satisfaction; therefore, it would seem that dissatisfaction could never occur except if the evaluative processes were to begin with negative user expectations (Anderson, 1973; Olson & Dover, 1979; Bitner, 1987), which is not always the case.

Contrast Theory

The Contrast Theory was first introduced by Hovland, Harvey and Sherif (1957). But Cardozo (1965) claimed that the theory presents an alternative view of the user post-usage evaluation process in contrast to the Assimilation Theory, which hypothesized that post-usage evaluation leads to outcomes in opposite predictions for the effects of expectations on satisfaction. The Contrast Theory posits that consumers would exaggerate any contrast between expectation and product evaluation. The Contrast Theory is centred on the propensity to magnify the discrepancy between one's own attitudes and the attitudes represented by opinion statements validated by persons with opposing views (Dawes, Singer & Lemons, 1972). Whereas Assimilation Theory suggests that users will seek to minimize the discrepancy between expectation and performance, Contrast Theory argues that a surprise effect arises leading to the discrepancy being exaggerated (Peyton, Pitts & Kamery, 2003). This theory was further developed into the Assimilation–Contrast Theory by Anderson in 1973.

Assimilation–Contrast Theory

The Assimilation-Contrast Model has been proposed as another way of explaining the relationship among the variables in the Disconfirmation Model. This model is a combination of both the Assimilation Theory and the Contrast Theory. This model postulates that satisfaction is a function of the magnitude of the discrepancy between expected and perceived performance (Peyton, Pitts & Kamery, 2003). Generally, users of any product have 'zones or latitudes of acceptance or rejection with respect to their perceptions' (Peyton, Pitts & Kamery, 2003: 43). As with Assimilation Theory, the user will tend to adjust differences in perceptions about product performance to bring it in line with prior expectations, but only if the discrepancy is relatively small. When there is a large discrepancy between expectations and perceived performance, contrast effects occur and the consumer tends to magnify the perceived difference (Peyton, Pitts & Kamery, 2003: 44). However, it should be noted that most discrepancies with a given product such as the case of state-subsidized low-income housing in South Africa are not just magnified or exaggerated, but they are simply the true evaluation of the products (houses), based on what the users have experienced. On the one hand, some evaluation can be an emotional expression of the user's judgement with regards to the functionality of the product. On the other hand, whether assimilation or contrast occurs depends upon the perceived disparity between expectations and actual product performance, which is both objective and subjective, based on the user's judgement.

The Assimilation–Contrast Theory argues that Cardozo's (1965) attempt in the Assimilation Theory at reconciling the two earlier theories was methodologically weak (Anderson, 1973). Anderson asserts that users possess a noticeable difference in the disconfirmation threshold. Further, Assimilation–Contrast Theory illustrates that both the Assimilation Theory and the Contrast Theory models have applicability in the study of user satisfaction. The approach makes it possible to

> hypothesize variables other than the magnitude of the discrepancy that might also influence whether the assimilation effect or the contrast effect would be observed ... when product performance is difficult to judge, expectations may dominate and assimilation effects will be observed ... contrast effects would result in high involvement circumstances. The strength of the expectations may also affect whether assimilation or contrast effects are observed.
>
> (Bitner, 1987: 13)

Attempts by researchers to empirically test the Assimilation–Contrast Model have met with varied results. For instance, Anderson (1973) and Olson and Dover (1979) found some evidence to support the Assimilation–Contrast Theory approach. In debating both of these studies, Oliver (1980b) argues that Anderson (1973) and Olson and Dover's (1979) findings cannot be accepted because they only measured expectations and supposed that there were perceptual differences between disconfirmation and satisfaction. This criticism is of some significance because most researchers do not actually measure satisfaction or dissatisfaction; instead, researchers usually assume that it is the perception of disconfirmation that leads to satisfaction or dissatisfaction (Forman, 1986). In contradiction to the findings supporting the Assimilation–Contrast Theory, negative correlation between expectation and disconfirmation do exist (Woodruff, Cadotte & Jenkins, 1983). Satisfaction is truly an additive function of the two concepts. For instance, uncertainty was created by the results of studies from the works of Oliver (1977a, 1977b, 1979), which found no relationship between expectation and disconfirmation. Moreover, Olshavsky and Miller (1972) in their study on consumer expectations, product performance and perceived product quality supported the Assimilation–Contrast Theory. However, it has been found that if the discrepancy was too large to be assimilated, then the contrast effect occurred.

Negativity Theory

Similar to the three previous models, Negativity Theory also has its foundations in the disconfirmation process. This theory was introduced into the consumer satisfaction literature by Anderson in 1973. Negativity Theory postulates that when expectations are strongly held, users will respond negatively to any disconfirmation. Therefore, dissatisfaction will occur if perceived performance is less than expectations or if perceived performance surpasses expectations (Carlsmith & Aronson, 1963; Anderson, 1973).

Further approaches to the study of satisfaction

The most well-known descendent of the Discrepancy Theory is the Expectancy Disconfirmation Paradigm (Oliver, 1981), which states that, on the one hand, if performance exceeds expectations, users will be positively disconfirmed or satisfied. On the other hand, if performance fails to meet expectations, users will be negatively disconfirmed or dissatisfied. Positive disconfirmation leads to increased satisfaction, with negative disconfirmation having the opposite effect, while zero disconfirmation occurs when performance matches expectations (no effect on satisfaction). This is because users' expectations are most times formed on the basis of past experience and statements made by friends and associates. Expectations could be exceeded in two different ways (Oliver, 1989; Mastura et al., 2007):

- the level of performance is within a normal range (product was better than expected); and
- the level of performance is surprisingly positive (one would not expect that the product would have performed so well and delights).

The Disconfirmation Paradigm is the most dominant theoretical paradigm used in many satisfaction research studies, and was likewise advocated for in this book. The paradigm has its roots in social and applied psychology (Oliver, 1977a). Hence, the Disconfirmation Paradigm presents satisfaction judgements in three ways: satisfaction; higher satisfaction; and dissatisfaction. But for the current book judgement will be related to satisfaction and dissatisfaction.

When performance is greater than the user's expected level of performance of a service, higher user satisfaction will result because the service performs better than expected. Whilst, user's dissatisfaction occurs when the performance is less than the user's expected level of service, as the service performs poorer than the user's expected level. A confirmation of expectations, or zero disconfirmation, is considered a state of satisfaction. A negative disconfirmation indicates that user expectations were not met and yields a state of dissatisfaction. The Expectancy Disconfirmation Model not only explains satisfaction with product performance, but also service satisfaction, as is the case of the government being responsible for the provision of low-income houses for the poor. There has been strong support for the Disconfirmation Paradigm as a measurement of satisfaction. However, some inconsistencies are found in some developed models whereby neither disconfirmation nor expectations have any effect on user satisfaction with durable products meaning that satisfaction is determined exclusively by the performance of the durable good. This again puts the burden of a genuine evaluation result of a typical low-income building or any other building product in the hands of the users because they are the ones who can determine if the building is durable in terms of how the different aspects of the building help to meet their needs.

Likewise, satisfaction can be viewed as a discrepancy between the observed and the desired (Poisz & van Grumbkow, 1988). This was found to have been consistent with the Value-Percept Disparity Theory in the work of Westbrook and Reilly (1983), which was developed in response to the problem that users could be satisfied by aspects for which expectations never existed (Yi, 1990). The Value-Percept Disparity Theory views satisfaction as an emotional reaction caused by a subjective evaluative process, which is the comparison of the 'object' to one's values rather than an expectation (Parker & Matthews, 2001). What users want is a zero disparity level between their values (needs, wants and desires) and the object of their evaluations. Recent developments in this study include the concept of desire congruency (Spreng, MacKenzie & Olshavsky, 1996). Besides discrepancy theories, Equity Theory has also been applied to model satisfaction (Parker & Mathews, 2001). Equity Theory holds that individuals compare their input/output ratios with those of others (Yi, 1990) and that the consumer will be satisfied if the net gain is perceived to be fair. Also, renewed attention has been focused on the nature of satisfaction to establish concrete attributes that determine satisfaction in low-income housing.

Due to the wide variance in the nature and meaning of satisfaction, many associations and firms are using different reference points as a standard to compare their own users' satisfaction figures. To resolve this, a number of organizationally harmonized national customer satisfaction indices has been developed (Hackl & Westlund, 2000). For example, the American Consumer Satisfaction Index (ACSI) and the European Customer Satisfaction Index represent the two major customer satisfaction indices for the United States and the European countries, respectively, on which the South African Satisfaction Index is based. The ACSI defines satisfaction as a weighted average of three survey ratings: perceived quality; perceived value; and customer expectations. This index has been used to measure satisfaction in the manufacturing/non-durables, manufacturing/durables, transportation, communications and utilities, retail, finance and insurance, services and public administration industries, and even in government establishments. Although the ACSI has an accepted satisfaction evaluation methodology, it has not been found suitable for the construction industry and it is has the lowest rating for government and public agencies (Fornell et al., 1996; Jyh-Bin & Sheng-Chi, 2006). This is because the evaluation result for customer satisfaction is highest for competitive products, lower for competitive services and retailers, and lowest for government and public agencies.

Figure 7.1 shows the model used by ACSI to measure satisfaction with government agencies. In the ACSI model, users' expectations influence the evaluation of quality and predict how well the product or service will perform. Perceived quality in the model is the extent to which a product or service meets the user's expectation and this normally has the greatest impact on user satisfaction. Lastly, satisfaction has an inverse relationship to customer complaints, which is measured as the percentage of respondents who reported a problem with the measured product or service within a specified time frame.

Another theoretical description of satisfaction is the Gap Analysis Model developed by Parasuraman, Zeithaml and Berry (1985). This is also referred to as the 'disconfirmation paradigm' in the customer satisfaction literature. The main theme of the Gap Analysis Theory is the fact that gaps between user expectations and user experiences lead to user dissatisfaction. Consequently, measuring gaps is the first step in enhancing user or service satisfaction, which results in a better understanding of users' or beneficiaries' perceptions. This is important for the establishment of policy performances. The Gap Analysis Model is used as a tool to narrow the gap between perceptions and reality, thus enhancing users' satisfaction. Hence, Parasuraman, Zeithaml and Berry (1985: 42) posits that housing satisfaction 'quality is a comparison between expectations and performance' and reiterated service quality as 'the discrepancy between users' expectations and perceptions'. Further, a service quality model based on the Gap Analysis Theory has been developed, which stated that the measurement of the product quality gap is attained in the same manner as service quality gap (Brown & Plenert, 2006). From the above discussion on the conceptualization of satisfaction, the present book tends towards the Gap Theory in ideology. However, the study conceptualized its own attributes in order to measure residential satisfaction.

Assessing residential satisfaction

This section discusses in detail residential satisfaction research and brings the theoretical framework that has been generalized in residential satisfaction studies to date.

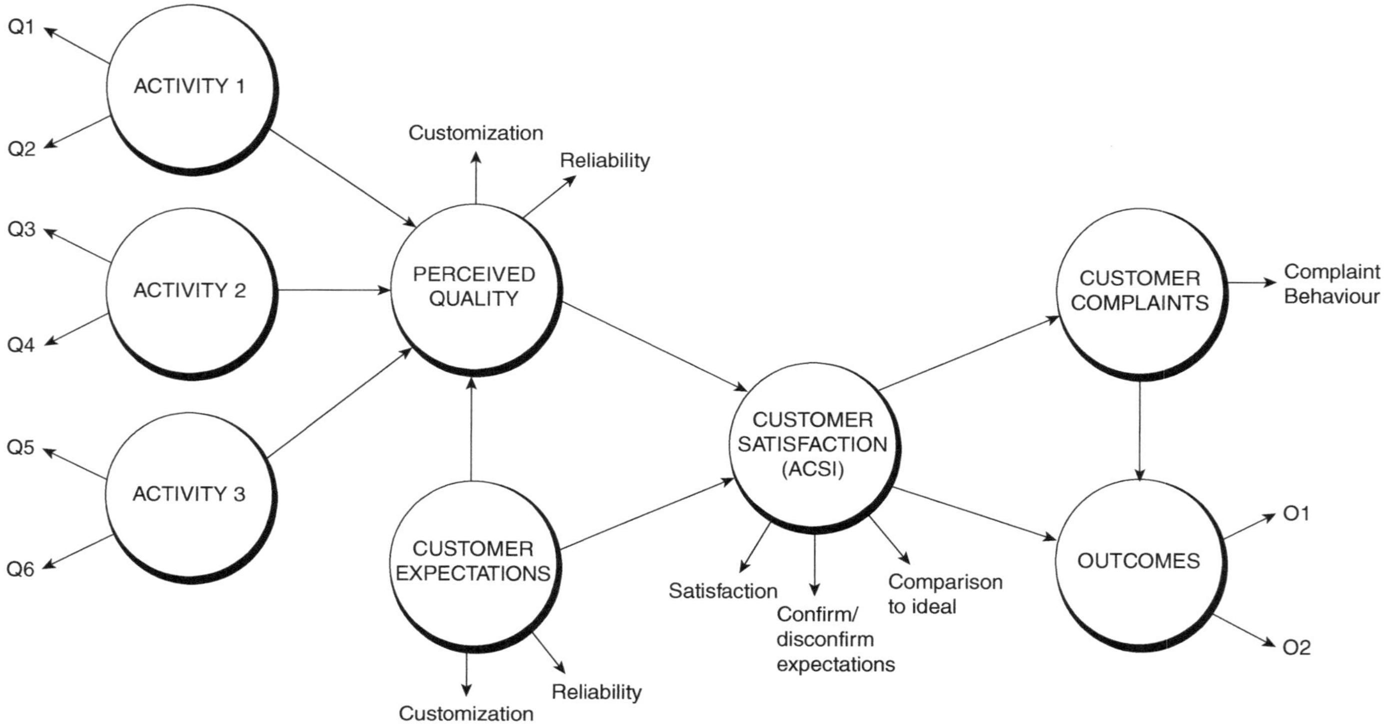

Figure 7.1 ACSI model for government agencies
Source: ASCI (2006).

Residential satisfaction research

Residential satisfaction describes an 'end-state', where an individual or household is satisfied with the residential status they have attained. This section of the book reviews in detail previous studies of residential satisfaction, bringing together a synthesized collection of housing and non-housing components that are related to the formation of housing satisfaction. This is because residential satisfaction is not one constant experience or state: it is an outcome, perceived by an individual or household, that their current housing status meets their needs and aspirations. Because residential satisfaction is based upon perception, the determinant factors essential to attain satisfaction will certainly be different in each case. Influencing this perception are factors such as expectation (as already discussed above), history, demographic characteristics and the employment situation among others. In addition, variables such as culture, age/older adults, individuals with severe handicap, low-income single-parent families, assisted living, life satisfaction, financial status, home-ownership, neighbourhood and environs, house and neighbours, perceived atmosphere, apartment evaluation, maintenance and friends nearby (Bruin & Cook, 1997; Weidemann & Anderson, 1982; Leder & Sayre, 1989; Amérigo, 1990; Montero, 1991; Taylor, 1995; Guney, 1997; Kim, 1997; Amérigo & Aragonés, 1997) have all been found significant to the study of resident satisfaction. Also, gender variances may appear with factors such as safety in the study of residential satisfaction (Potter, Chicoine & Speicher, 2001).

The study of 'satisfaction' dates back to the 1940s and is currently used in many disciplines such as housing, marketing, landscape architecture and medical fields but is dominated by social psychology scholars (Potter, Chicoine & Speicher, 2001). Residential satisfaction has been studied in a wide variety of housing settings, ranging from mini-suites or small self-contained apartments, gate-guarded neighbourhoods, low-income housing, owner-occupied homes, college residence halls, high-rise buildings and multi-family housing (Davis & Roizen, 1970; Weidemann & Anderson, 1982; Montero, 1991; Carvalho, 1995; Sidjak, 1995; Oseland & Raw, 1996; Guney, 1997; Amole, 2009).

The formation of residential satisfaction is not simply based upon freedom from dissatisfaction: it is more complex (Lu, 1999). Residential dissatisfaction is a differently composed construct; the causes of dissatisfaction are more likely to be a universal source of discontent for everyone (Hourihan, 1984), while the sources of satisfaction are much more diverse. This is the case with the beneficiaries of the South African low-income subsidy schemes, where there was a general dissatisfaction with the initially provided 30m^2 housing unit positioned in a 250m^2 plot of land, which has since been increased to a minimum of 40m^2. One of the main reasons of dissatisfaction was because the area estimation of the constructed housing units never took into consideration the housing life cycle of the beneficiaries and other dynamics that are relevant to the beneficiaries' optimal usage of the housing units. This is because a building's success depends not only on how effective the building provides for the setting of activities of daily living, but may also depend on the perceptions of its residents. To understand building occupants' satisfaction evaluations towards a product or a service, it is believed that improvements could thus be found and allocated to the right places and in the right direction (Yiping, 2005), which will thus enhance the efficacy of the production and service provision.

Residential satisfaction research deals with the housing products in terms of consumer satisfaction, and is aimed to inform housing policy, planning intervention and to enable future housing development to perform better than previously. Over the past decades, much research has been conducted on residential satisfaction (Campbell, Converse & Rogers, 1976; Weidemann & Anderson, 1985; Francescato, Weidemann & Anderson, 1987). These studies evaluate housing environments and the residents. The residents' satisfaction studies of their environment have had a tendency to focus on: research techniques; methods; and specific design/planning frameworks for a specific site but not on a more general basis. Also, most housing satisfaction studies have used a direct theoretical approach in relating to a person's beliefs, perceptions, or influences on their satisfaction with the housing environment. From this perspective, any belief, idea or fact is thus a potential predictor of residential satisfaction. However, this present study is geared towards an integrated holistic view of the study of residential satisfaction in state-subsidized low-income housing. Also, residential satisfaction has been discussed in numerous empirical scholarships that study characteristics of the users (either cognitive or behavioural) or characteristics of the environment, both physical and social (Amérigo & Aragonés, 1990). But very few scholars have organized these variables into a model so as to study and analyse, as a guide, the relationships produced among them.

There are two general approaches to empirical research studies about residential satisfaction according to the classification used by Weidemann and Anderson in 1985. One approach is to view residential satisfaction as a criterion of evaluation of residential quality. Amérigo in 1990 argued methodologically that the studies that fall into this category are characterized by their 'treatment of satisfaction as a criterion variable and, therefore, as a dependent variable'. The theoretical background guiding this type of research is displayed by the scholarly works of Marans and Rodgers (1975); Galster and Hesser (1981) and Cutter (1982). A second approach is to view residential satisfaction as a predictor of residential mobility. In this case, residential satisfaction is considered as a predictor of behaviour and, therefore, as an independent variable. The theoretical model developed by Speare in 1974 is a good example of the empirical research belonging to this second approach. The current research book emphasizes the former approach, where satisfaction is treated as a dependent variable.

Nevertheless, the concept of satisfaction has been used in at least four different ways (Lansing, Marans & Zehner, 1970; Speare, 1974; Marans & Rodgers, 1975; Campbell, Converse & Rogers, 1976; Michelson, 1977; Zehner, 1977; Varady, 1983):

- as a key predictor of an individual's perception of general quality of life;
- as an indicator of incipient residential mobility, and hence has altered housing demands and effected neighbourhood change;
- also as an ad hoc evaluative measure for judging the success of housing developments constructed by the private sector, and by the public sector; and
- also to assess residents' perceptions of inadequacies in their current housing environment so as to direct forthcoming private or public efforts to improve the status quo.

Nevertheless, a broader view on residential satisfaction is provided by Campbell, Converse and Rodgers (1976). They perceived housing satisfaction as one of the predictor's of life experience, where satisfaction with that variable might contribute to a person's quality of life. Developing from this same thinking were the more specific studies of a resident's housing satisfaction and the development of theoretical models explaining the sources of satisfaction (Marans & Rodgers, 1975). Together with these studies of housing satisfaction as a predictor of a person's quality of life, satisfaction was seen as a criterion for evaluation of the housing environment. Following the initial work by Francescato et al. (1979), Kim (1997) investigated the concept of users' satisfaction and focused primarily on a specific housing type – state-subsidized multi-family housing units. Although it was recognized that there are many different perspectives for housing evaluation, they viewed the occupant as the primary user and stated that evaluation from this perspective has been neglected.

Also, past models developed by numerous researchers reflect the use of both approaches and include affect, cognition and behaviour. The two approaches as stated above were first combined by Weidemann and Anderson in 1985 based on Fishbein and Ajzen's 1975 model of reasoned actions that considers how attitudes reflect beliefs and evaluations of residences (Amérigo, 1992; Kim & Anderson, 1997). Others have also supported integrated approaches (Michelson, 1977). An all-inclusive model of relationships among the environment, satisfaction and behaviour was proposed by Francescato et al. in 1989. While Amérigo in 1990 attempted to understand how the residential environment, the house, the neighbourhood and the neighbours related developed the systematic model of residential satisfaction. However, the integrated model as proposed by Weidemann and Anderson in 1985 deals with the complicated nature of housing quality. The integrated model embodies three basic components of housing quality evaluation. These are: objective attributes of the physical environment; residents' perception and beliefs regarding their housing quality; and satisfaction with the housing environment. The integrated model developed by Weidemann and Anderson in 1985 can serve as a framework for research on relationships that have not been empirically tested. The integrated model can also be used to organize the existing literature, which many feel is disjointed and unorganized. The perspective of this book is a proposed, organized relationship between publicly funded beneficiaries' dwelling units, neighbourhood features, building quality and services provided by the government, which are the essential variables that have all been measured in a majority of previous studies, together with the assessments of the beneficiaries' needs and expectations and meaningful participation in the housing development process.

Nonetheless, the theories of residential satisfaction are based on the notion that residential satisfaction measures the difference between households' actual and desired housing and neighbourhood situations (Galster & Hesser, 1981). It is believed that households make their judgement about residential conditions based on their needs and aspirations. Hence, on the one hand, satisfaction with their housing conditions indicates the absence of complaints as their needs meet their aspirations. On the other hand, they are likely to feel dissatisfied if their housing and neighbourhood do not meet their residential needs and aspirations. This notion supports the annexation of citizens' participation, needs and expectations on the proposed conceptual model advanced in this book, to allow a holistic view of beneficiaries' residential determinants in the evaluation of residential satisfaction.

There is considerable evidence in the literature which shows that residential satisfaction is influenced by a broad array of objective and subjective perceived conditions. Previous studies on residential satisfaction have analysed many variables such as housing, neighbourhood and users' characteristics that affect housing satisfaction (Galster, 1987; Lu, 1999). A buildings' physical and social features are also strongly related to housing satisfaction. Satisfaction with neighbourhood features has also been noted to be an important factor of housing satisfaction. These include neighbourhood facilities, such as schools, clinics, shops, community halls among others. However, numerous studies as carried out in developing countries have mainly analysed three main components of the identified residential satisfaction attributes such as the dwelling units, facilities and services, and the neighbourhood. For instance, a study by Husna and Nurizan (1987) found that the residents of low-cost flats in Malaysia were generally satisfied with their housing conditions and environments. Among the predictive variables that contributed to the overall housing satisfaction, neighbourhood satisfaction contributed the most. In another study by Savasdisara, Tips and Sumannodom (1989) the residents in a private low-income housing unit were generally satisfied with the dwelling units and the neighbourhood. In contrast, a study by Ukoha and Beamish (1997) found that the residents in a public housing unit in Abuja, Nigeria were dissatisfied with their overall housing situation but satisfied with the neighbourhood facilities. Overall, the concept of residential satisfaction does not lie on the individual's dwelling characteristics alone, but it is a composite of the overall physical and social components that make up the housing system. Hence, this book also places into context the effect of other variables that have not yet been studied collectively as to how they influence residential satisfaction.

Residential satisfaction, as a measure, has been criticized by some scholars as being subjective (Campbell, Converse & Rogers, 1976). Others have acknowledged the criticism but stated that all measures have limitations and satisfaction should not be dismissed as a measure because it is a useful concept. Another criticism of satisfaction is that operational definitions vary greatly because they are sometimes defined as cognitive, emotional and/or conative (Anderson & Weidemann, 1997). But all evolving models tend to support the belief that satisfaction can and does include all areas. Hence, satisfaction has been defined as an attitude, while satisfaction and responses to questions directed at measuring satisfaction could be considered affective, cognitive and conative (Francescato, Weidemann & Anderson, 1986). Therefore, as a construct, residential satisfaction must be both conceived and interpreted as multifaceted, including affective, cognitive and conative responses. However, social psychologists have suggested that there are three general categories of responses to any socio-physical object: the affective; the cognitive; and the conative or behavioural (Rosenberg & Hovland, 1960; Francescato, Weidemann & Anderson, 1986). This suggestion or environmental perception is also referred to as a process of knowing, feeling and doing (Rapoport, 1977). Thus, these categories create a useful framework in understanding the theoretical development of research satisfaction research (Francescato, Weidemann & Anderson, 1987; Weidemann & Anderson, 1985). As a result, residential satisfaction is not only used as an indicator of housing policy, but also as a predictor of housing mobility as many researchers have shown.

As already stated, satisfaction is a subjective response to an objective environment. As such, measures of satisfaction have been met with criticism. The criticisms, as outlined by Francescato, Weidemann and Anderson (1987: 48), include:

- a report that residential satisfaction tends to be uniformly high and, therefore, cannot be assumed to indicate the 'true' state of affairs;
- that subjective measures of satisfaction do not correlate with objective measures of context and behaviour, therefore they cannot be considered valid measures of the objective reality;
- satisfaction with an object varies, for the same individual or social group, with time and with personal and social norms and expectations, thus it is too fickle an indicator on which to base action;
- satisfaction tends to be higher where there is lower occupants' awareness of 'better' alternatives, which, it was argued, tends to reflect unenlightened assessments on which policy and decisions should not be based; and
- focusing on satisfaction rather than attacking 'real' problems may result in sub-optimal environments.

While the criticisms point to limitations that should be taken into account when interpreting results, they also seem to warrant using the construct of satisfaction (Francescato, Weidemann & Anderson, 1987; Potter, Chicoine & Speicher, 2001). Additionally, the exaggerated scepticism of subjective responses is not warranted based on extensive consideration of (among others) the following (Campbell, Converse & Rogers, 1976):

- the reliability and validity of measures;
- the comparison between objective and subjective indicators of well-being; and
- the levels of reality of domains being assessed, and the analytical intentions (Anderson & Weidemann, 1997).

Hence, it is important to be aware of these limitations. However, it is clear that they do not prevent satisfaction from being a useful concept. This is because there are limitations to all research investigations; for example, there are always limitations to the operationalization of a subjective concept. The criticisms in residential satisfaction research point out the need for research that addresses these criticisms, and illustrates the impact on theoretical models, and then proposes a research direction with a clear theoretical foundation. This is the idea behind the writing of this research book.

To this end, the next section will review the common problems that are mostly raised in residential satisfaction research and offer possible solutions that will guide future research. The present research book extends the idea that residential satisfaction should be studied as a criterion of evaluation, meaning that residential satisfaction should be treated as a dependent variable. This approach, when adopted, will assist to identify the most appropriate variables to be considered in the provision of housing for the low-income group by the governments in developing countries.

Problems raised in residential satisfaction study

When attempts are made to empirically prove models of residential satisfaction and the relationship between the individual and his/her environment, scholars have faced several kinds of problems. The problems that are mostly faced by researchers are usually grouped into three dimensions (Amérigo & Aragonés, 1997):

- The first relates to the definition of the terms of the interaction being studied, which is the residential environment. Most times, what is understood by residential environment is not clearly defined; or likely a clear assertion of how it has been empirically defined is necessary.
- The second dimension, according to Amérigo and Aragonés (1997: 52), raises the problem of the interaction between the individual and his/her residential environment, since the interaction is a dynamic two-way constantly changing process.
- Lastly, the above-mentioned problems, together with the social attractiveness inherent in the term 'satisfaction', result in the difficulty of formulating this variable.

Hence, it should be noted that it is important to highlight the theoretical and methodological queries that hinder research in this field, and the offering of possible solutions, which will guide future research. The next section of this chapter further discusses the above-listed three problems faced by researchers when studying the subject of residential satisfaction.

Definition of residential environment

Numerous studies of residential satisfaction have mostly been applied to the house and its surrounding neighbourhood; both have all been studied from two points of view namely (Amérigo & Aragonés, 1997):

- the physical: conforming to equipment and services; and
- the social: referring to the social linkages established both in communal areas of the building and in the neighbourhood.

There are common problem when attempts are made to outline the physical boundaries of the house and that of the neighbourhood. For example, when referring to a house, we should take into account not only its private space, but also the semi-public spaces immediately surrounding it. The appropriate definition of these areas is very significant at certain socio-economic levels due to the perceptions they involve, as spatial perceptions may vary substantially as a function of variables, like social and cultural status.

The concept of neighbourhood is even more confusing to define. Very few scholars have clearly defined this concept as to exactly which physical areas it involves, while most other scholars uses terms like community, district and neighbourhood among others, without defining them specifically (Lee, 1968; Rapoport, 1977; Amérigo & Aragonés, 1997). Only a few scholars, such as Marans and Rodger in 1975, provided clearly differentiated levels within the residential environment. In their work on the understanding of community satisfaction, they defined the environment as the intermediate zone between the macro-neighbourhood and micro-neighbourhood, including a more-or-less large area near the occupant's house, and where relationships are formed with other people living in it. This means that the individuals residing in a space and the physical objects they use are closely bound into one unit, thus forming an outline (Amérigo & Aragonés, 1997). According to this concept, neighbourhood cannot be specifically defined, rather the concept should be referred to as a personal category, which is what the residents' consider it to be. Another significant characteristic when trying to define the neighbourhood is given by the sense of belonging to it, or identification with it. Hence, this book presupposes that the definition of neighbourhood does not refer to the geographical area that limits it, but rather to the occupant's perception and to their sense of belonging. In this way, the neighbourhood does not have a fixed surface, but varies from one occupant to another.

Interaction between the residents and their residential environment

The study of residential satisfaction is most interesting when it is applied to residents of low-income housing, who cannot move away if they are dissatisfied with their present residential environment. When the degree of residential satisfaction is low in this type of residence, in most cases mental (cognitive) restructuring occurs in the resident, which keeps them in equilibrium with the residential environment. This interaction between the individual and the residential environment implies that all the residential environment intervening elements are considered as part of a process, which greatly complicates empirical treatment of conceptual models. This practice sets in motion internal mechanisms that determine the evaluations, which will make occupants experience a higher or lower degree of residential satisfaction. This internal mechanism is described as a standard of comparison when assessing the residential environment (Marans & Rodgers, 1975). This notion denotes issues such as expectations, levels of aspirations, degree of equity (participation), reference norms, needs and values.

Likewise, the description of the theoretical model of residential satisfaction refers to a similar element, which is essential when transforming the objective characteristics of the residential environment into subjective ones, since it is the latter that will primarily define the degree of residential satisfaction experienced by the individual (Amérigo, 1990). This element is called standard of residential quality, which is determined, among other things, by the occupant's norm of reference. For example, having an indoor toilet would be the maximum aspiration in housing quality for certain cultures or certain socio-economic levels, while for others it will have a much lower place on the scale. Hence, it is assumed that each occupant has a specific standard of residential quality, by which comparisons are made with the actual environment, so that as the gap between both decreases, satisfaction with the actual residential environment increases. This cognitive view is formed on the basis of the background of the occupant or household whose residential satisfaction is being studied. Thus, this element implicitly includes individual, social and cultural influences on the interaction with the residential environment.

The empirical demonstration of these internal processes in the assessment of the residential environment has not always been effectively clarified, given the complexity of interrelations posed by the processes themselves (Amérigo, 1990), although, Galster and Hesser's (1981) research on the model of residential satisfaction and the works of Lindberg et al. (1987, 1988) on residential preferences have both attempted to resolve the complexity of the interrelations. The work of Lindberg, Garling and Montgomery (1988) on the model of housing preferences, which was based on the Fishbein and Ajzen's (1975) theory of 'reasoned action', empirically supported the premise that the evaluations people make of a series of housing characteristics are defined by their structure of essential values and beliefs about the effects that certain types of behaviour will have on achieving these values (Amérigo & Aragonés, 1997).

Also, with the traditional approaches used for residential satisfaction data analysis such as multiple regression analysis, it is extremely difficult to prove empirically the intervention of mechanisms, such as those already mentioned. It has been found that it is not possible to derive cause–effect relations from the technique of regression models that bring out a serious weakness for previous models of residential satisfaction, which try to determine the causes that generate a certain degree of satisfaction and the effects they imply. Nevertheless, more and more reliable statistical techniques for multi-variant analysis are being developed that allow the extrapolation of causal relations between different variables. This considers the existence of the independent variables, which increase the reliability and validity of the relations established. For example, Galster and Hesser (1981) in their model of residential satisfaction used Path Analysis to analyse the relations produced among the variables. Also, Lu (1999) in his work on the determinants of residential satisfaction used the Ordered Logit Model, which is seen as a more appropriate method than the widely-used regression models due to the ordinal nature of the dependent variables. In order to overcome the above problems and thus achieving the desired cause and effect, the use of other robust statistical techniques – such as the use of structural equation modelling to determine the relationship between the exogenous variables and how they predict residential satisfaction – will be most ideal. This approach, when adopted, will assist to overcome the weaknesses that the use of regression models posed in residential satisfaction studies, though the techniques of analysis of structural equations were first applied to an attitudinal model by Bentler and Speckart (1979).

Methodological issues in the study of residential satisfaction

Despite the sizeable literature and the models that have been developed in the field of residential satisfaction, it has not proven easy to quantify residential satisfaction empirically. There are two general problems associated with the study of residential satisfaction: first, 'social desirability generated by direct questions of the type "to what extent are you satisfied with . . .?" and secondly, the difficulty of determining "objective" levels of residential satisfaction' (Amérigo & Aragonés, 1997: 54).

With regards to the first problem, there are many studies that obtain high levels of satisfaction, not only with the residential environment but also with life in general, and with other domains of life, when these are measured through items or scales that ask the residents directly about their degree of satisfaction (Campbell, Converse & Rogers, 1976; Argyle, 1987). However, solutions are with the use of indirect scales since they do not ask directly about the degree of satisfaction, but about the residents (Amérigo & Aragonés, 1997). In addition to the weaknesses of social desirability already mentioned, it may be noted that the word satisfaction has general connotations of meaning referring to the global state of the occupant, more than to a specific aspect of the residential environment, such as the neighbourhood, the house or the neighbours. This may obviously influence the judgements of satisfaction referring to these three components of the residential environment. In contrast, the indirect scale has the weakness of its validity in comparison with the direct scale, in so far as it is not certain that what is being measured is actually satisfaction and not some other concept. This book is oriented towards this measurement method that refers to a specific aspect of the occupant's residential environment and not to a global state of satisfaction. This is because more possibilities are offered when aiming at a more valid measurement of residential satisfaction.

The second problem, referring to the measurement of residential satisfaction, poses more problems and questions the traditional definitions of the concept of satisfaction. If the concept is defined as the gap existing between achievements and aspirations (Marans & Rodgers, 1975; Canter & Rees, 1982; Bardo & Hughey, 1984), how can the situation be explained of the individual who, despite having a wide gap between residential achievements and aspirations, professes to be satisfied with their residential environment when asked about it? The obvious answer is either that the question is influenced by 'social disability, as referred to above, or that these types of individuals have reduced the dissonance that their objective residential conditions generate'. In either case, this presumes that the outward expression of the degree of residential satisfaction experienced by this type of individual varies obviously from the actual residential situation they are in, and is determined by the gap that separates residential achievements from aspirations (Amérigo & Aragonés, 1997).

Consequently, the question of how to measure 'objectively' the degree of residential satisfaction has been a problem for most residential satisfaction researchers. However, the question of an accurate 'objective' measurement of residential satisfaction was first empirically proven by Amérigo in 1990, who asserted that a sample of housewives living in council housing in Spain obtained a higher degree of satisfaction when expressed directly than when it was obtained through the definition of satisfaction mentioned above. Specifically, the degree of satisfaction for the study was obtained by calculating the distance between the perceived residential environment and the ideal residential environment. Rationally, it was found that if this distance is small, the person is more satisfied than if it is greater. Besides, when a profile was established of those who claimed to be very satisfied, it was noted that those who lived in the areas that were shortly going to be rebuilt had very poor living conditions at the time (Amérigo, 1990). The high levels of residential satisfaction were achieved in cases where the objective residential conditions were predicted. While the opposite leads us to suspect that the measurement strategies used up to that moment are inadequate. However, to overcome these weaknesses, the use of indirect items and multi-term scales will help overcome this problem. To this end, the next section will discuss and review the previous residential satisfaction models and conceptual frameworks.

Residential satisfaction conceptual models

Previous models of residential satisfaction have been dedicated to three main components that constitute the environmental interrelationship between humans and their environment, that is, the residents (the human part of the system), the socio-physical environment and satisfaction (the regulator of this complex relationship). In explaining the residents' satisfaction, behaviour, choice and mobility, Michelson in 1977 came up with an integrated model.

Michelson's integrated model

In 1977 Michelson proposed an integrated model that explains residents' mobility and choice, user needs, environment and behaviour. The major constructs of Michelson's model were: aspirations; primary demands; expectations; the physical settings; perception and culture; and residents' behaviour. The theoretical framework of the model focuses on residents' satisfaction as a major determinant in residents' mobility from their homes. This model started by supposing that residents have aspirations and primary demands in interacting with their housing environment. Through residents' expectations, residents' aspirations and primary demands influence the physical and social characteristics of the physical settings.

After residents experience the physical setting, an assessment occurs through perception and culture, and spatial, social and psychological factors. Successively, this evaluation shapes residents' foreseen and unforeseen behaviour. The resultant behavioural pattern is a consequence of supportive or restrictive characteristics of the new physical setting (Ahmad, 1994). Michelson's model likewise assumes changes in the users' primary needs, as a result of actual contact with the physical setting. These changes in the users' primary needs affect the evaluation of the housing environment. The users' evaluations may yield negative or positive perception followed by an action in the physical setting. Actions related to negative perception, such as dissatisfaction, could be moving out of the neighbourhood, altering the use of space or adopting physical means to change or modify the design of the space. In addition, the model describes that the residents' action may not depend on the residents' evaluations of their housing setting, but rather on the ability to achieve their aspirations. In other words, a resident may not move because they cannot afford something better or it is simply not available. This model further states that the ability to achieve aspirations may lead to negative evaluation of present homes in favour of new or better ones. However, it can also be blocked by lack of affordance or absence of a better environment.

Onibokun 'Habitability' Model

In 1974 Onibokun postulated that assessing habitability means evaluating the satisfaction of a tenant living in a specific housing unit. This housing unit, according to Onibokun, would normally be part of a housing project located within a particular community under some type of institutional management. The model emphasized that the housing habitability systems usually involve four interacting subsystems, which include: the tenants subsystem; the dwelling subsystem; the environment subsystem; and the management subsystem. In the Onibokun 'Habitability' Model, it was hypothesized that the adequacy of a housing unit, as determined by the internal space, the structural quality, the household services, the amenities and the quality of the internal environment, will impact the extent to which the resident is satisfied with the unit. It was argued that the housing unit by itself is not the only variable or the only determinant of housing needs satisfaction. The unit subsystem according to this model is only a part of the whole system, which constitutes housing habitability.

The 'Habitability' Model thus emphasized that the variables that will affect the satisfaction level with a housing unit are tenants, external environment, management and dwelling variables. In particular the model singled out the tenant as the recipient of all the feedbacks from the subsystems and the inhabitant is therefore the central focus of the conceptual model of habitability on which a study on housing habitability should be based (Falah, Al-Abed & Stan, 1995). However, this concept remains limited with respect to the real and complex situation of housing satisfaction.

Marans–Rodgers Model

Another conceptual model of residential satisfaction was that developed by Marans and Rodgers in 1975. The model conceptualized that an individual's satisfaction with housing depends on their perception of the various neighbourhood characteristics and their assessment thereof. The neighbourhood attributes include several aspects of the physical environment and the quality of local or community services. The Marans–Rodgers Model conceptualized that both the perpetual evaluative process and the overall satisfaction level are related to the person's own characteristics, such as social class and housing status, among others. These socio-demographic variables involve a smaller portion of residential satisfaction than does the assessment of neighbourhood features. However, when personal characteristics were combined with valuation variables as predictors of residential satisfaction, it was found that the former were largely taken into account through the latter, and did not have much independent influence on the level of satisfaction.

Nevertheless, in spite of adding new factors that will have an impact on satisfaction (neighbourhood and community), Marans and Rodgers in 1975 assessed personal characteristics through the assessments of housing and neighbourhood attributes. The assessed variables were found to be insufficient to fully assess personal characteristics. This limitation in the model was what led to the development of the Path Analysis Model, which emphasizes the impact of other significant variables such as neighbourhood and community variables. The Marans–Rodgers (1975) model measured satisfaction with the community, the macro-neighbourhood and the micro-neighbourhood, and found that satisfaction with community is related more to social factors, while satisfaction with neighbourhood is related more to physical factors.

Path Analysis Model

The Path Analysis Model as proposed by Hourihan in 1984 hypothesizes that personal characteristics are inter-related. The principal concern of the Path

Analysis Model is the relationship between the personal characteristics of residents and their levels of satisfaction. The model specifies that residential satisfaction begins with residents' personal characteristics. These comprise the measure of social class, local social attachments, residential experience, life-cycle stages and housing type. For example, housing type is dependent on social class, and social attachment, in turn, may well be related to housing type. Only social class and length of residence were treated as being totally predetermined variables, and these would then influence all other personal indices.

Neighbourhood attributes have also been found to have a direct contribution to housing satisfaction. Attributes, such as safety, design of dwelling unit, stability and friendliness, were found to form a fairly comprehensive profile of each resident's perception and assessment of the neighbourhood. The model confirms the importance of personal and neighbourhood variables.

Housing Adjustment Model

The Normative Model (Housing Adjustment Model) was first proposed by Morris and Winter in 1978. This model used the notion of housing deficit to hypothesize residential (dis)satisfaction. The Housing Adjustment Model of residential mobility theorized that individuals judge their housing conditions according to normatively defined norms. These are dictated by societal standards or rules for life conditions, and family/personal norms, which amount to households' own standards for housing. Thus, families evaluate their own residential situation and that of others using definite culturally derivative benchmarks as norms. However, a family whose housing does not meet these standards experiences one or more deficits. The Housing Adjustment Theory contends that if a household's current housing meets the norms, the household is likely to express a high level of satisfaction with housing and neighbourhood. Thus, an incongruity between the actual housing situation and the cultural and/or familiar housing norms results in a housing deficit, which in turn gives rise to residential dissatisfaction. Households with a housing deficit who are dissatisfied are likely to consider some form of housing adjustment to meet the known norm. The occupants' needs are defined in terms of both cultural and housing norms. Cultural norms are the standards by which the behaviour or conditions experienced by members of a culture are evaluated as 'good' or 'bad'. Housing norms are standards related to the dwelling and its environment. They vary from zoning regulations that specify, among other things, the minimum distance a house must be set back from the street to very informal rules about having a quiet place to live in (Falah, Al-Abed & Stan, 1995).

The Normative Model emphasizes, in addition to the many variables common to the previous models, the significance of culture, which is a very important factor in satisfaction research and in all research involving developing countries. But the factor (culture) in the study of satisfaction should not be considered as a separate factor, since every subjective decision made by the occupants is influenced by their cultural background, although the Normative Model postulates that a standard (good or bad) should be set according to the cultural environment of each country. Standards should be set in relation to local housing needs, which take into account cultural and ethnic factors, rather than using some universal standards set in different countries. In a developing nation like South Africa, and in most developing countries where housing standards for the low-income are fully regulated, it is essential to measure, as objectively as possible, the physical quality of housing and its environment without predetermined ideas of housing standards derived from the developed nations of the world. However, a number of empirical studies has demonstrated that housing deficit is a useful notion in explaining residential satisfaction and mobility behaviour (Cook, Bruin & Laux, 1994; Bruin & Cook, 1997).

Francescato et al. model

In an attempt to understand the relationship of humans to their environment, which was a question of an understanding of the 'users' needs' by the design and planning professions during the 1960s, Francescato et al. in 1974 examined residents' satisfaction with their housing environment. In this model, issues important to residents were identified and self-report measures for these issues and for satisfaction were developed. The empirically derived causal model revealed a range of issues to be direct and indirect predictors of housing satisfaction. The empirically derived causal model has been a prototype for later housing satisfaction studies and has been used as framework by several housing evaluation researchers. The 1974 Francescato et al. model shows the multifaceted character of the housing environment. The model identifies important predictors of residents' satisfaction with their housing environment, such as safety, physical convenience and social interaction. Some of the predictors related to the physical environment, some to the social environment and some to the housing environment. This brought about the notion that residential satisfaction can be conceived in three levels, which are: the residential (physical) environment; the social environment; and housing (individual) environment or characteristics. The Francescato et al. model assumes a direct functional relationship between satisfaction and each of the above components, that is, residents' characteristics and socio-physical components. Although the model includes all the basic components for measuring satisfaction, residents' behaviour and values were not included in the model (Ahmad, 1994). The model also ignores the various levels of the physical environment, such as the home, neighbourhood and city. Another criticism of this model is that it focuses on satisfaction as an outcome of one side of the equation, while the human behavioural aspects were completely ignored.

Weidemann and Anderson model

In 1985 Weidemann and Anderson, seeking a more advanced understanding of resident housing satisfaction, developed a conceptual framework for housing satisfaction by drawing on other theories and models. This led to their development of a conceptual framework for residential satisfaction. The model was based on the concept found in general Theory of Reasoned Action (Fishbein & Ajzen, 1975). The conceptual framework makes explicit several of the theoretical orientations and the assumptions that underline the housing satisfaction approach.

The model explicitly recognizes the causative role of the physical and social environment by indicating these as categories of 'objective attributes' of the particular environment. The objective environmental attributes have an influence upon a person's satisfaction, which is defined as an attitude and affect on the physical and social environment – through the person's perceptions and beliefs about those environmental attributes. In addition, this model recognizes that the person's affective attitude towards the environment influences the person's intentions to behave with respect towards the environment. Subsequently, the occupant's intention to behave has an influence upon behaviour related to the environment (Weidemann & Anderson, 1985). The model therefore proposed an interpretation of satisfaction in purely affective terms, informing that housing satisfaction is the subjective response to the dwelling, the positive or negative feeling that the occupants have towards the place they live in. This means that it is a global representation of the affective response of people to the social-physical environment in which they live.

The theoretical model explicitly includes personal and social information, which many social researchers have neglected. However, the characteristics of the individual resident in relation to personal and social attributes should be considered as potential predictors of housing satisfaction. Therefore, with respect to housing satisfaction, inputs of resident's characteristics with personal and social attributes are important, and housing satisfaction cannot be properly interpreted without them, which are also advocated for in this book.

Marans and Sprecklemeyer 'inclusive' model

In 1981 Marans and Sprecklemeyer further suggested a theoretical framework that attempts to clarify the relationship between objective conditions, subjective experience and residential satisfaction. The basic three components of the Marans and Sprecklemeyer conceptual model are: the physical environment; the perception and attitude of the residents towards their housing environment; and residents' satisfaction. The model assumed a linear relationship between objective attributes of the physical environment and residents' satisfaction. The model posits that satisfaction is a function of the physical environment through one's perception and beliefs of the physical environment. Hence, residential satisfaction is a result of an integrated relationship between environment and the human perception of beliefs. Additionally, the model assumes that human behaviour is a result of the satisfactory or dissatisfactory outcome of the relationships produced among the variables. Further to the above presentation of the previous models of residential satisfaction, Table 7.1 gives a summary of the previous models' conceptualizations.

Table 7.1 Conceptualization of residential satisfaction models

Model	*Conceptualization*
Francescato et al. (1979) Francescato et al.'s model of housing satisfaction	The Francescato et al. model shows the multifaceted character of the housing environment. The model identifies important predictors of residents' satisfaction with their housing environment, such as safety, physical convenience and social interaction. Some of the predictors relate to the physical environment, some to the social environment and some to the housing environment. This brought about the notion that residential satisfaction can be conceived in three levels, which are: the residential (physical) environment; the social environment; and the housing (individual) environment or characteristics.
Hourihan (1984) Path Analysis Model	Personal characteristics are inter-related i.e. the relationship between the personal characteristics of residents and their levels of satisfaction. The model specifies that residential satisfaction begins with residents' personal characteristics. These comprise the measure of social class, local social attachments, residential experience, life-cycle stages and housing type.
Marans and Rodgers (1975) Marans–Rodgers Model	An individual's satisfaction with housing depends on their perception of the various neighbourhood characteristics and their assessment of them.
Marans and Sprecklemeyer (1981) Inclusive model (basic conceptual model)	This model posits that satisfaction is a function of the physical environment through one's perception and beliefs of the physical environment. Hence, housing satisfaction is as a result of an integrated relationship between environment and the human perception of beliefs.
Michelson (1977) Michelson's integrated model	Residents' satisfaction is a major determinant in resident's mobility from their homes. Residents' expectations, residents' aspirations and primary demands influence the physical and social characteristics of the physical settings.
Morris and Winter (1978) Housing Adjustment Model	The notion of 'housing deficit'. They theorize that individuals judge their housing conditions according to normatively defined norms, which are dictated by societal standards or rules for life conditions, and family/personal norms, which amount to households' own standards for housing.
Onibokun (1974) 'Habitability' Model	The adequacy of a housing unit is determined by the internal space, the structural quality, the household services, the amenities and quality of the internal environment impact and the extent to which the resident is satisfied with the unit.

(*Continued*)

Table 7.1 (Continued)

Model	*Conceptualization*
Weidemann and Anderson (1985) Integrated conceptual model	They proposed an interpretation of satisfaction in purely affective terms, stating that housing satisfaction is the 'emotional response to the dwelling, the positive or negative feeling that the occupants have for where they live'. Hence, it is a global representation of the affective response of people to the socio-physical environment in which they live. The model explicitly recognizes the causative role of physical and social environment by indicating these as categories of 'objective attributes' of the particular environment. The Model recognizes that the person's affective attitude towards the environment influences the person's intentions to behave with respect to the environment.

Source: Author's literature review.

Measuring residential satisfaction

From the conceptualized models discussed above, the work of Marans and Rodgers (1975) and Marans and Sprecklemeyer (1981) are the most comprehensive conceptual models of residential satisfaction and many other studies have been based them. All previous models suggest a general sense of causality with the exception of the Marans and Sprecklemeyer's (1981) conceptual model. Likewise, all models suggested the indirect associations between objective attributes and satisfaction through other components in the model, which was not in their model. Marans and Sprecklemeyer's model was the only one that stressed the direct effects of objective environmental attributes on overall neighbourhood satisfaction. The direct association between these two variables is considered in the current study. Both Marans and Sprecklemeyer's (1981) and Marans and Rodgers' (1975) models posited that residential satisfaction together with satisfaction with other domains can influence the quality of life as an individual experiences it. Despite the robustness of both models, they excluded beneficiary participation, needs and expectation as significant factors, which have been considered in the conceptual model developed in this book as a robust holistically integrated model of residential satisfaction.

Marans and Rodgers' (1975) model hypothesized that the residents' satisfaction depends on their perception of three domains (the dwelling unit, the neighbourhood and community facilities). In contrast, the Path Analysis and the Onibokun 'Habitability' models specify that housing satisfaction is based on the occupants' personal characteristics. This meant that the central focus of their models is the inhabitant. This is a limited assessment of the nature of housing satisfaction, which in practice has several other dimensions. In addition, the Marans–Rodgers (1975) model further postulates that overall satisfaction should be related to the person's characteristics and other variables. However, socio-demographic variables account for a smaller proportion of housing satisfaction level, than do the assessments of the three domains of measurement (Hourihan, 1984). The Normative and Marans–Rodgers models emphasized that as well as looking out from the inside, residential satisfaction should be evaluated by looking in from the outside by measuring the eccentricities of actual environments from norms or standards (Michelson, 1977; Falah, Al-Abed & Stan, 1995).

Studying these previous satisfaction models leads to the conclusion that certain essential variables that have an impact on residential satisfaction are contained within the following four main domains:

- personal characteristics (socio-economic variables);
- dwelling unit;
- neighbourhood; and
- community services.

Because of the disagreement between researchers as to the relative importance of these four different variables, the conceptual framework described in this book assesses the four variables and likewise takes into consideration the impact of two new variables (occupants' participation; needs and expectations).

Measuring residential quality and adequacy (satisfaction)

It is worth noting that previous theories of residential satisfaction all centre around the concept that residential satisfaction measures the difference between households' actual and desired (or aspired-to) housing and neighbourhood characteristics (Galster & Hesser, 1981; Galster, 1987). A significant issue in all models of residential satisfaction is how the housing attributes are measured. There are commonly two types of measurements available, namely objective and subjective measures of housing attributes (Wiedemann & Anderson, 1985; Francescato, 2002). All models discussed above assess the level of housing satisfaction subjectively, which is only one indicator of beneficiaries' satisfaction as defined already. Consequently, an objective measure of housing adequacy is essential to get a holistic understanding of its formation. Objective measures refer to the actual measurements, such as the presence, the lack of, or quantities of attributes, while subjective measures refer to perceptions, emotions, attitudes and intentions towards the housing attributes. The objective measures of the attributes of housing satisfaction have been shown to be weaker predictors than the subjective measures (Wiedemann & Anderson, 1985; Francescato, Weidemann & Anderson, 1989). The main objective measuring technique, which has been used in assessing housing satisfaction quality, was first adopted by Morris et al. in 1976 and classified three areas of housing quality:

- structural quality, which refers primarily to durability of the shell;
- service quality, which is concerned with the kinds of equipment, facilities and conveniences the dwelling provides; and
- the state of maintenance and caretaking.

The measure of quality as used in the work of Morris et al. of 1976 consisted of 26 items that measured these three identical areas. The presence or absence of a particular characteristic was used as the prime basis for the assignment of a score to the various items. The total resulting item score was used to provide a measure of housing quality. The procedure was based on traditional scaling techniques. However, the work of Duncan (1971), titled *Measuring Housing Quality*, presented a number of different models for measuring housing quality in the United Kingdom and in America, though these vary significantly in their origins and scope because of the cultural differences. To incorporate a more flexible and practical approach, Duncan (1971) in his study developed the Housing and Environment Defects Index, which has been used in the Scottish Development Department, and is similar to the work of Morris, Crull and Winter (1976). The categorized dimensions of housing quality are (Duncan, 1971):

- basis of the dwelling interior schedule;
- basis of the dwelling exterior schedule; and
- basis of the environment schedule.

The method used a weighting system to distinguish between defects of greater and lesser significance so that the aggregate result can be meaningful and capable of comparison. The rationale behind this method is that when some element or condition in the housing environment deviates from its set point or standard, a deficit results. This is what the general principle of housing satisfaction is based on in all the models reviewed previously. This technique was found to be flexible for measuring quality under different housing standards. Because of the setting, the specific indices developed by Duncan in 1971 are equally applicable to developing countries in some respects. The method of measuring the quality of housing schemes is recommended for use in developing countries, but with the necessary adaptations to fit the particular context when measuring the quality of a particular dwelling units.

Also, it has become common, in measuring residential satisfaction, to use an index of highly correlated items rather than a single-item variable of how satisfied you are with your housing unit. This is insufficient to illustrate satisfaction as a multifaceted constructs. This issue can be addressed in two ways as proposed by the work of Francescato et al. (1986). First, it is proposed that a list or index of four questions reflecting overall satisfaction with the housing unit should be asked:

- How satisfied are you with living here?
- How long do you want to live in this housing development?

- If you move again, would you like to live in another place like this?
- Would you recommend this place to one of your friends if they were looking for a place to live?

Second, it is important to recognize that interpretation of responses to the questions above could have affective, cognitive and conative components. This index of satisfaction would best be described if many questions reflecting this multiplicity were used in the evaluation. This system helps to increase the reliability of the criterion since an index is essentially better than a single item (Wiedemann & Anderson, 1985; Carvalho, George & Anthony, 1997). Hence, when residential satisfaction is being considered in developing countries, the use of the domain's objective and subjective characteristics should be strongly considered.

Determinants of residential satisfaction

Most empirical studies of residential satisfaction have been based on one of the conceptual frameworks discussed above. The emphases of these studies have been to establish the effects of various housing, neighbourhood and household features on residential satisfaction (Bonnes, Bonaiuto & Ercolani, 1991; Lu, 1999). Various studies have analysed the correlates of observed residential satisfaction for specific population groups, as already described above. Also, a host of variables representing housing and neighbourhood characteristics, individuals' socio-demographic attributes, as well as their perceptions of housing and neighbourhood conditions has been analysed in previous studies. They vary from the home size to personal collections. Likewise, differences in model specification and data type could also prevent a direct comparison of the empirical results (Lu, 1999). Two features have arisen from empirical studies on residential satisfaction. First, the significance of the perceptual variables has been emphasized because of the belief that what is important in determining individuals' residential satisfaction is their perception rather than the actual structure of the residential surroundings (Weidemann & Anderson, 1982). In other words, objective measures of housing and neighbourhood attributes alone do not provide an adequate explanation of satisfaction. Second, dwelling satisfaction and neighbourhood satisfaction are measured differently and are often analysed separately (Crull, Bode & Morris, 1991) but it must be noted that the two types of satisfaction are also inter-related. This is because the assessment of one's housing unit, for example, is likely to include its immediate surroundings, even one's relationship with one's neighbours.

Overall, empirical studies have identified a number of important determinants of residential satisfaction, such as income, tenure, life-cycle stages, house size and housing quality. For instance, being older, having a higher income and having a smaller family have all been related to higher housing satisfaction (Campbell, Converse & Rogers, 1976; Morris & Winter, 1978; Galster & Hesser, 1981). Home-owners, particularly owners of single family homes, are almost always more satisfied with their homes and neighbourhoods than are renters (Rohe & Basolo, 1997). Also, available space in the house has a significant positive effect on residents' dwelling satisfaction. Neighbourhood satisfaction has also been found to be an important predictor of dwelling satisfaction; but there are also inconsistent and conflicting results in the literature on several variables. Some scholars have argued that the residential satisfaction (habitability) of a house is influenced not only by the engineering elements, but also by social, behavioural, cultural and other elements in the entire socio-environmental system (Onibokun, 1974) because the house is only one link in a chain of factors that determines beneficiaries' relative satisfaction with their accommodation.

Furthermore, housing characteristics, neighbourhood characteristics and household characteristics have also been viewed as the essential determinants of residential satisfaction (Galster & Hesser, 1981; Lu, 1999; Amérigo & Aragonés, 1997). Housing characteristics such as the age of the house, interior and proximal exterior environments, and other aspects of housing such as building quality and disrepair, neighbourhood, social, economic and physical features are also major determinants of residential satisfaction (Amérigo & Aragonés, 1990; Sirgy & Cornwell, 2002; Phillips et al., 2005; Paris & Kangari, 2006; He, 2009). The social features most often regarded as important include interaction with neighbours, attachment to the communities, perceptions of privacy and safety at home, among others (Weidemanh & Anderson, 1982; Bruin & Cook, 1997). Neighbourhood socio-economic status, home values and community cost of living are typical factors used to measure the economic features of a neighbourhood (Lu, 1999; He, 2009). Physical features such as the infrastructural and equipment settings and the quality of the environment of the community, such as lighting of streets, crowding and noise levels, and green areas or open space among others, are also determinants of residential satisfaction (Dahmann, 1983; Bonnes, Bonaiuto & Ercolani, 1991; Gomez-Jacinto & Hombrados-Mendieta, 2002; Turner, 2005).

Largely, the concept of housing does not lie in the individual's dwelling alone. It is a composite of the overall physical and social components that make up the housing system (Francescato, Weidemann & Anderson, 1987). Furthermore, housing satisfaction is influenced by the numerous components in the system and the background characteristics of the occupants. Other factors that have been found related to housing satisfaction include marital status, number of children and family size, socio-economic status, education, employment and welfare, physical characteristics of the house, satisfaction with the physical condition of the house and management services, social participation and interaction, and past living conditions, as well as residential mobility and future intention to move (Yeh, 1972; Miller & Crader, 1979; Morshidi et al., 1999; Varady & Carrozza, 2000; Theodori, 2001; Varady, Walker & Wang, 2001).

However, there is little agreement on the effect of these factors on residential satisfaction. The inconsistence in empirical findings may be attributed to the fact that such key variables such as residential satisfaction are often defined differently in different studies as well as the inappropriate statistical techniques that were employed in measuring the determinants (Lu, 1999). The most widely used method in the previous studies has been multiple regression analysis, with levels of residential satisfaction being the dependent variable. Because residential satisfaction is usually measured at the ordinal level even though it actually has an interval scale, regression models have been found not to be appropriate. Other robust statistical methods that consider covariation of constructs, such as structural equation modelling, will be better suited to measuring residential satisfaction. This method, when used, will help to overcome the limitations of other measurement techniques that have so far been used. This is because structural equation modelling is a statistical methodology that takes a confirmatory approach, rather than an exploratory approach, to the analysis of a structural theory, which represents causal processes that generate observations on multiple variables (Bentler, 1988).

Summary

This chapter of the book was focused on the discussion of theoretical and conceptual perspectives of residential satisfaction studies, thus addressing the second focus of the book, which explores the theories underpinning residential satisfaction revealed in the work of Marans and Rodgers (1975) and that of Marans and Sprecklemeyer (1981). These are the most comprehensive conceptual models of residential satisfaction and as such many studies of residential satisfaction have been based on them. This chapter of the book also revealed that the past theories of residential satisfaction all centre upon the concept of residential satisfaction measuring the difference between households' actual and desired (or aspired-to) housing and neighbourhood characteristics. This is because a significant issue in all models of residential satisfaction is the actual measurement of housing attributes. However, it was also found that the two common types of measurement available in satisfaction study are objective and subjective measures. All previous models have all tended to assess the level of housing satisfaction subjectively, which is only one aspect of occupants' satisfaction as discussed.

Hence, the current study hopes to describe the formation of residential satisfaction in houses through the development of a conceptual framework, which is the subject of the next chapter of this book. The approach describes residential satisfaction objectively and subjectively because objective measures of housing adequacy are essential to have a holistic understanding of the subject.

References

ACSI (2006). Customer satisfaction study. Available online: www.fs.fed.us/research/pdf/2006_fs_rd_customer_satisfaction_survey_final_report.pdf (accessed 23 October 2013).

Ahmad, H.H. (1994). *Residential satisfaction and social integration in public low cost housing in Malaysia*. Birmingham: University of Birmingham.

Amérigo, M.A. (1990). The perception of residential environment and environment role. In R. Pamir, V. Iuramoglu & N. Teymur (eds) *Culture, space and history*. Ankara: METV, Faculty of Architecture.

Amérigo, M.A. (1992). A model of residential satisfaction. In *Socio-environmental metamorphoses: Builtscape, landscape, eethnoscape, euroscape. Proceedings of 12th IAPS conference.* Karaletsou, Salonica: Aristotle University of Thessaloniki.

Amérigo, M. and Aragonés, J.I. (1990). Residential satisfaction in council housing. *Journal of environmental psychology*, 10(4):313–325.

Amérigo, M.A. & Aragonés, I.J. (1997). A theoretical and methodological approach to the study of residential satisfaction. *Journal of environmental psychology*, 17:47–57.

Amole, D. (2009). Residential satisfaction in students' housing. *Journal of environmental psychology*, 29:76–85.

Anderson, E.W. & Fornell, C. (1994). A customer satisfaction research prospectus. In R.T. Rust & R.L. Oliver (eds) *Service quality: New directions in theory and practice*. Thousand Oaks, CA: Sage, pp. 241–268.

Anderson, J. & Weidemann, S. (1997). Developing and utilizing models of resident satisfaction. In G. Moore & R. Marans (eds) *Advances in environment behavior design*. New York: Plenum, pp. 287–314.

Anderson, R. (1973). Consumer Dissatisfaction: The effect of disconfirmed expectancy on perceived product performance. *Journal of marketing research*, 10(2):38–44.

Argyle, M. (1987). *The psychology of happiness*. London: Methuen & Co. Ltd.

Bardo, J.W. & Hughey, J.B. (1984). The structure of community satisfaction in a British and an American community. *Journal of social psychology*, 124:151–157.

Bentler, P.M. (1988). Causal modeling via structural equation systems. In J.R. Nesselroade & R.B. Cattell (eds) *Handbook of multivariate experimental psychology, perspectives on individual differences*. New York: Plenum Press, pp. 317–335.

Bentler, P.M. & Speckart, G. (1979). Models of attitude–behavior relations. *Psychological review*, 86:452–464.

Bitner, M. (1987). Contextual cues and consumer satisfaction: The role of physical surroundings and employee behaviors in service settings. Unpublished paper, University of Washington.

Bonnes, M., Bonaiuto, M. & Ercolani, A.P. (1991). Crowding and residential satisfaction in the urban environment: A contextual approach. *Environment and behavior*, 23(5):531–552.

Brown, G. & Plenert, G. (2006). Gap analysis. In M. Helms (ed.) *Encyclopedia of management*. Detroit: Gale, pp. 319–321.

Bruin, M. & Cook, C. (1997). Understanding constraints and residential satisfaction among low-income single-parent families. *Environment and behavior*, 29(4):532–553.

Campbell, A., Converse, P.E. & Rogers, W.J. (1976). *The quality of the American life: Perceptions, evaluations, and satisfaction*. New York: Russell Sage Foundation.

Canter, D. & Ress, K.A. (1982). Multivariate model of housing satisfaction. *International review of applied psychology*, 32:185–208.

Cardozo, R. (1965). An experimental study of customer effort, expectation, and satisfaction. *Journal of marketing research*, 2(8):244–249.

Carlsmith, J. & Aronson, E. (1963). Some hedonic consequences of the confirmation and disconfirmation of expectations. *Journal of abnormal and social psychology*, 66(2):151–156.

Carvalho, M. (1995). Residential satisfaction in condominios exclusivos (gate-guarded neighborhoods) in Brazil. *EDRA Proceedings*, p. 169.

Carvalho, M., George, V.R. & Anthony, K.H. (1997). Residential satisfaction in *condominios exclusivos* (gate-guarded neighborhoods) in Brazil. *Environment and behavior*, 29:734–768.

Churchill, G. & Surprenant, C. (1982). An investigation into the determinants of customer satisfaction. *Journal of marketing research*, 19(4):491–504.

Cook, C.C., Bruin, M.J. & Laux, S. (1994). Housing assistance and residential satisfaction among single-parent women. *Housing and society*, 21(2):62–75.

Crull, S.R., Bode, M.E. & Morris, E. (1991). Two tests of the housing adjustment model of residential mobility. *Housing and society*, 18(3):53–64.

Cutter, S. (1982). Residential satisfaction and the suburban homeowner. *Urban geography*, 3(4):315–327.

Dahmann, D.C. (1983). Subjective assessments of neighborhood quality by size of place. *Urban studies*, 20(1):31–45.

Davis, G. & Roizen, R. (1970). Architectural determinants of student satisfaction in college residence halls. *Environment design and research association*, 2:28–44.

Dawes, R., Singer, D. & Lemons, P. (1972). An experimental analysis of the contrast effect and its implications for intergroup communication and indirect assessment of attitude. *Journal of personality and social psychology*, 21(3):281–295.

Day, R. (1980). How satisfactory is research on consumer satisfaction? In J. Olson (ed.) *Advances in consumer research*. Ann Arbor: Association for Consumer Research, pp. 593–597.

Duncan, T.L.C. (1971). Measuring housing quality: A study of methods. Birmingham: Centre for Urban and Regional Studies, University of Birmingham.

Engel, J., Kollat, D. & Blackwell, R. (1968). *Consumer behavior*. New York: Holt, Rinehart and Winston.

Falah, M., Al-Abed, A. & Stan, W. (1995). A model for assessing the effectiveness of public housing in Sana'a (Republic of Yemen). *Construction management and economics*, 13:457–465.

Festinger, L. (1957). *A theory of cognitive dissonance*. Stanford, CA: Stanford Press.

Fishbein, M. & Ajzen, I. (1975). *Belief, attitude, intention and behavior: An introduction to theory and research*. Reading, MA: Addison-Wesley.

Forman, A. (1986). The impact of purchase decision confidence on the process of consumer satisfaction/dissatisfaction. Unpublished Ph.D. dissertation, Knoxville: The University of Tennessee.

Fornell, C., Johnson, M., Anderson, E., Cha, J. & Bryant, B. (1996). The American customer satisfaction index: Nature, purpose, and findings. *Journal of marketing*, 60(4):7–18.

Francescato, G. (2002). Residential satisfaction research: The case for and against. In J.I. Aragonés, G. Francescato & T. Gärling (eds) *Residential environments: Choice, satisfaction and behaviour*. London: Bergin and Garvey, pp. 15–34.

Francescato, G., Weidemann, S., Anderson, J. & Chenoweth, R. (1974). Evaluating residents' satisfaction in housing for low and moderate income families: A multi-method approach. In D.H. Carson (ed.) *Man–environment interactions: Evaluation & applications* (vol. 5). Washington, DC: Environmental Design Research Association, pp. 285–295.

Francescato, G., Weidemann, S. & Anderson, J.R. (1986). Residential satisfaction and residential quality: An overview of recent applications. 21st International Congress of Applied Psychology, Jerusalem, Israel.

Francescato, G., Weidemann, S. & Anderson, J.R. (1987). Residential satisfaction: Its uses and limitations in housing research. In W.V. Vliet, H. Choldin, W. Michelson & P.

Popene (eds) *Housing and neighbourhood: Theoretical and empirical contributions*, Westport, CT: Greenwood Press, pp. 43–57.

Francescato, G., Weidemann, S. & Anderson, J.R. (1989). *Evaluating the built environment from the users' point of view: An attitudinal model of residential satisfaction*. New York: Plenum Press.

Francescato, G., Weidemann, S., Anderson, J.R. et al. (1979). *Satisfaction in HUD-assisted housing: Design and management*. Washington, DC: US Department of Housing and Urban Development.

Galster, G.C. (1987). Identifying the correlates of dwelling satisfaction: An empirical critique. *Environment and behavior*, 19(5):539–568.

Galster, G.C. & Hesser, G.W. (1981). Residential satisfaction: An empirical critique. *Environment and behavior*, 13(6):735–758.

Ge, J. & Hokao, K. (2006). Research on residential lifestyles in Japanese cities from the viewpoints of residential preference, residential choice and residential satisfaction. *Landscape urban plan*, 78(3):165–178.

Gomez-Jacinto, L. & Hombrados-Mendieta, I. (2002). Multiple effects of community and household crowing. *Journal of environmental psychology*, 22:233–246.

Guney, Y. (1997). The evaluation of high-rise residents' satisfaction in Turkey. *Proceedings*, EDRA 28, Space design and management for place making, University of Quebec, Montreal.

Hackl, P. & Westlund, A. (2000). On structural equation modelling for customer satisfaction measurement. *Total quality management*, 11(4–6):820–826.

Hansemark, O.C. & Albinson, M. (2004). Customer satisfaction and retention: The experiences of individual employees. *Managing service quality*, 14(1):40–57.

He, X. (2009). Residential satisfaction with home location: Examination of the relationship between location- embedded benefits and risk perception. Unpublished doctoral dissertation, Texas State University-San Marcos.

Hourihan, K. (1984). Context-dependent models of residential satisfaction: An analysis of housing groups in Cork, Ireland. *Environment and behavior*, 16:369–393.

Hovland, C., Harvey, O. & Sherif, M. (1957). Assimilation and contrast effects in reaction to communication and attitude change. *Journal of abnormal and social psychology*, 55(7):244–252.

Hoyer, W.D. & MacInnis, D.J. (2001). *Consumer behaviour*. Boston: Houghton Mifflin Company.

Hunt, H. (1977). *CS/D: Bits and pieces: Consumer satisfaction/dissatisfaction and complaining behavior*. Bloomington: Indiana University Conference, April 1977, pp. 38–41.

Husna, S. & Nurizan, Y. (1987). Housing provision and satisfaction of low-income households in Kuala Lumpur. *Habitat international*, 11(4):27–38.

Iacobucci, D. & Oston, A. (1995). Distinguishing service quality and customer satisfaction: The voice of the customer. *Journal of consumer psychology*, 4(3):277–303.

Jyh-Bin, Y. & Sheng-Chi, P. (2006). Development of a customer satisfaction evaluation model for construction project management. *Building and environment*, 43:458–468.

Kim, S. (1997). Outdoor environment satisfaction: Contributions of landscape design to multi- family housing residents' satisfaction. Unpublished dissertation. Urbana-Champaign: Environmental Design and Research Association, University of Illinois.

Kim, S. & Anderson, J. (1997). Modeling residents' satisfaction: Comparison of the Francescato and Fishbein and Ajzen models. Urbana-Champaign: Environmental Design and Research Association, University of Illinois.

Kotler, P. (2000). *Marketing management: Analysis, planning, implementation and control.* Upper Saddle River, NJ: Prentice Hall.

Lansing, J., Marans, R.W. & Zehner, R.B. (1970). *Planned residential environment.* Ann Arbor: Institute for Social Research, the University of Michigan.

Leder, D. & Sayre, T. (1989). Adapting the bedroom of individuals with severe handicaps: Improving life satisfaction and self-sufficiency. *EDRA Proceedings*, p. 320.

Lee, T. (1968). Urban neighbourhood as a socio-spatial schema. *Human relations*, 21:241–267.

Lindberg, E., Garling, T. & Montgomery, H. (1988). *Subjective belief-value structures as determinants of preferences for and choices among housing alternatives.* Umea: University of Umea.

Lindberg, E., Garling, T., Montgomery, H. & Waara, R. (1987). People's evaluation of housing attributes. A study of underlying beliefs and values. *Scandinavian housing and planning research*, 481–103.

Lu, M. (1999). Determinants of residential satisfaction: Ordered logit vs. regression models. *Growth and change*, 30(Spring):264–287.

McQuitty, S., Finn, A. & Wiley, J.B. (2000). Systematically varying customer satisfaction and its implications for product choice. *Academy of marketing science review*, 10 (1):231–254.

Marans, R. & Rodgers, S. (1975). *Toward an understanding of community satisfaction.* New York: Halstead Press.

Marans, R. & Sprecklemeyer, K. (1981). *Evaluating built environment: A behavioral approach.* Ann Arbor: The University of Michigan.

Mastura, J., Noor, L.H., Osman, M., & Ramayah, T. (2007). The determinants of housing satisfaction level: A study on residential development projects. Pulau Pinang, Malaysia: Penang Development Corporation.

Michelson, W. (1977). *Environment choice, human behaviour, and residential satisfaction.* Oxford: Oxford University Press.

Miller, M.K. & Crader, K.W. (1979). Rural–urban differences in two dimensions of community satisfaction. *Rural sociology*, 44:489–504.

Montero, M. (1991). Residential satisfaction in low interest housing in Mexico city. *Environmental design and research association*, 22:68–74.

Morris, E.W. & Winter, M. (1978). *Housing, family and society.* New York: John Wiley and Sons.

Morris, E.W., Crull, S.R. & Winter, M. (1976). Housing norms, housing satisfaction and the propensity to move. *Journal of marriage and family*, 38(2):309–320.

Morshidi, S., Abdul Fatah, C.H., Abdul Rashid, A.A., Alip, R., Halim, S. and Usman, Y. (1999). *Low-cost housing in urban-industrial centres of Malaysia: Issues and challenges.* Penang: Penerbit Universiti Sains Malaysia.

Oliver, R.L. (1977a). A theoretical reinterpretation of expectation and disconfirmation effects on postexposure product evaluations: Experience in the field. In Ralph L. Day (ed.) *Consumer satisfaction, dissatisfaction, and complaining behavior.* Bloomington: Indiana University Division of Business Research, pp. 2–9.

Oliver, R.L. (1977b). Effect of expectation and disconfirmation on post-exposure product evaluations: An alternative interpretation. *Journal of applied psychology*, 62(8):480–486.

Oliver, R.L. (1979). *Product satisfaction as a function of prior expectation and subsequent disconfirmation: New evidence.* Bloomington: Indiana University.

Oliver, R.L. (1980a). Theoretical bases of consumer satisfaction research: Review, critique and future direction In C. Lamb & P. Dunne (eds) *Theoretical developments in marketing*. Chicago: American Marketing Association, pp. 206–210.

Oliver, R.L. (1980b). A cognitive model of the antecedents and consequences of satisfaction decisions. *Journal of marketing research*, 17(11):460–469.

Oliver, R.L. (1981). Measurement and evaluation of satisfaction process in retail setting. *Journal of retailing*, 57:25–48.

Oliver, R.L. (1989). Processing of the satisfaction response in consumption: A suggested framework and research propositions. *Journal of satisfaction, dissatisfaction and complaining behavior*, 2:1–16.

Oliver, R.L. (1993). A conceptual model of service quality and service satisfaction: Compatible goals, different concepts. *Advances in services marketing and management*, 2:65–85.

Olshavsky, R.W. & Miller, J.A. (1972). Consumer expectation, product performance and perceived product quality. *Journal of marketing research*, 9(February):19–21.

Olson, J.C. & Dover, P. (1979). Disconfirmation of consumer expectation through product trial. *Journal of applied psychology*, 641:79–89.

Onibokun, A.G. (1974). Evaluating consumers' satisfaction with housing: An application of a system approach. *Journal of American institute of planners*, 40(3):189–200.

Oseland, N. & Raw, G. (1996). Satisfaction with privacy in modern owner-occupied UK homes. *Environment design and research association*, 27:106–112.

Parasuraman, A., Zeithaml, V. & Berry, L. (1985). A conceptual model of service quality and its implications for future research. *Journal of marketing*, 49(4):41–50.

Paris, E. & Kangari, R. (2006). Multifamily affordable housing: Residential satisfaction. *Journal of performance of constructed facilities*, 19(2):138–145.

Parker, C. & Matthews, B.P. (2001). Customer satisfaction: Contrasting academic and consumers' interpretations. *Marketing intelligence and planning*, 19(1):38–44.

Peyton, R.M., Pitts, S. & Kamery, R.H. (2003). Consumer Satisfaction/Dissatisfaction (CS/D): A review of the literature prior to the 1990s. *Proceedings of the Academy of Organizational Culture, Communication and Conflict*, 7(2):41–46.

Phillips, D.R., Siu, O.L., Yeh, A.G. & Cheng, K.H. (2005). The impacts of dwelling conditions on older persons' psychological well-being in Hong Kong: The mediating role of residential satisfaction. *Social science & medicine*, 60(12):2785–2797.

Poisz, T.B.C. & Van Grumbkow, J. (1988). Economic wellbeing, job satisfaction, income evaluation and consumer satisfaction: An integrative attempt. In W.F. Raaij, G.M. Veldhoven & K.E. Warnyerd (eds) *Handbook of economics psychology*. Dordrecht: Kluwer Academic Publishers.

Porter, L.W. (1961). A study of perceived need satisfaction in bottom and middle management jobs. *Journal of applied psychology*, 4:1–10.

Potter, J., Chicoine, L. & Speicher, E. (2001). Predicting residential satisfaction: A comparative case study. *EDRA 32 Proceedings*. Lincoln: University of Nebraska.

Rapoport, A. (1977). *Human aspects of urban form*. Oxford: Pergamon.

Rohe, W.M. & Basolo, V. (1997). Long-term effects of homeownership on the self-perceptions and social interaction of low-income persons. *Environment and behavior*, 29(6):793–819.

Rosenberg, M.J. & Hovland, C.I. (1960). *Cognitive, effective, and behavioral components of attitude*. New Haven: Yale University Press.

Savasdisara, T., Tips, W.E.J. & Sumannodom, S. (1989). Residential satisfaction in private estates in Bangkok: A comparison of low-income housing estates and determinant factors. *Habitat international*, 13(1):65–73.

Sidjak, C. (1995). Are mini-suites a viable housing alternative? Two independent studies on residential satisfaction with small, self-contained apartments. *EDRA Proceedings*, p. 169.

Sirgy, M.J. & Cornwell, T. (2002). How neighborhood features affect quality of life. *Social indicators research*, 59(1):79–114.

Smith, M.K. (2001). Kurt Lewin, groups, experiential learning and action research: The encyclopedia of informal education. Available from: www.infed.org/thinkers/et-lewin.htm (accessed 23 December 2011).

Speare, A. (1974). Residential satisfaction as an intervening variable in residential mobility. *Demography*, 11:173–188.

Spreng, R., MacKenzie, S. & Olshavsky, R. (1996). A reexamination of the determinants of consumer satisfaction. *Journal of marketing*, 60(July):15–18.

Taylor, P. (1995). Social and environmental contexts of aging in place. *EDRA Proceedings*, pp. 107–112.

Theodori, G.L. (2001). Examining the effects of community satisfaction and attachment on individual well-being. *Rural sociology*, 66(4):618–628.

The Oxford Library of Words and Phrases (1993). *The Oxford library of words and phrases: Concise Oxford dictionary of proverbs, concise Oxford dictionary of quotations and concise Oxford dictionary of word origins*. Oxford: BCA.

Tse, D.K. & Wilton, P.C. (1988). Models of consumer satisfaction formation: An extension. *Journal of marketing research*, 25(2):204–212.

Turner, M.A. (2005). Landscape preferences and patterns of residential development. *Journal of urban economics*, 57:19–54.

Ukoha, O.M. & Beamish, J.O. (1997). Assessment of residents' satisfaction with public housing in Abuja, Nigeria. *Habitat International*, 21(4):445–460.

Varady, D. (1983). Determinates of residential mobility decisions. *Journal of the American planning association*, 491:84–99.

Varady, D.P. & Carrozza, M.A. (2000). Towards a better way to measure customer satisfaction levels in public housing: A report from Cincinnati. *Housing studies*, 15(6):797–825.

Varady, D.P., Walker, C.C. & Wang, X. (2001). Voucher recipient achievement of improved housing conditions in the US: Do moving distance and relocation services matter? *Urban studies*, 38(8):1273–1305.

Weidemann, S. & Anderson, J. (1982). Residents' perceptions of satisfaction and safety: A basis for change in multifamily housing. *Environment and behavior*, 14(6):695–724.

Weidemann, S. & Anderson, J.R.A. (1985). A conceptual framework for residential satisfaction. In I. Atman & R. Werner (eds) *Home environment*. New York: Plenum Press, pp. 154–182.

Westbrook, R. & Reilly, M.D. (1983). Value percept disparity: An alternative to the disconfirmation of expectation theory of consumer satisfaction. In R.P. Bagozzi & A.M. Tybout (eds) *Advances in consumer research*. Ann Arbor: Association for consumer Research, pp. 256–261.

Wilton, P. & Nicosia, I. (1986). Emerging paradigms for the study of consumer satisfaction. *European research*, 14(1):4–11.

Woodruff, R., Cadotte, E. & Jenkins, R. (1983). Modeling consumer satisfaction processes using experience-based norms. *Journal of marketing research*, 20:296–304.

Yeh, S.H.K. (1972). *Homes for the people: A study of tenant's views on public housing in Singapore*. Singapore: Economic Research Center, University of Singapore.

Yi, Y. (1990). A critical review of consumer satisfaction. Working paper. Available from: https://deepblue.lib.umich.edu/bitstream/handle/2027.42/36290/b1412322.0001.001.pdf?sequence=2&isAllowed=y (accessed 2 May 2018).

Yiping, F. (2005). Residential satisfaction conceptual framework revisited – A study on redeveloped neighbourhood in inner-city Beijing. Unpublished doctoral dissertation, University of Colorado at Denver.

Zehner, R. (1977). *Indicators of the quality of life in new communities*. Cambridge: Ballinger.

8 Conceptual perspective of residential satisfaction formation

Introduction

Chapter 7 focused on the review of theoretical and conceptual perspectives on residential satisfaction research. Also discussed are previous residential satisfaction models and theories, residential satisfaction research (conceptual issues on residential satisfaction), such as the appropriate ways of measuring residential satisfaction, followed by the discussion on the determinants of residential satisfaction. In view of this, this chapter discusses the formation of residential satisfaction through the development of a conceptual perspective. A hypothesized integrated residential satisfaction model is presented that is based on the discussion of theoretical underpinnings of the previous models presented in Chapter 7 of this book. This chapter also describes the selection of the variables adopted for the conceptual model. Also presented in this chapter is the model identification and justification for the selected variables, thereafter a conclusion is drawn for the chapter.

Variable selection for residential satisfaction conceptual framework

From the conceptual frameworks of Marans and Rodgers (1975) and Weidemann and Anderson (1985), it is notable that a majority of the research findings relating to residential satisfaction is done in the developed Western countries. Studies on residential satisfaction completed in developing countries mostly relate to public housing provided by private developers. However, these studies have not adequately provided an overview of the concept compared to those done in developed countries. Hence, the application and relevance of the results of the studies conducted in the developed countries are not consistent with those of the developing countries, as a result of the peculiarity of the developing countries' housing situations. This section of the study identifies the gaps in the residential satisfaction conceptual framework. Since the conceptual framework provides the perspectives from which problems are highlighted, it is most likely that there are some gaps in the Western conceptual framework that have failed to capture the factors affecting residential satisfaction in a developing country like South Africa, in other developing countries and in public housing studies in general. This section attempts to address the two gaps that have been identified, namely: lack of understanding of occupants' needs and expectations; and the lack of practical involvement of occupants' in meaningful participation prior to the housing development process. It is of importance to inform the reader that the houses being evaluated and referred to in this study are subsidized government-allocated housing units. These houses are built by the government and allocated to the poor and low-income groups within a certain category, as recommended by the human settlement department allocation guidelines. The consideration of these identified gaps is based on the notion that residential satisfaction cannot be achieved without good internal (needs and expectations) and external (participation in the housing process) assessment of the occupants. This is because residential satisfaction is not a simple, single-track factor assessment but a combination of numerous variables.

Most residential satisfaction study models have combined both objective and subjective attributes for the assessment of residential satisfaction. For instance, Francescato, Weidemann and Anderson (1987) suggest that residents' satisfaction with any residential dwelling depends on three elements, which are: the design of the house (i.e. the dwelling space organization, layout and facilities provided); the management practices; and the surrounding social aspects. However, residential satisfaction can also encompass four distinct types of satisfaction, which include: satisfaction with the dwelling unit; satisfaction with the services provided, including repair services; satisfaction with the whole package received, as in the case of public housing, where no rent is paid (dwelling and service); and satisfaction with the neighbourhood or area (Varady & Carrozza, 2000; Salleh et al., 2011). These four constructs were considered in the formation of the conceptual framework described in this chapter. Furthermore, facilities outside the house also influence the formation of residential satisfaction for a given setting. Other basic facilities such as shops, markets, schools, clinics, mailing systems, community halls, playgrounds and others are important to support the daily life of the occupants, and enhancing their quality of life. Overall, scholars of housing studies have also identified three main qualities that bring about residential satisfaction, which are: the quality of the dwelling; the quality of the close environment; and the quality of the urban site, which impacts on the quality of housing (Oh, 2000; Nurizan & Hashim, 2001).

Therefore, based on the extant discussion of the previous frameworks and models as detailed in Chapter 7 above, the conceptual framework described in this chapter considers the residential satisfaction bundle in a typical low-income housing development to contain the dwelling unit features with 17 variables; neighbourhood and environmental features with 22 variables; services provided by the government with 13 variables; and building quality features with 16 variables. These are the constructs that have been frequently conceptualized in most residential satisfaction studies. However, the present work brings into focus the impact of needs and expectations features with four variables and beneficiaries' participation features with five variables. These two additions are the gaps identified from the review of literature, which were found peculiar to the developing nation's situation. The next section of this chapter will present a detailed explanation of the different constructs influencing the level of satisfaction towards housing.

Understanding occupants' needs and expectations

Before a conclusion can be reached on how residential satisfaction of subsidized low-income housing beneficiaries in South Africa is formed, it is important to explore why there is a contrast in residential satisfaction research findings and whether the existing theoretical framework proposed by Western researchers has some gaps that have not fully accommodated the developing nation's context.

Residential satisfaction is an individual evaluation of living conditions. Collectively in social research, an individual's evaluation has the power to appraise the housing policy's performance, and possibly predicting housing mobility. In order to examine the difference in residential satisfaction research as a combination of residents' individual housing evaluations, it is essential to explore it both independently and collectively. As a result, this calls for research on residential satisfaction across individual and social perceptions, which study this at both psychological and sociological level. So far, most residential satisfaction studies have focused on certain social goals, such as assessing housing policy as a measure and also forecasting housing mobility as a predictor. The supposition behind housing policy research is that higher satisfaction levels are a good indication of the success of specific policies, programmes or designs such as the South African housing subsidy scheme among others. While for housing mobility research, mobility results from the increase in dissatisfaction beyond a person's threshold of tolerance level. It is assumed that satisfied residents choose to stay, rather than move out without a thorough examination of other factors that could have contributed to the zero-mobility decision. In contrast to the previous uses of residential satisfaction, the focus should be primarily to determine which components of the housing system most strongly and consistently predict residential satisfaction, so that it can be used to direct efforts in those directions (outcomes) and to those aspects in which an intervention is likely to yield the most beneficial effect for the occupants of the houses, which is the focus of the current book. The idea of aiming to intervene in some components of the housing system has tilted most research focus towards the physical and social setting of the housing system, away from the occupants' needs and expectations.

Aside the above, some residential satisfaction conceptual frameworks have included needs and expectations as part of the factors researched. Needs and expectation data have been found to be better determinant of residential satisfaction, as opposed to socio-demographic data (Bruin & Cook, 1997; Greenberg, 1999; Parkes, Kearns & Atkinson, 2002). Some proven and useful personal needs and expectation variables researched during the housing development process include mistrust of authority, negative emotions and pessimism amongst others (Greenberg, 1999). Moreover, because there is a lack of psychological understanding in most residential satisfaction research, the focus has been put on sociological understanding alone (Yiping, 2005). However, psychological understanding in residential satisfaction research has increasingly incorporated proven situational and contextual variables but fundamental exploration from a psychological perspective is still lagging behind in most conceptual frameworks. As a result, the effort to understand the individual psychological differences in the residential satisfaction evaluation process is necessary.

In addressing the gap of understanding personal needs, Maslow's (1970) needs theory was drawn upon, while for the gap of residents' expectations, the expectancy disconfirmation theoretical framework postulated by Oliver in 1981, as discussed in the previous chapter, was used. As already discussed, research in residential satisfaction is a valid way of assessing the overall performance of the housing system as a criterion, and it is useful to explore the meaning of satisfaction from the residents' perspectives in order to have a holistic view of the housing system. Studying satisfaction requires real understanding of the individual needs and expectations; and according to the Merriam-Webster dictionary, satisfaction means the fulfilment of a need or want. Thus, an understanding of occupants' housing needs and expectations is useful to investigate the gaps in previous residential satisfaction research.

The 1970 work of Maslow conceptualized the well-known Needs Order Theory. Maslow theorizes that basic human needs are organized into an order of relative importance. Maslow also believed that human needs arrange themselves in order of 'pre-potency'. The Needs Order Theory further postulates that the appearance of one need usually rests on the prior satisfaction of another more pre-potent need. Also, no need or drive can be treated as if it were isolated or discrete; thus every drive is related to the state of satisfaction or dissatisfaction of another drive. It is believed that once a need is satisfied, it ceases to motivate behaviour. But man being an 'ever-wanting' creature, as soon as one need is satisfied, another appears in its place. Thus 'human needs' form a hierarchy according to Maslow's work of 1970, which includes the physiological needs, safety needs, social needs, esteem needs and self-actualization needs. The Maslow's Needs Order Theory postulates that each need must be satisfied in turn, starting with the first, which deals with the most obvious needs for survival. It is only when the lower-order needs of physical and emotional well-being are satisfied that a concern can be placed on the higher-order needs of influence and personal development. However, if the things that satisfy the lower-order needs are swept away, people are no longer concerned about the attainment and satisfaction of the higher-order needs.

The Maslow's Needs Order Theory has been extensively used in many fields but mainly in the business and management domain to provide help on how to stimulate employees' motivation. However, the Needs Order Theory clearly sets up the levels of order that individuals have tried to pursue, as each level's need satisfaction will motivate the desire for the next level. This theory has also been tested to be useful in job satisfaction and customer satisfaction and, as such, it has the potential to help in addressing the gap in residential satisfaction research. Using Maslow's Needs Order Theory suggests that material and existential needs and priorities exist in housing choices, in which the existential functions include identity, security and opportunity. In any given context, housing priorities across different income groups show difference in their vital need (Turner, 1972). However, Greenberg in 1999 attempted to combine Maslow's needs order but failed to explore the full coverage of the theory and only indicated that controlling crime and physical problems are the two basic criterion for a satisfied neighbourhood. This is right in conceptualization, but when it only touches upon the holistic understanding of complex human needs in relation to their environment, then it is insufficient.

It must be recognized that a housing need exists, in which studies are mostly focused on different levels of the need. The work of Taylor (1995) claims that the fear of crime, or the feeling of safety, is the dominant predictor of satisfaction. Also, Greenberg in 1999 found that crime and severe physical problems are the necessity need of any given neighbourhood. Furthermore, to achieve a satisfied living environment, there exists the needs order in the resident's housing consumption, but little attention has been paid on researching this order. However, the work of McCray and Day (1977) on housing satisfaction based on Maslow's Theory of Needs evaluated individuals' needs towards housing. McCray and Day found that when housing needs are fulfilled, individuals will indirectly be satisfied with their houses. Despite the general acceptance that housing is the primary component for quality life, housing construction rarely refers to the needs and types of families who are going to inhabit the houses, whereas these criteria are critical in the establishment of human habitats. The emphasis in most housing construction that involves the low-income is on the delivery at scale (quantity), which has compromised the principles enacted in most housing edicts that are committed to the provision of low-income housing.

In another work by Maslow (1998), he posits that the housing order is constructed to understand factors that lead to a satisfied or dissatisfied neighbourhood, which is a major ideology of the current book. Residential satisfaction is determined by the fulfilment of individual housing needs, which is fundamentally determined under the condition of what level of housing need is pursued. This is because unless one level of needs is satisfied, it remains in the consciousness and becomes the prime determinant of behaviour towards the neighbourhood. Also, the effects of satisfying higher-order needs will be neutralized if the lower-order needs are not fulfilled or when only partially fulfilled. In other words, the residents who do not have sufficient living space in their apartment will care little about how the historic design of their building could affect their satisfaction. Figure 8.1 shows the housing needs based on Maslow's Needs Hierarchy Theory.

Physiological needs refer to the quality of the shelter provided by the housing unit and the location the house is situated in. The location of the housing unit should be within an acceptable distance from the resident's work place. Using the available transportation type, the daily commute distance should be acceptable to a majority of the residents, and the house has to be a permanent

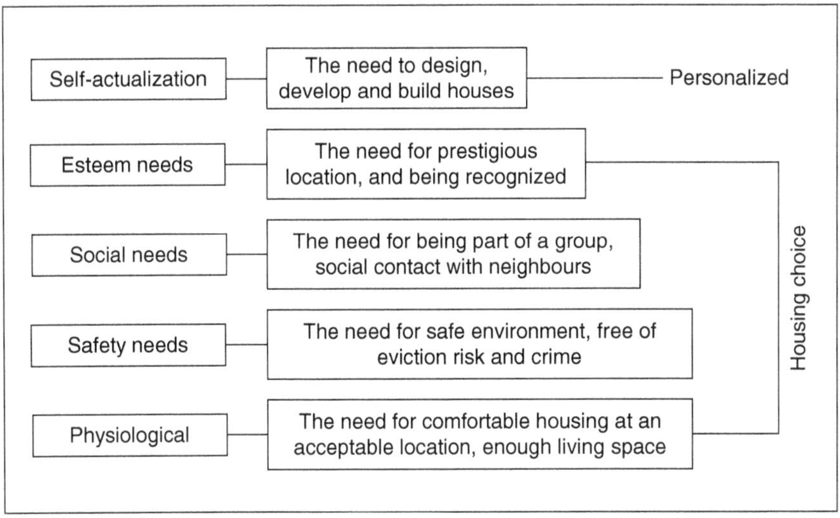

Figure 8.1 Housing needs order
Source: Yiping (2005).

structure, with the necessary ventilation, of an acceptable climate according to the prevailing weather conditions in its particular place, have access to water and an electricity supply. All these services can vary by different societies and geographical locations, and should be among the prerequisite norm in the housing selection process. Also, the size of the housing units should be big enough to accommodate all family members, providing necessary separation of rooms for different generations and different genders.

When the minimum (physiological) needs for housing are satisfied residents will start pursuing the next level, which is the security need. The safety need includes physical, emotional and financial security. Residents would then want their living condition to be secured with the appropriate structure and supply. For instance, the low-income groups prefer a safe, orderly, predictable, lawful and organized dwelling environment where they feel emotionally safe and secure. It means a safe environment free of crime and the risk of eviction. They want their properties to remain free from damage or theft. When crimes happen to a resident's neighbours, they could generate a feeling of insecurity. The broader aspects of the attempts to seek safety and stability in the world are seen in the common preference for familiar rather than unfamiliar things, or for the known rather than the unknown (Yiping, 2005). When residents already have satisfied their minimum living needs and the fulfilment of their safety needs, they start considering the social needs.

The desire for social needs comes after the security needs. When the first two order needs are fairly well satisfied, there will emerge the love and affection and belonging (social) needs. Within the living environment, these third-order needs will be typically exhibited towards family members and neighbours. Residents expect affectionate relations with family members and look for friends among their neighbours. It is the need to become part of the small society, a feeling of belonging to a group and associating with it. This will enable the residents to participate in activities and have contact with their neighbours. Especially for newcomers to a neighbourhood, whose lower order needs are all satisfied, this level order need will start developing. Moreover, the aspect of beneficiaries' housing participation will only happen when their physiological and safety needs have been met. This social need is followed by the esteem need.

The esteem need is the desire for a stable, firmly based and usually high evaluation from others. It is the need for being recognized and respected by people around you. In the living environment, it relates to the desire for regard, reputation, prestige, authority and appreciation from others. The form of the esteem need includes the desire for living in a neighbourhood with a good reputation and being respected by neighbours. Satisfaction of the esteem need leads to the feeling of self-confidence, being useful and necessary within the society.

Self-actualization is a term that has been used in various psychological theories, often in slightly different ways. The term was originally introduced by Goldstein in 1934, in his work on organism theory for the motive to realize one's full potential. In his view, it is the organism's master motive, the only real motive, to actualize itself as fully as possible in the basic drive of self-actualization. Similarly, Rogers further shed light on the concept through his 1951 work *Client-Centered Therapy*, informing the curative force in psychotherapy, which is man's tendency to actualize himself. This is the ability to become his inherent potential and to express and activate all the capacities of the organism. However, the concept was brought fully to prominence in Maslow's Hierarchy of Needs Theory as the final level of psychological development that can be achieved when all other basic and mental needs are fulfilled and the 'actualization' of the full personal potential takes place. When all of the above-mentioned needs are satisfied then, and only then, are the needs for self-actualization activated.

Maslow's Needs Theory describes self-actualization as a person's need to be and do that which the person was born to do. Self-actualization needs refer to the human need for self-fulfilment, such as to the tendency to actualize what is inherent in his/her potential. Within the housing needs order, self-actualization refers to the desire of achieving a living environment true to the residents' own nature. Possible forms of self-actualization might include the personalization of the interior design of the dwelling unit and the customized designing or construction of his own house. Nevertheless, a clear emergence of these needs usually rests upon some prior satisfaction of the lower-order needs.

The housing needs order is only a framework for general residents. It thus has different meanings to different groups of people such as children, older people or even the low-income groups that are being considered in the development of the conceptual framework. For instance, a lower-income resident in a subsidized housing unit will not have the need for self-actualization, when the lower-order needs of good-quality housing close to their place of work and with enough rooms to cater for his/her needs and that of the family have not yet been met. However, the change and progression of peoples' needs as the society develops are clearly evident. For example, the South African experience on evaluating quality of life has shown that the indicators of quality of life have shifted from goals, which are basically a concern for food and shelter, as well as needs for equity and racial respect, to the need for participation, challenge and personal development.

In addressing the gap of residents' expectations, the Expectancy Disconfirmation Theoretical Framework postulated by Oliver in 1981 was drawn upon. Research on satisfaction using disconfirmation of expectations suggests that satisfaction is the result of a comparison of that which was expected and that which was received (Woodruff, Cadotte & Jenkins, 1983). A fundamental premise of disconfirmation of expectation is that expectation is related to satisfaction. Erevelles and Leavitt in 1992 describe that post-purchase evaluation of a product can be explained, at least in part, by a comparison of the pre-purchase performance. Tse and Wilton in 1988 suggest that in addition to the influences from expected performance and subjective disconfirmation, 'perceived performance exerts direct influence on satisfaction'. Hence, the Expectancy Disconfirmation Model claims that user's satisfaction is a response to the congruency between an individual's expectations and the actual performance of a product (Oliver, 1981). When applied to the public housing subsidy scheme, satisfaction is viewed as a function of the interrelationship between what housing occupants expect from the government and their perceptions of the housing unit they have received, that is, the quality of the houses received and the satisfaction derived from the housing services provided.

The Expectancy Disconfirmation Model can be conceptualized in a four-stage process. First, the user formulates expectations regarding a product. Expectations contrast across users (Tse & Wilton, 1988; Reisig & Chandek, 2001). For example, based on occupant knowledge of the product, an individual may estimate what the performance will be. However, expectations may also be more normative in nature, and thought of as what the user believes performance ought to be (Woodruff, Cadotte & Jenkins, 1983; Tse & Wilton, 1988). Second, the individual makes certain attributions regarding the performance of that product. Third, the individual compares the perception of the product's performance against the initial expectations. The last stage in the Expectancy Disconfirmation Process is the user's determination of how well the product measures up to initial expectations. Here, expectations provide a standard from which to compare perceptions of product performance. Consequently, the individual may judge product performance to be better than, worse than or equal to what he/she expected. The extent to which perceptions of performance match expectations dictates the type of disconfirmation the occupant experiences, and has a direct effect on satisfaction. For example, an individual might experience positive disconfirmation, wherein the expectations are exceeded (increases likelihood of satisfaction). Negative disconfirmation is another probability, and arises when the user's expectations are not met by the product or service performance (decreases likelihood of satisfaction). Lastly, zero disconfirmation can also occur when performance of the product matches expectations (no effect on satisfaction).

While disconfirmation is assumed to have a major effect on user satisfaction, research shows that disconfirmation is not the only direct outcome. Expectations have also been found to directly affect satisfaction. For instance, individuals with lower expectations often report higher levels of satisfaction. Similarly, the second component of disconfirmation, which is performance, has also been interrelated to outcome satisfaction. Hence, Oliver in 1981 maintained that as performance increases, so too do levels of user satisfaction. Expectations and performance, therefore, are believed to have both direct and indirect effects on user's satisfaction (Reisig & Chandek, 2001).

The Expectancy Disconfirmation Theory not only explains satisfaction with product expectation performance, but also service satisfaction (Churchill & Surprenant, 1982). For example, Caughey, Francis and Kolodziej (1998) found that expectations have a significant effect on overall satisfaction of occupants, as satisfaction normally occurs based on a comparison of that which is expected with that which is received. Also, prior exposure to what is to be received has the tendency to influence occupant's satisfaction towards a property, while a negative prior experience can generate a lower expectation, which will result in lower satisfaction. So, an understanding of how residents' expectations are formed is significant in ascertaining how residential satisfaction is ultimately formed. However, the dominant hypothesis guiding recent research on satisfaction has been disconfirmation of expectations. Some researchers have been challenging and expanding the disconfirmation theory and suggesting that many other determinants also affect satisfaction apart from expectation (Woodruff, Cadotte & Jenkins, 1983; Erevelles & Leavitt, 1992), which is a proposition that the current conceptual framework advocates. Based on this assertion, expectation together with needs is considered as one of the exogenous variables included in the development of the conceptual model described in this book to ascertain how occupants' satisfaction in subsidized low-income housing is formed in a developing country context, using South Africa as a case study.

As part of the conceptual framework of residential satisfaction research, the gratifications of housing needs and expectations should have noteworthy prominence. For people with different housing needs and expectations, the same housing condition could bring different satisfaction levels because their needs and expectation are different. Residential satisfaction is in most cases shaped under the conditions of what the level of housing needs are right now and the prior expectations held by the beneficiaries. Unless the first-order needs are sufficiently satisfied, they will remain in the occupants' consciousness and will thus become the prime determinants of housing behaviour. The living conditions that are currently pursued form the housing expectation of the individual, which influences the overall residential satisfaction.

From the literature on housing research, from various perspectives, there have been many studies separately addressing different levels of needs of individuals and social groups, or their significance in informing policies on how best to deal with the needs of a particular social group. For instance, Marcus (1995) studies the self-actualization level and states that housing is like a mirror that has a powerful effect on our sojourn towards a state of wholeness. Furthermore, research on social needs in the housing environment has increased to such an extent that social capital is the focus (Putnam, 1995). Social capital refers to social trust, norms and networks that people can draw upon to resolve common problems such as a housing problem. All over the world, and in South Africa, there is a growing agreement that social capital constitutes a significant new dimension of community development and establishment as occupants are directly involved. This means that their needs and expectations would have been taken care of through their active participation in the housing development process (Lang & Hornburg, 1998), which is the second gap addressed in this book. Furthermore, the security needs of housing extend to another large area of research. For example, Newman in 1972 addressed the relationship between the built environment and security using his theory of defensible space. Related to the security issue, there have been proposals and projects on urban renewals, as well as debate on the gated community and on social issues of residential segregation (Smith, 1996; Wilson-Doenges, 2000; Hamnett, 2001; Landman, 2004). Housing needs, as shelter, are mostly concerned with those who struggle for these needs, such as the homeless, or those previously disadvantaged from owning property, as a result of the previous South African government rule, defined as those constituting the low-income groups.

All this social research on housing can be grouped within a system relating to a different order of needs. Individually, every household is inspired to pursue a higher level of needs in the housing needs order, when the lower needs have been satisfied. Collectively, it brings out social issues regarding the processes of different levels of housing need satisfaction. Discrepancies in housing priorities are so big that housing provision sectors have to provide a wide variety of dwelling types with all forms of tenure to meet the demand. This is because residents are only satisfied when their current housing needs and expectations are satisfied. However, it must be noted that satisfaction will not stay unchanged because soon there will be other higher level needs and expectations that will have to be satisfied.

More so, households who are dissatisfied are likely to consider some form of adjustment. They may attempt to make adjustments to reduce dissatisfaction by revising their needs and expectations to reconcile the incongruity, or by improving their housing conditions through remodelling. They may also move to another place to bring their housing into conformity with their needs and expectations. Both mobility and adjustments are subject to the constraints posed by financial resources at one's disposal and by the information given regarding alternative adaptation opportunities (Lu, 1999; Morris, Crull & Winter, 1976). Thus, moving behaviour is only one type of adjustment residents perform during the time of dissatisfaction with housing needs but, in the case of the low-income groups, it might not be possible, as most cannot access housing on their own and the subsidized houses received might be their only lifetime opportunity of access to housing. Therefore, in this present conceptual formation, needs and expectation features that have been hypothesized for the development of an integrated residential satisfaction model are summarized in Table 8.1.

Understanding participation of beneficiaries

As already discussed, research in residential satisfaction is a valid way to assess the overall performance of the housing system. Hence, it is useful to explore the meaning of satisfaction from the residents' perspective in order to have a holistic view of the housing system. Studying satisfaction requires the real understanding of housing occupants' meaningful participation, as housing issues affect an entire community or group of people who in the present context are the low-income and disadvantaged groups.

The occupants' participation offers an opportunity to engage those who are affected by housing issues in a dialogue, defining problems and creating solutions. The inclusion of community stakeholders in the housing process helps ensure appropriate housing strategies and policies are developed through more efficient evaluation, development and implementation to guarantee the satisfaction of the beneficiaries. Inadequate beneficiary participation in the process can lead to community conflict or, as a worst-case scenario, anti-development initiatives and ultimately housing dissatisfaction, which impacts on the quality of life of the final beneficiaries. Successful beneficiary participation is important because a mixed cross-section of the population that has a housing need can be involved in defining the housing problem and in crafting community-sensitive solutions. However, there is disagreement among planners and professionals about the contribution of beneficiary participation in improving the lives of the people, particularly the poor and disadvantaged (Rifkin & Kangere, 2002). Some scholars completely dismiss its value altogether, while others believe that it is the 'magic bullet', (Rifkin & Kangere, 2002: 39) that will ensure improvements especially in the context of poverty alleviation and community ownership.

Too frequently, development initiatives have been designed by those who have no real knowledgeable understanding of the real needs of a specific community. Hence, most times, the produced 'housing plan' is based on the different stakeholders' perceived needs of the low-income groups instead of the beneficiaries' true needs (Davy, 2006). This can be attributed to the fact that the idea that development consists of a transfer of skills or information creates a role for the expert as the only person capable of facilitating the transfer of these skills from them to the community or society. In order to create developmental efforts that echo the real needs and expectations of specific groups, inclusive of development that will satisfy the people, a paradigm shift is needed in the current conceptualization of residential satisfaction research. This is a shift from the so-called blueprint approach to development towards a more process- and people-centred development that will produce beneficiary participation. The role of beneficiary participation in South Africa cannot be undermined or may not override economic, personal or technological aspirations in the South African public sector as the country's past governance situation should compel the government to correct injustices by actively involving those affected in policy development.

In addressing the gap of understanding beneficiary participation as identified in the work of Meyer and Theron (2000), the building blocks of development were drawn upon as criteria against which to assess beneficiaries' participative role in predicting housing satisfaction. The building blocks include beneficiary participation, social learning, empowerment, sustainable development, capacity building and self-reliance. The above-listed building blocks should be present for development to be considered a success. This is because beneficiary participation has since been envisaged as a diminution of the state's involvement and a strengthening of the role of the civil society, as a means to empower ordinary citizens, and the poor in particular, and to promote more sustainable and satisfying forms of development (Meyer & Theron, 2000; Tapscott & Thompson, 2010). Likewise the objectives of beneficiary participation as an active process are: empowering the residents; building beneficiary capacity; increasing project effectiveness; improving project efficiency; and sharing of project costs. These frameworks identify four levels of intensity of participation: information sharing; consulting; decision-making; and initiating action (Abbott, 1996). According to Thwala (2009) the framework has been largely accepted by development agencies worldwide. However, a criticism of the model is that it is project-based and does not include the full spectrum of community participation approaches.

Beneficiary participation in public-sector organizations has undergone a significant change. Prior to this, people were more tolerant of poor service deliveries, more patient in long queues and enduring of inefficient public administration than they are now (Olivier, 2003). Nowadays, people expect quality delivery of public services and are beginning to hold elected representatives increasingly accountable when their expectations are not met. Hence, the origin of beneficiary participation can probably be traced to three root sources, which are: participation as good development project practice; participation as good governance; and participation as political empowerment (Abbott, 1996; Bond, 2001; Freire, 2000).

When implementing a participatory process, beneficiary participation should be considered right from the onset, from concept development and planning, through to implementation, to monitoring and evaluation of outcomes. Engagement with the beneficiaries should commence as early as possible in the decision-making process, which is very essential if participatory processes are to lead to higher quality and durable decisions (Chess & Purcell, 1999; Reed, Fraser & Dougill, 2006; Reed, Dougill & Baker, 2008). Normally, beneficiaries only get involved in decision-making at the implementation phase of the project cycle, and not in earlier project identification and preparation phases. Gradually, they may also be involved in monitoring and evaluating the outcomes of the decision-making process, to see how the process is undertaken for subsequent empowerment to participate meaningfully in other developments that will concern them. However, unless flexibility can be built into the project design, this can mean that beneficiaries are invited to get involved in a project that is at variance with their own needs and priorities. This can make it a problem to motivate beneficiaries to engage with the decision-making process, and those who are engaged may be placed in a responsive position, where they are asked to respond to proposals that they perceive have already been concluded (Chess & Purcell, 1999; Reed, Dougill & Baker, 2008). The beneficiary participation features considered for the present study are summarized in Table 8.1.

Dwelling unit features

In some situations, pleasant dwelling features are the main parameters used in describing quality of housing. In order to distinguish if a house is of good quality or not, the dwelling unit's features from the internal and external aspects and also the nearby area are used to qualify the house (Salleh et al., 2011). Dwelling unit features refer to the floor plan of internal spaces within the dwelling unit and include the living room, dining room, bedroom, kitchen, bathroom, toilet and drying areas, including ventilation of the house. These can also be classified as internal dwelling unit features. Dwelling unit features also include: dwelling size; size of the living room, bedroom, kitchen, toilets and washing area; number of bedrooms; location of bedrooms; and size of dining room, laundry and washing area (Ukoha & Beamish, 1997; Lu, 1999; Ilesanmi, 2010; Mohit, Ibrahim & Rashid, 2010; Opoku & Abdul-Muhmin, 2010; Ibem & Amole, 2011; Salleh et al., 2011).

Over time, some of the above dwelling unit's features have been combined to estimate the level of residents' satisfaction with their dwelling units, thus informing housing authorities of the necessary changes to be made in order for the occupants to be satisfied with their houses. For instance, Husna and Nurizan's (1987) study on satisfaction on public housing was used by the Malaysian government to redesign its public housing dwelling unit feature to a new standard. Also, the number and location of the bedrooms, availability of laundry facilities and the provision of a washing line are also dwelling unit factors that are considered in order to bring about a quality housing units. In this present conceptual formation, the dwelling unit features that have been hypothesized for the development of an integrated residential satisfaction model are summarized in Table 8.1.

Neighbourhood features

A neighbourhood can be defined in several ways. Neighbourhood forms are derived from patterns of activities, the existence of a common visual motif, an area with

Table 8.1 Conceptual model latent constructs

Latent variable constructs	*Measurement variables*
Dwelling unit features	Location of bedrooms Number of bedrooms Size of the bedrooms Location of living room Location of dining room Location of kitchen Size of the kitchen Size of bathroom(s) Size of wardrobe/closet Size of children's play space Size of children's study space Amount of privacy within the house Amount of brightness/sunshine in the house Quality of ventilation in the house Quality of floor level in the house Overall appearance of the house Overall size of the house
Neighbourhood features	Location of the dwelling unit in the neighbourhood Quality of relationship with neighbours Quality of landscape in the neighbourhood Quality of walkways Ease of access to main roads Amount of privacy from other neighbours Quality of street lighting at night Amount of security in the neighbourhood Physical condition and appearance of the neighbourhood Cleanliness of the neighbourhood Proximity of house to workplace Proximity of house to shopping areas Proximity of house to the nursery school Proximity of house to the high school Proximity of house to hospitals/clinics proximity of house to place of worship Proximity of house to police services Proximity of house to parking facilities Proximity of house to disabled facilities Proximity of house to the community hall Proximity of house to playground/recreational facility Proximity of house to public transportation and services
Building quality features	External construction quality Internal construction quality Water pressure Wall quality

(*Continued*)

Table 8.1 (Continued)

Latent variable constructs	*Measurement variables*
	Floor quality Window quality Door quality Internal painting quality External painting quality Plumbing quality The finished quality of sanitary system Electrical wiring quality Electrical fittings quality Numbers of electrical sockets Level of sockets Overall unit quality
Services provided by government	The drainage system Garbage and waste collection Fire protection services Electricity supply Water supply Telephone service Safety How well resident complaints are handled Housing department rules and regulations Enforcement of rules by the Department of Human Settlement (Housing) Overall services provided by the government
Beneficiary participation	Owners should be consulted about the housing location Owners should be consulted about the house design Owners should be consulted about the house construction Owners should be consulted about the internal finishes of the house Owners should be consulted about the external finishes of the house
Needs and expectation	Owners should be told beforehand the type of house they will receive Owners should be asked the type of house they need Owners expect good-quality houses Houses should meet family needs
Residential satisfaction	I am satisfied living here I am taking proper care of my house I am taking proper care of my neighbourhood I am constantly maintaining my house I am not intending to move to another place in the future I would like to live in another place like this I would recommend to my friend to obtain a house in the same way that I did

continuous boundaries or a network of often-travelled streets (Brower, 1996). Diverse definitions of neighbourhood serve different interests, so that the neighbourhood may be seen as a source of place-identity, an element of urban form or a unit of decision-making. It is presumed that research uses multiple definitions of a neighbourhood simultaneously to reflect the fact that neighbourhood is not a static concept but rather a dynamic one (Talen & Shah, 2007). Likewise, planners and designers have also thought of the neighbourhood setting as a fixed, controllable and imaginable physical area. Researchers generally have agreed that a neighbourhood should comprise of a walkable distance (the distance that a person could pleasantly walk at a 3mph pace in 5 minutes). However, the actual walkable distance considered has varied from a quarter-mile to one mile from centre to edge (Colabianchi et al., 2007; Talen & Shah, 2007).

Previous studies on residential satisfaction revealed that several features are required to determine the satisfaction of a given household or individual. For instance, the availability of desired features and structure types are related; accordingly, as different services are provided by different structure types, this also affects satisfaction with housing units (Johnson & Abernathy, 1983). Also, the availability of space depends on the structure type, and the amount of space in a dwelling unit has also been found to correlate with the housing satisfaction level (Kinsey & Lane, 1983). Satisfaction with neighbourhood features has been observed as a vital determinant of residential satisfaction (Vrbka & Combs, 1991) to the extent that residents are willing to compromise on inefficiencies within the dwelling unit because of the satisfaction that is provided by the neighbourhood facilities and features (Ukoha & Beamish, 1997). Neighbourhood features refer to the location of the dwelling unit, neighbourhood relations, distance to the shopping areas, distance to the workplace or school, distance to the police services, distance to recreational facilities secure and clean environment, the building image and parking facilities among others (Awotona, 1991). Hence, residents of a given housing scheme are most likely to be dissatisfied with housing facilities that require residents to travel or walk long distances to school, workplaces, shopping areas, medical centres and the geographical areas around their dwelling units. Easy access to good public transportation, community and shopping facilities and physical environment variables will increase residents' satisfaction with their housing units.

For instance, research conducted by Bjorklund and Klingborg (2005) in eight Swedish municipalities found the following top neighbourhood factors among others to be related to residential satisfaction. These include:

- proximity to commercial areas;
- building exteriors with high aesthetic values;
- proximity to open spaces;
- less noisy environments with no traffic congestion;
- good reputation;
- good quality along the housing surroundings; and
- proximity to town centres and a conducive environment.

However, findings of a study conducted by Abdul and Yusof in 2008 on residential satisfaction show that neighbourhood facility factors are the most dominant factors in determining the level of satisfaction towards housing. The study further revealed that factors of neighbourhood facilities that caused a low level of satisfaction were poor public transport, lack of sport fields, lack of multi-purpose halls, lack of parking areas and lack of safe facilities for the disabled. Also, Ramdane and Abdullah's 2000 study on the factors of neighbourhood facilities to evaluate the level of residential satisfaction found that neighbourhood factors have a huge impact on the overall satisfaction with the housing facilities. Research has pointed out the complex characteristics of neighbourhood satisfaction (Marans & Rodgers, 1975; Marans & Sprecklemeyer, 1981; Amérigo & Aragonés, 1997; Francescato, 2002). It has also been identified that aesthetics, or pleasantness to the eye, is one of the most important factors in neighbourhood satisfaction (Sirgy & Cornwell, 2002). While social and personal characteristics, such as neighbourhood cohesion, or networks, were other factors associated with neighbourhood satisfaction (Okun, 1993; Morrow-Jones, Wenning & Li, 2005; Westaway, 2006; Chapman & Lombard, 2006). The neighbourhood and environmental features, which are considered for the present study, are summarized in Table 8.1.

Building quality features

Residents' satisfaction towards a given housing unit is also derived from the satisfaction with the building quality and the housing condition features in the buildings. Onibokun (1974) classified building condition features as dwelling subsystems to the human habitat, which influence the level of housing satisfaction. This position was further supported by McCray and Day (1977) who informed that low-income housing construction is rarely developed to reflect the needs and types of families who are going to inhabit the houses, as the building condition/quality elements are seldom considered in the establishment of human habitats. Whereas the quality of low-income housing should be a combination of both the user's requirements and the principles that define adequate housing. But because public low-income housing is built for the poor and disadvantaged, with the cost being covered by the government, the choices of design and materials used during construction are only based on an affordable budget, which compromises best practices with regards to adequate housing for the low-income groups. A good building structure with good quality is an important indicator that determines the residents' satisfaction with the building and the value they place on the dwelling.

Three dimensions of housing quality are usually considered with regards to dwellings, which include (Duncan, 1971; Ramdane & Abdullah, 2000): internal aspects of a dwelling unit; its external aspects; as well the surrounding area. The higher quality a dwelling is, the higher the resident's satisfaction with it. Housing quality and condition should not be assessed based on one variable only, but from objective and subjective dimensions. Housing quality can be classified into five critical factors, namely: basic housing quality factor; dwelling unit quality factor; surrounding property quality factor; non-residential land use quality factor; and structural average quality factor (Kain & Quigley, 1970; Elsinga & Hoekstra, 2005). Basic housing quality factors refer to the index used to measure the surrounding areas and the external physical quality of the unit. While the dwelling unit quality factor is assessed from the structural aspects and internal hygiene of the dwelling unit, the surrounding property quality factor is assessed from the general cleanliness of the surrounding area, its ambience and landscaping. The factor of quality for non-residential uses is measured from the effects of industrial and commercial uses in residential areas. These effects are assessed based on the level of discernible noise, air quality and traffic flow in the area. The structural average quality factor is assessed based on the structural quality on the building façade (Kain & Quigley, 1970).

In addition, the main cause of occupants' problems with their health, safety and physical issues is building quality (Salleh et al., 2011). Building quality factors that contribute to residents' satisfaction with their dwelling units include: walls, floors, windows, rooves, doors and painting quality, among others (Ukoha & Beamish, 1997; Salleh et al., 2011). For instance, the materials used for wall construction give effect to the building temperature. The quality of windows should provide good ventilation and air circulation in the units, because if the windows are unable to open it will increase the heat in the unit, hence residents will be uncomfortable in their houses. The building quality features considered for the present study are summarized in Table 8.1.

Services provided by government

The relationship between the government departments responsible for public housing and the occupants has a large influence on residential satisfaction with the housing units. For instance, the response to occupants' complaints and building defects and repair services carried out by the government in a public housing environment influences the level of the occupants' satisfaction towards their dwellings. Also, the time taken by the management in handling the complaints is a major factor that influences occupants' satisfaction with a given public housing unit (Ukoha & Beamish, 1997; Varady & Carrozza, 2000; James, Carswell & Sweaney, 2009). Also issues such as prompt plumbing and building repairs, electrical wiring, water supply, garbage disposal and security are vital services when provided, which influences the level of satisfaction among residents of low-income housing. As already established, services provided by the government in low-income housing play an important role in producing housing quality, which brings about satisfaction with the dwelling unit. The indicator variables included in this component are likewise summarized in Table 8.1.

Model specification and justification

The residential satisfaction conceptual framework developed in this book is centred on the subsidized low-income housing scheme. The theoretical conceptual framework for the current research builds on the work of Marans and Rodgers (1975) and Marans and Sprecklemeyer (1981). Their models of satisfaction were discussed in Chapter 7. Marans and Rodgers in 1975 conceptualized that an individual's overall satisfaction with housing depends on their perception of the various neighbourhood characteristics and their assessment of them. Marans and Rodgers' 1975 model also conceptualized that both the perpetual evaluative process and the overall satisfaction level are related to the residents' own characteristics, such as social class and housing status among others (see Table 8.2). Similarly, Marans and Sprecklemeyer in 1981 further determined that residents' satisfaction is a function of the physical environment through one's perception and beliefs of the physical environment. In this particular framework, residential satisfaction was derived as a result of an integrated relationship between the environment and the human perception of beliefs. The three basic components of the model were: the physical environment; the perception and attitude of residents towards their housing environment; and residents' satisfaction. Based on the fundamental underpinning of these two frameworks and the incorporated theoretical perspectives, which has been adopted in other similar studies, they are therefore useful for conceptualizing the present conceptual framework as a variety of satisfaction studies with urban housing living being conceptualized within the broad theoretical framework.

Therefore, the conceptual framework for this book is primarily based on the approach used by Marans and Rodgers in 1975 when they view residential satisfaction as a criterion of evaluation of residential quality and, at the same time, as a variable predicting certain behaviour. In this regard, residential satisfaction was treated as a criterion variable and, therefore, as a dependent variable. The approach was also used by Galster and Hesser in 1981, Cutter in 1982 and by Weidemann and Anderson in 1985, which has also been adopted in the developed framework for this book. Based on the fundamental factors and constructs associated with all the previous models as revealed in Table 8.2, the present conceptual framework model for the study looks at the relationship of the dwelling unit, neighbourhood and environmental features, services provided by government, building quality, which are the essential variables that have been measured in a majority of the previous studies, with the inclusive consideration of the impact of needs and expectations and beneficiary participation, which have been classified as the exogenous variables and their role in predicting overall beneficiary residential satisfaction, the endogenous variable. These will, in turn, predict the beneficiaries' satisfaction towards the housing stock, behaviour to maintain the housing stocks and their overall responsibility in the low-income neighbourhood, or likelihood to move and eventually place attachment. This present book does not empirically forecast the relative predictive power of these different variables for beneficiaries' residential satisfaction in order to test/determine if residential satisfaction depends on the supposed features of the variables, taking into account the effects of the beneficiaries' needs, expectations and meaningful participation prior to construction in alliance with the South African Housing Policy and Codes, and as emphasized by

Table 8.2 Factors of residential satisfaction

Residential satisfaction elements	*Aspiration*	*Expectations*	*Physical settings*	*Perception*	*Culture*	*Residential behaviour*	*Personal or residential features*	*Neighbourhood features*	*Neighbourhood and environmental features*	*Community services*	*Dwelling unit features*	*Socioeconomic characteristics*	*Housing type*	*Users' needs*
Michelson (1977) – Michelson's integrated model	X	X	X	X	X	X								X
Onibokun (1974) – Habitability Model							X	X		X	X			
Marans and Rodgers (1975) – Marans–Rodgers model							X		X	X	X			
Hourihan (1984) – Path Analysis Model							X	X					X	
Morris and Winter (1978) – Housing adjustment model					X		X			X	X	X		
Francescato et al. (1979) – Francescato et al.'s model of housing satisfaction				X			X		X		X			
Weidemann and Anderson (1985) – integrated conceptual model				X		X	X		X	X	X			
Marans and Sprecklemeyer (1981) – inclusive model (basic conceptual model)				X		X		X	X	X	X			

Source: Author's literature review.

other frameworks. It is envisaged that another work will consider the exploration of an empirical relationship among the variables.

In order to empirically determine the relationship among these variables, it is apparent that some of the variables discussed above should be measured by objective means, some by subjective means and some will include both forms of measurement. The reason for combining both objective and subjective indicators within the proposed model is supported by the scholars such as Campbell, Converse and Rogers (1976) and Falah, Al-Abed and Stan (1995) who stated that, by themselves, objective indicators are often misleading and will remain so until indicators that human beings attached to them are obtained. Likewise, by themselves, subjective indicators are insufficient as guides to policy.

The theoretical conceptual model theorizes that residential satisfaction is established by the relationship that exists between the exogenous variables, which include the basic elements by which the subjective and objective measurements are linked. These variables are considered the major determinants of residential satisfaction in subsidized low-income housing. These have been adopted to fit with the peculiar housing and other socio-economic characteristics of the South African society. Hence, the combination of the objective and subjective measures will then produce a measure of residential satisfaction for the beneficiaries of the low-income units, as defined in the previous sections.

Structural and measurement components of the conceptual framework

The present conceptual model hypothesis is that housing occupants' residential satisfaction with publicly provided low-income housing in South Africa (and other developing countries) is derived from residents' overall satisfaction with their dwelling unit features, neighbourhood and environment features, building quality features, services provided by the government, beneficiaries' needs and expectations and the assessment of the beneficiary participation in the housing process. The model hypothesis postulates a priori that residential satisfaction is a multi-dimensional structure composed of dwelling unit features, neighbourhood features, building quality features, services provided by the government, beneficiaries' needs and expectations and the assessment of the beneficiary participation. This is presented schematically in Figure 8.2. The theoretical underpinning of this is derived from the works of Marans and Rodgers (1975) and Marans and Sprecklemeyer's (1981) models of satisfaction and the approaches as adopted by Galster and Hesser (1981), Cutter (1982) and Weidemann and Anderson (1985), as discussed above.

Inherent in the conceptualized model is the notion that satisfaction with housing provision is related to the evaluation of many variables. While the principal variable under consideration is the dwelling unit that has been received by the housing occupants, it is difficult to discuss it without reference to the variables of neighbourhood, service provided by the government and inclusion of the other exogenous variables deemed relevant to the South African/developing economies setting. The satisfaction level is expressed by the

Figure 8.2 An integrated conceptual framework of residential satisfaction

households' subjective evaluation of their housing environment and will be defined by them.

The evaluation will depend on the beneficiaries' assessment of several indicator variables under each of the exogenous variables as captured in Table 8.1. Which attributes are most relevant is an empirical question and may differ under different circumstances. How households assess a particular aspect of their housing environment, for instance, is/will be considered dependent on their personal characteristics. This is meant to include all characteristics and experiences of the beneficiaries that influence their evaluations. For example, beneficiaries of different cultures, races, incomes or genders may have diverse evaluations of the same dwelling unit they have received. As such, depending on an individual's diverse value system, experiences and aspirations, certain residential features can generate in residents feelings of convenience, beauty, health and accessibility, or otherwise (Ebong, 1983). Thus it is possible for one to see in any residential environment what one is supposed to see, turning a blind eye to much that is actually present in that particular environment.

In order to adequately measure the hypothesized framework, the measurement component of the model should comprise of the following residential satisfaction factors: dwelling unit features = 17 measurement variables; neighbourhood features = 22 measurement variables; building quality features = 16 measurement variables; services provided by government = 13 measurement variables; beneficiary participation = 5 measurement variables; needs and expectations = 4 measurement variables and residential satisfaction = 7 measurement variables. In the present model, it is therefore theorized that residential satisfaction is to be considered as a sufficient indication to show the success of state-subsidized housing provision in meeting the beneficiaries' needs and giving them a good start in the housing market.

Summary

In this chapter, a residential conceptual framework was theorized, which postulates a theoretical and notional priori that residential satisfaction is a multidimensional structure composed of the six latent variables of dwelling unit features, neighbourhood features, building quality features, services provided by the government, beneficiary participation and needs and expectations of the housing occupants. Also highlighted in this chapter is the theoretical framework for the explanation of the variables selected for the construction of the integrated conceptual model of residential satisfaction. This chapter also describes the selection of the variables adopted for the conceptual model and the framework identification and justification for the selected variables.

References

Abbott, J. (1996). *Sharing the city: Community participation in urban management*. London: Earthscan.

Amérigo, M.A. & Aragonés, I.J. (1997). A theoretical and methodological approach to the study of residential satisfaction. *Journal of environmental psychology*, 17:47–57.

Awotona, A. (1991). Nigerian government participation in housing: 1970–1980, Nigeria. *Social indicators research*, 25:63–98.

Bjorklund, K. & Klingborg, K. (2005). Correlation between negotiated rents and neighbourhood quality: A case study of two cities in Sweden. *Housing studies*, 20(4):627–647.

Bond, P. (2001). *Against global apartheid: South Africa meets the World Bank, IMF and international finance*. London and New York: University of Cape Town Press.

Brower, S. (1996). *Good neighborhoods: Study of in-town and suburban residential environments*. Westport, CT: Praeger Publishers.

Bruin, M. & Cook, C. (1997). Understanding constraints and residential satisfaction among low-income single-parent families. *Environment and behavior*, 29(4):532–553.

Campbell, A., Converse, P.E. & Rogers, W.J. (1976). *The quality of the America life: Perceptions, evaluations, and satisfaction*. New York: Russell Sage Foundation.

Caughey, C., Francis, S. & Kolodziej, A. (1998). Effects of expectations on user satisfaction with a remodeled university dining facility. *Journal of consumer satisfaction, dissatisfaction and complaining behavior*, 11:180–185.

Chapman, D.W. & Lombard, J.R. (2006). Determinants of neighborhood satisfaction in fee-based gated and nongated communities. *Urban affairs review*, 41(6):769–799.

Chess, C. & Purcell, K. (1999). Public participation and the environment – Do we know what works? *Environmental science and technology*, 33: 2685–2692.

Churchill, G. & Surprenant, C. (1982). An investigation into the determinants of customer satisfaction. *Journal of marketing research*, 19(4):491–504.

Colabianchi, N., Dowda, M., Pfeiffer, K.A., Porter, D.E., Almeida, M.J. & Pate, R.R. (2007). Towards an understanding of salient neighborhood boundaries: Adolescent reports of an easy walking distance and convenient driving distance. *International journal of behavioral nutrition and physical activity*, 1(3):S99–S117.

Cutter, S. (1982). Residential satisfaction and the suburban homeowner. *Urban geography*, 3(4):315–327.

Davy, J. (2006). *Assessing public participation strategies in low-income housing: The Mamre housing project*. Stellenbosch: Stellenbosch University.

Duncan, T.L.C. (1971). *Measuring housing quality: A study of methods*. Birmingham: Centre for Urban and Regional Studies, University of Birmingham.

Ebong, M.O. (1983). The perception of residential quality: A case study of Calabar, Nigeria. *Third world planning review*, 5(3):273–285.

Elsinga, M. & Hoekstra, J. (2005). Homeownership and housing satisfaction. *Journal of housing and the built environment*, 20:401–424.

Erevelles, S. & Leavitt, C. (1992). A comparison of current models of consumer satisfaction/dissatisfaction. *Journal of consumer satisfaction, dissatisfaction and complaining behavior*, 5:104–114.

Falah, M., Al-Abed, A. & Stan, W. (1995). A model for assessing the effectiveness of public housing in Sana'a (Republic of Yemen). *Construction management and economics*, 13:457–465.

Francescato, G. (2002). Residential satisfaction research: The case for and against. In J.I. Aragonés, G. Francescato & T. Gärling (eds) *Residential environments: Choice, satisfaction and behaviour*. London: Bergin and Garvey, pp. 15–34.

Francescato, G., Weidemann, S. & Anderson, J.R. (1987). Residential satisfaction: Its uses and limitations in housing research. In W.V. Vliet, H. Choldin, W. Michelson & P. Popene (eds) *Housing and neighbourhood: Theoretical and empirical contributions*. Westport, CT: Greenwood Press, pp. 43–57.

Francescato, G., Weidemann, S., Anderson, J.R. et al. (1979). *Satisfaction in HUD-assisted housing: Design and management*. Washington, DC: US Department of Housing and Urban Development.

Freire, P. (2000). *The pedagogy of the oppressed*. New York: The Continuum International Publishing Group Ltd.

Greenberg, P. (1999). Improving neighbourhood quality. A hierarchy of needs. *Housing policy debate*, 10(3):601–624.

Hamnett, C. (2001). Social segregation and social polarization. In R. Paddison (ed.) *Handbook of urban studies*. London: Sage, pp. 162–176.

Hourihan, K. (1984). Context-dependent models of residential satisfaction: An analysis of housing groups in Cork, Ireland. *Environment and behavior*, 16: 369–393.

Husna, S. & Nurizan, Y. (1987). Housing provision and satisfaction of low-income households in Kuala Lumpur. *Habitat international*, 11(4):27–38.

Ibem, E.O. & Amole, O.O. (2011). Evaluation of public housing programmes in Nigeria: A theoretical and conceptual approach. *The built & human environment review*, 3:88–117.

Ilesanmi, A.O. (2010). Post-occupancy evaluation and residents' satisfaction with public housing in Lagos, Nigeria. *Journal of building appraisal*, 6(2):153–169.

James, R.N., Carswell, A.T. & Sweaney, A.L. (2009). Sources of discontent: Residential satisfaction of tenants from an internet ratings site. *Environment & behavior*, 41(1):43–59.

Johnson, P.J. & Abernathy, T.J. (1983). Sources of urban multifamily housing satisfaction. *Housing and society*, 10:36–48.

Kain, J.F. & Quigley, J.M. (1970). Measuring the value of housing quality. *Journal of the American Statistical Association*, 65(330):532–548.

Kinsey, J. & Lane, S. (1983). Race, housing attributes and satisfaction with housing. *Housing and society*, 10: 98–116.

Landman, K. (2004). Gated communities in South Africa: Comparison of four case studies in Gauteng. Pretoria, CSIR Report, BOU/I 347.

Lang, R.E. & Hornburg, S.P. (1998). What is social capital and why is it important to public policy? *Housing policy debate*, 9(1):1–16.

Lu, M. (1999). Determinants of residential satisfaction: Ordered logit vs. regression models. *Growth and change*, 30(Spring):264–287.

McCray, J.W. & Day, S.S. (1977). Housing values, aspirations, and satisfactions as indicators of housing needs. *Home economics research journal*, 5:244–254.

Marcus, C.C. (1995). *Home as a mirror of self: Exploring the deeper meaning of home*. Berkeley, CA: Conari Press.

Maslow, A.H. (1970). *Motivation and personality*. New York: Harper and Row.

Maslow, A.H. (1998). *Towards a psychology of being*. New York: J. Wiley and Sons.

Marans, R. & Rodgers, S. (1975). *Toward an understanding of community satisfaction*. New York: Halstead Press.

Marans, R. & Sprecklemeyer, K. (1981). *Evaluating built environment: A behavioral approach*. Ann Arbor: The University of Michigan Press.

Meyer, I. & Theron, F. (2000). *A framework for action*. Bellville: School of Public Management and Planning, University of Stellenbosch.

Michelson, W. (1977). *Environment choice, human behaviour, and residential satisfaction*. Oxford: Oxford University Press.

Mohit, M.A., Ibrahim, M. & Rashid, Y.R. (2010). Assessment of residential satisfaction in newly designed public low-cost housing in Kuala Lumpur, Malaysia. *Habitat international*, 34(1):18–27.

Morris, E.W., Crull, S. R., & Winter, M. (1976). Housing norms, housing satisfaction and the propensity to move. *Journal of marriage and the family*, 38: 309–320.

Morrow-Jones, H. Wenning, M.V. & Li, Y. (2005). *Differences in neighborhood satisfaction between African American and white homeowners*. Kansas City, MO: Association of Collegiate Schools of Planning (ACSP46).

Morris, E.W. & Winter, M. (1978). *Housing, family and society*. New York: John Wiley and Sons.

Nurizan, Y. and Hashim, A. H. (2001). *Perumahan dan Kediaman*. Selangor: Universiti Putra Malaysia.

Oh, L. S. (2000). *Housing satisfaction of middle income households in Bandar Baru Bangi.* Selangor: Universiti Pertanian Malaysia.

Okun, M.A. (1993). Predictors of volunteer status in a retirement community. *International journal of aging and human development*, 36(1):57–74.

Olivier, A. (2003). A critical review of public participation in development planning within South African local governments. Occasional paper. Cape Town: Organisation Development Africa.

Oliver, R.L. (1981). Measurement and evaluation of satisfaction process in retail setting. *Journal of retailing*, 57:25–48.

Onibokun, A.G. (1974). Evaluating consumers' satisfaction with housing: An application of a system approach. *Journal of American Institute of Planners*, 40(3): 189–200.

Opoku, R.A. & Abdul-Muhmin, A.G. (2010). Housing preferences and attribute importance among low-income consumers in Saudi Arabia. *Habitat international*, 34(2):219–227.

Parkes, A., Kearns, A. & Atkinson, R. (2002). What makes people dissatisfied with their neighborhoods? *Urban studies*, 39(13):2413–2438.

Putnam, R.D. (1995). *Bowling alone*, revisited. *Responsive community*, 5(2):18–33.

Ukoha, O.M. & Beamish, J.O. (1997). Assessment of residents' satisfaction with public housing in Abuja, Nigeria. *Habitat international*, 21(4):445–460.

Ramdane, D. & Abdullah, A.A. (2000). Satisfaction level with neighborhood's in low-income public housing in Yemen. *Property management*, 18(4):230–242.

Reed, M.S., Fraser, E.D.G. & Dougill, A.J. (2006). An adaptive learning process for developing and applying sustainability indicators with local communities. *Ecological economics*, 59: 406–418.

Reed, M.S., Dougill, A.J. & Baker, T. (2008). Participatory indicator development: What can ecologists and local communities learn from each other? *Ecological applications*, 18: 1253–1269.

Reisig, D.M. & Chandek, M.S. (2001). The effects of expectancy disconfirmation on outcome satisfaction in police–citizen encounters. *An international journal of police strategies & management*, 24(1):88–99.

Rifkin, S.B. & Kangere, M. (2002). What is participation? In S. Hartley (ed.) *CBR: A participatory strategy in Africa*. London: Centre for International Child Health, pp. 37–49.

Rogers, C. (1951). *Client-centered therapy: Its current practice, implications and theory*. London: Constable.

Salleh, A., Yusof, N.A., Salleh, A.G. & Johan Noraire, D. (2011). Tenant satisfaction in public housing and its relationships with rent arrears: Majlis Badaraya Ipoh, Oerak, Malaysia. *International journal of trade economics and finance*, 2(1):10–18.

Sirgy, M.J. & Cornwell, T. (2002). How neighborhood features affect quality of life. *Social indicators research*, 59(1):79–114.

Smith, N. (1996). *The urban frontier: Gentrification and the revanchist city*. London and New York: Routledge.

Talen, E. & Shah, S. (2007). Neighborhood evaluation using GIS: An exploratory study. *Environment and behavior*, 39(5):583–615.

Tapscott, C. & Thompson, L. (2010). Participatory development in South Africa – Between rhetoric and practice. 14th International Research Society for Public Management Conference, Bern, Switzerland.

Taylor, R.B. (1995). The impact of crime on communities. *Annals of the American academy of political and social science*, 539:28–45.

Thwala, W.D. (2009). Experiences and challenges of community participation in urban renewal projects: The case of Johannesburg, South Africa. *Journal of construction in developing countries*, 14(2):37–54.

Tse, D.K. & Wilton, P.C. (1988). Models of consumer satisfaction formation: An extension. *Journal of marketing research*, 25(2):204–212.

Turner, J.F.C. (1972). Housing as a verb. In J.F.C. Turner & R. Fichter (eds) *Freedom to build, dwellers control of the housing process*. New York: Macmillan, pp. 148–175.

Varady, D.P. & Carrozza, M.A. (2000). Towards a better way to measure customer satisfaction levels in public housing: A report from Cincinnati. *Housing studies*, 15(6):797–825.

Vrbka, S.J. & Combs, E.R. (1991). Predictors of neighborhood and community satisfaction. Referred papers of the American Association of Housing Educators annual conference, Durham, NH.

Weidemann, S. & Anderson, J.R.A. (1985). A conceptual framework for residential satisfaction. In I. Atman & R. Werner (eds) *Home environment*. New York: Plenum Press, pp. 154–182.

Westaway, M.S. (2006). A longitudinal investigation of satisfaction with personal and environmental quality of life in an informal South Africa housing settlement, Doornkop, Soweto. *Habitat international*, 30:175–189.

Wilson-Doenges, G. (2000). An exploration of sense of community and fear of crime in gated communities. *Environment and behavior*, 32(5):597–611.

Woodruff, R., Cadotte, E. & Jenkins, R. (1983). Modeling consumer satisfaction processes using experience-based norms. *Journal of marketing research*, 20:296–304.

Yiping, F. (2005). Residential satisfaction conceptual framework revisited: A study on redeveloped neighbourhood in inner-city Beijing. An unpublished doctoral dissertation, University of Colorado at Denver.

Index

For Product Safety Concerns and Information please contact our EU
representative GPSR@taylorandfrancis.com
Taylor & Francis Verlag GmbH, Kaufingerstraße 24, 80331 München, Germany

www.ingramcontent.com/pod-product-compliance
Ingram Content Group UK Ltd.
Pitfield, Milton Keynes, MK11 3LW, UK
UKHW021301190926
475701UK00009B/573

* 9 7 8 1 0 3 2 0 9 5 0 9 7 *